ALLEGORIES OF FARMING FROM GREECE AND ROME

In this book Professor Kronenberg shows that Xenophon's *Oeconomicus*, Varro's *De Re Rustica*, and Virgil's *Georgics* are not simply works on farming but belong to a tradition of philosophical satire which uses allegory and irony to question the meaning of morality and the right way to live. These works metaphorically connect farming and its related arts to political life; but instead of presenting farming in its traditional guise as a positive symbol, they use it to model the materialistic foundations and deficiencies of conventional morality and politics. In turn, they juxtapose a contemplative model of life that is superior to the active life in its access to knowledge and lack of hypocrisy. Although these three texts are not usually treated together, and each section can be taken as a stand-alone analysis, this book convincingly connects them with an original and provocative interpretation of their allegorical use of farming. It also fills an important gap in our understanding of the literary influences on the *Georgics* by showing that it is shaped not just by its poetic predecessors but by philosophical dialogue.

LEAH KRONENBERG is Assistant Professor of Classics at Rutgers University.

ALLEGORIES OF FARMING FROM GREECE AND ROME

Philosophical Satire in Xenophon, Varro, and Virgil

LEAH KRONENBERG

Rutgers University

CAMBRIDGE
UNIVERSITY PRESS

CAMBRIDGE UNIVERSITY PRESS
Cambridge, New York, Melbourne, Madrid, Cape Town, Singapore, São Paulo, Delhi

Cambridge University Press
The Edinburgh Building, Cambridge CB2 8RU, UK

Published in the United States of America by Cambridge University Press, New York

www.cambridge.org
Information on this title: www.cambridge.org/9780521517263

First published 2009

Printed in the United Kingdom at the University Press, Cambridge

A catalogue record for this publication is available from the British Library

Library of Congress Cataloguing in Publication data
Kronenberg, Leah, 1976–
Allegories of farming from Greece and Rome : philosophical satire in Xenophon, Varro, and Virgil /
Leah Kronenberg.
p.   cm.
Includes bibliographical references and index.
ISBN 978-0-521-51726-3 (hardback)
1. Agriculture in literature.   2. Satire, Greek – History and criticism.   3. Satire, Latin – History
and criticism.   4. Agriculture, Ancient – Greece.   5. Agriculture, Ancient – Rome.
6. Xenophon. Oeconomicus.   7. Varro, Marcus Terentius. Rerum rusticarum libri tres.
8. Virgil. Georgica.   I. Title.
PA3015.A37K76 2009
881′.01 – dc22   2008055930

ISBN 978-0-521-51726-3 hardback

89881

For Chris

ἀλλὰ πιαίνειν οἴει αὐτὸν τὰ πρόβατα, καθ᾽ ὅσον ποιμήν ἐστιν,
οὐ πρὸς τὸ τῶν προβάτων βέλτιστον βλέποντα ἀλλ᾽, ὥσπερ
δαιτυμόνα τινὰ καὶ μέλλοντα ἐστιάσεσθαι, πρὸς τὴν εὐωχίαν, ἢ
αὖ πρὸς τὸ ἀποδόσθαι, ὥσπερ χρηματιστὴν ἀλλ᾽ οὐ ποιμένα.
τῇ δὲ ποιμενικῇ οὐ δήπου ἄλλου του μέλει ἢ ἐφ᾽ ᾧ τέτακται,
ὅπως τούτῳ τὸ βέλτιστον ἐκποριεῖ.

But you think that the shepherd, in his capacity as shepherd, fattens
the flock not with a view to what is best for the flock but, as if he
were some guest about to feast, with a view to good cheer, or, in
turn, with a view to selling them, as if he were a money-maker, not
a shepherd. But surely the concern of the shepherding art is
nothing other than to provide what is best for its charge.

Socrates to Thrasymachus, Plato's *Republic* 345c–d

Νὴ τοὺς θεούς, ἀτεχνῶς γε ἀεὶ σκυτέας τε καὶ κναφέας καὶ
μαγείρους λέγων καὶ ἰατροὺς οὐδὲν παύῃ, ὡς περὶ τούτων ἡμῖν
ὄντα τὸν λόγον.

By the Gods, you simply never cease talking about cobblers,
clothes-cleaners, cooks, and doctors, as if our discussion were about
them.

Callicles to Socrates, Plato's *Gorgias* 491a

Contents

Acknowledgments

I have many people to thank for their help and support in bringing this book to completion. My largest debt of gratitude goes to Richard Thomas, who directed the dissertation from which this book grew, and who has provided constant friendship, advice, and inspiration throughout my college, graduate, and post-graduate years. I am also very grateful to the members of my dissertation committee, Albert Henrichs, Andreola Rossi, and the dearly missed Charles Segal, and to my other friends and colleagues at Harvard University. My current colleagues at Rutgers University have provided invaluable advice and encouragement in the later stages of the work, and I would particularly single out for thanks Corey Brennan, Lowell Edmunds, Tom Figueira and Kathryn Neal.

Completion of this book was made possible by generous research support along the way from the Whiting Foundation, the American Council of Learned Societies, the Loeb Classical Library Foundation and Rutgers University.

Many thanks are also due to Michael Sharp, Elizabeth Noden, and Jodie Barnes for their excellent editorial guidance, to Linda Woodward for her meticulous copy-editing, and to the two anonymous readers, whose extremely helpful and detailed comments on my manuscript improved it in numerous ways.

Finally, I am above all grateful for the love and support of my family and especially my husband Chris, to whom this book is dedicated.

Abbreviations and editions

Abbreviations to ancient authors and works are based on those used in the LSJ and *OLD*. Abbreviations to classical journals are based on those used in the *L'Année Philologique*, with the customary alterations for English usage. In addition, the following abbreviations are used:

DK   Diels, H. ed. (1952) *Fragmente der Vorsokratiker*. 6th edn., rev. W. Kranz. Berlin: Weidmann.

LSJ   Liddell, H. G. and R. Scott, eds. (1940) *A Greek–English Lexicon*. 9th edn., rev. H. S. Jones. Oxford: Clarendon Press.

OCD   Hornblower, S. and A. Spawforth, eds. (1996). *Oxford Classical Dictionary*. 3rd edn. New York: Oxford University Press.

OLD   Glare P. W., ed. (1968–82) *Oxford Latin Dictionary*. Oxford: Clarendon Press.

RE   Pauly, A., G. Wissowa and W. Kroll, eds. (1894–1980) *Paulys Real-Encyclopädie der classischen Altertumswissenschaft*. Stuttgart: J. B. Metzler.

The editions used for the major primary texts discussed are as follows. Translations are my own.

B. Mandeville   Kaye, F. B., ed. (1924) *Bernard Mandeville: The Fable of the Bees, Or Private Vices, Publick Benefits*. 2 vols. Oxford: Clarendon Press.
Note: The first numbers for the Mandeville references indicate volume and page number of Kaye's edition, and the number in brackets is Kaye's reference to the original pagination of Mandeville's text.

Varro   Flach, D., ed. (2006) *Über die Landwirtschaft.* Darmstadt: Wissenschaftliche Buchgesellschaft.

Virgil   Mynors, R. A. B., ed. (1969) *P. Vergili Maronis Opera.* Oxford: Clarendon Press.

Xenophon   Marchant, E. C. (1921) *Xenophontis opera omnia.* 2nd edn. Oxford: Clarendon Press.

Introduction

> T'enjoy the World's Conveniencies,
> Be fam'd in War, yet live in Ease,
> Without great Vices, is a vain
> EUTOPIA seated in the Brain.
>
> Bernard Mandeville, *The Fable of the Bees* (1.36 [23])

In the early eighteenth century, the Dutch writer and philosopher Bernard Mandeville produced a satire of human society via an allegorical description of a bee state entitled *The Fable of the Bees: or Private Vices, Publick Benefits*. His fable originated as a 433-line poem entitled *The Grumbling Hive: or Knaves turn'd Honest*, which attracted little attention from the reading public when it was first published in 1705. However, his subsequent expansion and prose elaboration of the poem in 1723 so scandalized European society that the Grand Jury of Middlesex recommended that Mandeville be prosecuted, the French translation of the *Fable of the Bees* was burned by the public hangman, and published critiques of his work abounded.[1] Mandeville attracted infamy because, instead of using bees to represent an orderly and virtuous monarchy,[2] he used the hive to model the rampant vices that he believed are responsible for a flourishing human society, namely greed, luxury, and other self-interested appetites.[3] As such, his work flouted the moralizers of Augustan England, epitomized by the

---

[1] On the hostile reception of the *Fable of the Bees* in the eighteenth century, see most recently Hundert (1994), Stafford (1997), and Goldsmith (2000).

[2] On the usual idealization of the bee in Augustan England, see Johnson (1961) and Allen (2004).

[3] Cf. Mandeville's explanation of his purpose in the preface to the fable: "For the main Design of the Fable (as it is briefly explain'd in the Moral) is to shew the Impossibility of enjoying all the most elegant Comforts of Life that are to be met with in an industrious, wealthy and powerful Nation, and at the same time be bless'd with all the Virtue and Innocence that can be wish'd for in a Golden Age; from thence to expose the Unreasonableness and Folly of those, that desirous of being an opulent and flourishing People, and wonderfully greedy after all the Benefits they can receive as such, are yet always murmuring at and exclaiming against those Vices and Inconveniences, that from the Beginning of the World to this present Day, have been inseparable from all Kingdoms and States that ever were fam'd for Strength, Riches, and Politeness, at the same time" (1.6–7 [vii]).

Society for the Reformation of Manners, who sought to police private life and eradicate immorality.[4] In contrast to these moralizers, Mandeville exposed virtue to be a mask or a delusion and set out a genealogy of society and morality based on the natural, self-interested passions that drive human beings.[5]

Mandeville's ultimate intentions and the ethical implications of his work are still debated, and his many published attempts to clarify and defend his position have only added to the controversy since many see his language as consistently pervaded with irony.[6] Still, if one does give weight to his words in the preface, it seems that his overall goal is not to praise the vices that have made a country like England prosperous so much as to point to the hypocrisy of those who are "always murmuring at and exclaiming against those Vices" (1.7 [vii]) while at the same time enjoying the conveniences of a country like England.[7] Mandeville himself espouses a preference not for the supposed greatness of a city like London but for a retired life in the country: "But if, without any regard to the Interest or Happiness of the City, the Question was put, What Place I thought most pleasant to walk in? No body can doubt but, before the stinking streets of *London*, I would esteem a fragrant Garden or a shady Grove in the country" (1.12 [xiii]).

Danielle Allen suggests that Mandeville was the first to invert the bee trope and use it to model vices instead of virtues.[8] The goal of this book, however, is to suggest that, in fact, his ideas and methods had been anticipated by writers in antiquity.[9] In particular, I argue that Xenophon's

---

[4] On the moral climate of Mandeville's England, see Horne (1978), Goldsmith (1985) 1–27, Hundert (1994) 1–15 and Jack (2000).

[5] On Mandeville's genealogy of morals and the intellectual influences on his conception of morality and human society, see Kaye (1924) 1.lxxvii–cxiii, Jack (1987) 98–113, Schneider (1987) 67–100, Hundert (1994) and Allen (2004).

[6] Monro (1975) 178 notes, "At least five distinct, and indeed widely different, moral theories have been attributed to Mandeville: moral scepticism…immoralism…rigorism or asceticism… utilitarianism…and ethical egoism." On Mandeville's irony and ambiguity, cf. Stumpf (2000) 115: "It is important to remember that Mandeville is a great literary figure, especially in the first volume of *The Fable of the Bees*, and that we should be as reluctant to impose ideological consistency upon him as we would be to impose it upon Swift. Librarians have difficulty putting Mandeville in one place, and so should we. His irony is both pervasive and elusive, and, like most great writers, he can entertain the truth of opposites." See also Hind (1968) and Schneider (1987) 194–231.

[7] As Allen (2004) 80 n. 16 notes, "The point that Mandeville's satire is aimed at hypocrisy was first made by Harth ("Satiric Purpose" [note 14], 328) and has been very influential in Mandeville studies." Her reference is to Harth (1969).

[8] Allen (2004) 78: "And indeed, his inversion of the bee trope was prodigious, in the sense of being without prior example."

[9] The classical influences on Mandeville have been well noted. In particular, Hundert (1994) emphasizes the influence of Epicureanism on his thought. Stumpf (2000) notes many connections between *The Fable of the Bees* and the *Georgics*, though he does not see any irony or satire in Virgil's own version of the bee state.

Oeconomicus, Varro's *De Re Rustica*, and Virgil's *Georgics* all utilize bee imagery, as well as broader agricultural allegory, to expose the greedy and self-interested underpinnings of human societies and conventional morality. Like the virtuous bee, the virtuous farmer is a familiar cultural trope from Greece and Rome.[10] While recent studies have brought out the complexity of the country–city dichotomy in ancient thought, with the result that one cannot simply equate the country with "good" and the city with "bad," the negatives generally attached to the life of the rustic farmer are qualities like boorishness or lack of sophistication.[11] Thus, the equation of farming with a materialistic value system, which I suggest informs the agricultural works of Xenophon, Varro, and Virgil, is as shocking as the equation of the beehive with greed and luxury. Like the beehive, the farmer's world in these works has metaphorical connections to political society, and these three writers use these connections to juxtapose the active, political life to a preferred contemplative ideal, perhaps akin to Mandeville's preference for a "fragrant Garden" or "shady Grove." Thus, far from being simple didactic manuals on farming, these works use allegory, irony, and satire to rethink the meaning of morality and critique the hypocrisy of politicians, moralizers, and anyone with pretensions to knowledge.

MENIPPEAN SATIRE, ANCIENT AND MODERN

There are some major differences, of course, between Mandeville's work and the works of Xenophon, Varro, and Virgil. None of the ancient works met with the kind of hostile reception that Mandeville's eventually did, and none of the ancient writers went out of their way to court the infamy that Mandeville enjoyed or to unpack the meaning of their works in explanatory essays. Indeed, many readers do not see irony or satire in their works at all, and none of them is classified generically as a satire. On the other hand, recent works on satire have sought to expand our notion of the genre to

[10] On the ideology of farming and country life in Greece and Rome, see most recently Rosen and Sluiter (2006). See also Martin (1971) *passim*, Dover (1974) 112–14, White (1977), Cossarini (1976–77), (1979–80), Miles (1980) 1–63, Hunter (1985) 109–13, Ross (1987) 10–25, Braund (1989a), Vasaly (1993) 156–90, Connors (1997), Nelson (1998) 88–91, Reay (2005), and Diederich (2007) 327–29. White (1977) 5 suggests that "this powerful, almost obsessive, morality myth is peculiar to the Romans. In the Greek tradition, from Hesiod's *Works and Days* onwards there are few signs of illusion on the subject." While the myth is more firmly entrenched in Rome, Hunter (1985) 109 points out that after the Peloponnesian war, "an opposition between 'town' and 'country' became an increasingly common structuring device in drama and literature" and that the "most common form of the city-country contrast in comedy is between the frivolity and luxury of the city and the virtue and stern morality of the country" (110).

[11] On the complexities of the city–country dichotomy in the ancient world, see esp. Rosen and Sluiter (2006) 1–12.

include works other than the generically self-conscious poems of Horace, Persius, and Juvenal.[12] In particular, more attention is being paid to the Menippean tradition of satire, a genre whose characteristics are much less fixed than those in formal verse satire; it is this type of satire that I believe is relevant to the agricultural works of Xenophon, Varro, and Virgil, as well as to Mandeville's *Fable of the Bees*.[13]

Many modern theorists of Menippean satire have connected this genre to Socratic dialogue, though generally to Plato's version and not Xenophon's.[14] Thus, my suggestion that Xenophon's dialogue might have a genetic relationship to Menippean satire is not outlandish, especially since many believe that Xenophon's Socratic dialogues were influenced by those of Antisthenes, the purported founder of Cynicism, and Menippus himself was a famous Cynic.[15] Connections between Varro's *De Re Rustica* and Menippean satire are even more reasonable to suppose since Varro is known to be the author of 150 *Menippean Satires*, which survive in fragments, and so was clearly drawn to a Menippean frame of mind. Virgil's didactic poem, then, is the only work without a potential tie to Menippean satire; however, depending on how one defines this genre, many connections still might be made.

There seems to have been little notion of a fixed genre of Menippean satire in antiquity, and the various definitions that modern critics have come up with are wide ranging and diverse.[16] Menippus himself, the Greek

---

[12] E.g. Hooley (2007) 142: "Yet there is much more 'satire' out there, and even in Rome, the hexameter form was not the only way into this modality: comedy, philosophy, streetcorner diatribe, verse invective all did this thing we popularly call satire, if not exclusively, at least some of the time and in some ways."

[13] On the importance of integrating the study of Menippean satire with formal verse satire, see Griffin (1994) esp. ch. 1. On classifying Mandeville's *Fable of the Bees* as Menippean satire, see Hind (1968).

[14] Most famously, Bakhtin (1981) 26: "A few words now about Menippean satire. Its folklore roots are identical with those of the Socratic dialogue, to which it is genetically related (it is usually considered a product of the disintegration of the Socratic dialogue)." See also Frye (1957) 310, Bakhtin (1984) 106–22, Relihan (1993) 6, 11, 25–26, 33, 180–86 and Dentith (2000) 45–58. Relihan (1993) 180 calls "Plato's narrator and self-deprecating naïf, Socrates, the most important model for Menippus's own literary personality."

[15] Bakhtin (1984) 113 even suggests that the "first representative" of Menippean satire was "perhaps Antisthenes." On Antisthenes' influence on Xenophon, see Branham and Goulet-Cazé (1996) 7 and Long (1996a) 32. For the modern critique of the Hellenistic belief that Antisthenes was the founder of Cynicism, as well as a moderate defense of the connections between Antisthenes and Cynicism, see Tsouna McKirahan (1994).

[16] Cf. Relihan (1984) 227: "That such a genre existed is evident from the lines of influence and tradition that can be traced in Varro, Seneca, Petronius, and others, but antiquity does not acknowledge the genre which modern literary acumen has uncovered and named on its own." See also Rimell (2005) 164–69, Henderson (2005) 316–18, and Hooley (2007) 143. For surveys of various modern definitions of the genre, see Kirk (1980) 223–84, Relihan (1993) 3–11, Griffin (1994) 31–34, Kaplan (2000) 47–58, Rimell (2005) 166–69, and Weinbrot (2005) 1–19.

founder of the genre in the third century BC, has left us no surviving works, though a few titles and fragments are recorded in Diogenes Laertius and Athenaeus. The only two ancient writers who explicitly connect their works to Menippus are Varro, who wrote what Jerome labels *Satirarum Menippearum Libros CL*, and Lucian, who wrote several dialogues with Menippus as a character.[17] Quintilian does mention "another kind" (*alterum . . . genus*) of satire, written by Varro, which uses not just different meters, but prose and verse (10.1.95), but it is unclear if he is talking about an actual genre or simply a variation of Ennian satire.[18] Whatever its import for the ancient conception of the genre of Menippean satire, Quintilian's description of Varro's satire has been influential among classicists, who usually consider the mixture of prose and verse an essential feature of the genre.[19] Accordingly, Seneca's *Apocolocyntosis* and Petronius' *Satyricon* are usually considered Menippean, even though they seem to have little in common with Varro's satires or Lucian's dialogues, which, incidentally, have little verse in them. Thus, if there was a tacitly recognized genre of Menippean satire in antiquity, then it was also recognized to be a genre with immense variety in form and content.[20] If one adds in the works that scholars of various modern literatures have considered Menippean, the diversity grows even more daunting, to the extent that some have questioned whether the name "Menippean satire" has any use at all as a marker of genre.[21]

[17] For an inclusive list of all potentially Menippean works and fragments from antiquity, see Kirk (1980) 3–37. Relihan (1993) limits the list of authors to Menippus, Varro, Seneca, Petronius and Lucian, as well as later writers like Julian, Martianus Capella, Fulgentius, and Ennodius.

[18] On the various interpretations of this controversial line of Quintilian, see Relihan (1984), who argues that Quintilian is grouping Varro's satires with the Ennian model instead of suggesting that Varro invented a new genre of satire. Relihan (1984) also points out that the term "Menippean satire" was not used as a marker of genre until 1581, in Justus Lipsius' *Somnium*.

[19] See, for instance, Duff's (1936) 84 traditional description: "Menippean Satire, which Quintilian regarded as an older type than Lucilian, has been touched upon in connection with Menippus of Gadara, after whom this blend of various meters with prose has been named. It had three exponents in the Roman classical period: first, M. Terentius Varro . . . secondly, Seneca, the philosopher, in his skit on the recently deceased Emperor Claudius; and, thirdly, Petronius, Nero's master of ceremonies, who wrote in his *Satyricon* the first picaresque novel."

[20] As Relihan (1993) 50–51 notes regarding Varro's *Menippeans*, "It is inconceivable that all of the *Menippeans* would formally belong to the same genre . . . Menippean satire likes to appropriate various genres of literature as grist for its mill." See also Weinbrot (2005) 4: "[Menippean satire] often attaches itself to other kinds of works within other dominant genres, and peers in as occasion requires. It is perhaps less a clearly defined genre than a set of variable but compatible devices whose traits support an authorial theme."

[21] Cf. Relihan (1993) 3: "Outside of classical circles Menippean satire has become a critical term used to discuss a vast genre of world literature, comprising practically the full range of seriocomic and learned fiction, and denotes, in very general terms, an unsettling or subversive combination

Most scholars of Menippean satire, however, find something useful about the term and are drawn to attempts at definition and classification, despite what Kirk (1980) calls the "inherent circularity of such a procedure" since "the members and the class would define each other" (x). As Rimell (2005) notes, "one of the most convincing arguments for genre is simply that it is a useful critical tool that facilitates debate on the relation between literary texts" (166). While there is much diversity in modern definitions of the genre, there is also interesting common ground that I think justifies the endeavor to look for resemblances among works that either declare themselves Menippean or have led readers to think that they are. For instance, since Cicero, it has been recognized that Menippean satire involves both humor and philosophy,[22] and one of the most consistent elements of modern definitions of Menippean satire is the presence of parody of philosophy, or of prevalent orthodoxies or of those who profess to be knowledgeable.[23] In general, it seems that what Dryden said about Lucian's satires could be said about most representatives of the genre: "his business . . . was rather to pull down every thing, than to set up any thing."[24] This destructive, rather than constructive, tendency of Menippean satire makes sense for a genre with deep roots in Cynicism, a philosophy that never developed a formal school or doctrines but whose motto was to "deface the currency,"

---

of fantasy, learning, and philosophy. Within its categories are included, with varying degrees of persuasiveness, Erasmus and humanistic literature, Rabelais and Burton and Swift, *Tristram Shandy*, *Moby Dick*, *Alice in Wonderland*, and *Ulysses* . . . What was once novel is now a somewhat discredited commonplace; the term has been long enough in vogue that it has been expanded beyond what many would consider its reasonable bounds, and its usefulness has justly been questioned" (see also 221 n. 3).

[22] Cf. Cicero's rendition of Varro describing his Menippean satires (*Ac.* 1.8): "And yet in those old works of ours, which we interspersed with a certain humor, in imitation (not translation) of Menippus, there are many things mixed in from profound philosophy and many things said dialectically" (*et tamen in illis veteribus nostris quae Menippum imitati, non interpretati, quadam hilaritate conspersimus, multa admixta ex intima philosophia, multa dicta dialectice*).

[23] E.g. Frye (1957) 309: "A constant theme in the tradition is the ridicule of the *philosophus gloriosus*"; Bakhtin (1984) 114: "The most important characteristic of the menippea as a genre is the fact that its bold and unrestrained use of the fantastic and adventure is internally motivated, justified by and devoted to a purely ideational and philosophical end: the creation of *extraordinary situations* for the provoking and testing of a philosophical idea, a discourse, a *truth*, embodied in the image of a wise man, the seeker of this truth"; Relihan (1993) 10: "But I urge that the genre is primarily a parody of philosophical thought and forms of writing, a parody of the habits of civilized discourse in general, and that it ultimately turns into the parody of the author who has dared to write in such an orthodox way"; Weinbrot (2005) 6: "Menippean satire, then, is a form that uses at least two other genres, languages, cultures, or changes of voice to oppose a dangerous, false, or specious and threatening orthodoxy."

[24] Dryden, *Life of Lucian*. The quotation is from vol. 11.420 of the 1844 edition of *The Works of John Dryden*, ed. J. Mitford (New York: Harper & Brothers).

or to subvert tradition and convention.[25] It is also a philosophy intimately connected with the literary modes of satire and parody and known for its innovative creation of new types of satirical genres.[26]

IRONY IN XENOPHON, VARRO, AND VIRGIL

To return, then, to Xenophon, Varro, and Virgil: I would argue that this tradition of destructive, not constructive, satire, which gives voice to traditional beliefs or professional dogma only to subvert them through techniques of irony and parody,[27] informs the *Oeconomicus*, the *De Re Rustica*, and the *Georgics*, even if they do not fulfill all the formal features of the genre as it has been variously defined over the centuries.[28] While no one has labeled the *Oeconomicus* or *Georgics* "Menippean" before, and only superficial aspects of Menippean satire have been granted the *De Re Rustica*,[29] several of the fundamental characteristics that I believe connect

[25] Diogenes' mission to "deface the currency" (παραχάραττειν τὸ νόμισμα) is connected by Diogenes Laertius to a literal act of defacing coinage (D.L. 6.20–21), which led to the philosopher's exile, though most give it a symbolic sense. E.g. Bosman (2006) 101: "Cynicism attempts to redefine the relationship between human nature and human behaviour, which naturally leads to conflict with generally accepted norms. This is the meaning of the programmatic Cynic slogan, παραχάραττειν τὸ νόμισμα (D.L. 6.20; 56; 71): 'reminting the coinage', the 'transvaluation of values'." See also Dudley (1937) 22, Branham (1996), and Prince (2006) 89–90.

[26] Cf. Branham and Goulet-Cazé (1996) 2: "Menippean satire is probably the most familiar Cynic genre, but in antiquity Cynics were known for innovating forms of parody, satire, dialogue, diatribe, and aphorism"; Branham (1996) 93: "The Cynic motto – 'Deface the Current Coin' (*parakharattein to nomisma*) – makes joking, parody, and satire not merely a useful rhetorical tool, but an indispensable one, constitutive of Cynic ideology as such. Humor is the chisel stamp of Cynic discourse." See also Bosman (2006).

[27] While there is certainly much overlap between parody and satire, particularly in "their common use of irony as a rhetorical strategy" (Hutcheon [1985]/[2000] 52), Rose's (1993) 81 distinction is useful: "One major factor which distinguishes the parody from satire is . . . the parody's use of the preformed material of its 'target' as a constituent part of its own structure. Satire, on the other hand, need not be restricted to the imitation, distortion, or quotation of other literary texts or preformed artistic materials."

[28] This destructive, satiric spirit characterizes Mandeville, as well. Cf. Jack (1975) 37: "Mandeville was not concerned with advancing a substantive moral view when he advanced his paradox, 'private vices, public benefits'; rather he was concerned with exposing the inconsistency and hypocrisy of those who in his own society did try to retain an ascetic and utilitarian ethic simultaneously." Cf. also Jack (1987) 151–52 and Adolph (1975) 162: "He should be regarded as a kind of compulsive debunker of received opinion rather than as a satirist in the great tradition . . . Mandeville has the sociologist's instinct to reveal 'what really goes on' under the surface rather than the outrage emanating from a moral center which characterizes most satire."

[29] E.g. Hirzel (1895) 1.560–62, Heisterhagen (1952) 63–105, Green (1997) 429, Flach (1997) 42, Rösch-Binde (1998) 345 and Diederich (2007) 199–203. Of these, Heisterhagen gives the most detailed analysis of Menippean elements in the *De Re Rustica* and focuses on its use of parody, word-play and moral critique, though his interpretation of Varro's Menippean spirit is very different from the one I discuss further below and presents Varro as a traditional Roman moralist, not a subversive and self-parodic satirist.

these works to the genre have been noticed by other readers. Thus, I will briefly lay out the schools of interpretation of each author, with particular attention to interpretations which grant their works a high degree of irony, before suggesting why I think it is useful to bring all three works in conjunction with each other and Menippean satire.

Xenophon's current readers can be divided into three different camps: those who believe Xenophon is *not* capable of irony or philosophy, those who find him a capable philosopher and literary stylist but not an ironist, and those who see his works as deeply philosophical, literary, and laden with complex irony. Until fairly recently, the first group was ascendant, despite the high regard in which previous centuries held Xenophon.[30] Vlastos' low opinion of Xenophon is often cited as representative of this group, though there are many others who would join him in reviling Xenophon's philosophical talent.[31] In the last quarter century, however, there has been, as Tuplin notes (2004b), "not only a renaissance but a metamorphosis" in Xenophontic scholarship, both because of the increased scholarly activity on Xenophon and because of the change in attitude towards him by a series of scholars who have "conceded that [Xenophon] should be taken seriously as a distinctive voice on the history, society and thought-world of the later classical (and pre-hellenistic) era."[32] Within this group of scholars who take Xenophon seriously, there are still fierce debates over how to read Xenophon, with most of the disagreements centering on the nature and extent of Xenophon's use of irony.[33]

---

[30] On earlier centuries' esteem of Xenophon, see Bartlett (1996) 3, Howland (2000) 875–76, and Nadon (2001) 3. It is also interesting to note that it is only modern scholars who have seen Xenophon as more of a historian than a philosopher. See Pomeroy (1994) 21–22: "Greek and Roman authors did not question Xenophon's affiliation with Socrates, nor did they hesitate to call him a philosopher. In fact, they classified him more often among philosophers than among historians." See also Gray (1998) 4–5 and Long (1996b) 7: "In fact Plato, or what we call Plato's Socratic dialogues, appears to have been widely regarded [in antiquity] as neither a more nor a less authentic witness to Socrates than Xenophon's writings." In addition, Xenophon's rhetorical skills were highly regarded. See Bartlett (1996) 3 and Pomeroy (1994) 22 for the ancient references.

[31] E.g. Vlastos (1991) 99: "One could hardly imagine a man who in taste, temperament, and critical equipment (or lack of it) would differ as much as did Xenophon from leading members of the inner Socratic circle. The most important difference, of course, is that people like Plato, Aristippus, Antisthenes, Euclid, Phaedo were philosophers with aggressively original doctrines of their own, one of them a very great philosopher, while Xenophon, versatile and innovative litterateur, creator of whole new literary genres, does not seem versed nearly as well as they in philosophy or as talented in this area." For discussion and rebuttal of Vlastos' Xenophon, see Morrison (1987). For further examples of negative judgment about Xenophon's philosophical abilities, see Gray (1998) 1–6.

[32] Both quotations are from Tuplin (2004b) 13. See also Tuplin (2004b) 13 n. 1 for a list of the many books and commentaries published on Xenophon in the last few decades.

[33] Cf. Tuplin (1996) 1629: "A (perhaps *the*) central question, which divides modern readers into two camps, is how far style and content are really *faux-naif* and informed by humour and irony."

The "ironic" approach to reading Xenophon is strongly associated with the polarizing figure of Leo Strauss. Strauss was the first scholar to read Xenophon's Socratic works as containing the sort of complex and pervasive irony more often associated with Plato's Socrates, and his approach to Xenophon has been influential. The first major study of Xenophon to openly acknowledge its Straussian influence and focus extensively on Xenophon's use of irony is Higgins' 1977 book *Xenophon the Athenian*. While it garnered mixed reviews upon its initial publication, it has recently been credited with an important role in the course of Xenophontic scholarship in the decades since its publication.[34] Indeed, its ironic approach is now less revisionist and nearly mainstream, despite the vigorous debates still being waged about Xenophontic irony.[35] Along with this greater popularity of the ironic Xenophon has come perhaps a greater reticence about the influence of Strauss because of the negative baggage that comes with his name, especially among non-political scientists.[36] Indeed, the term "Straussian" is frequently used to dismiss ironic interpretations of Xenophon or Plato without having to grapple with them or even to define what is meant by the term Straussian.[37] As Smith (2006) points out in his recent book on Strauss, there are many misconceptions about what Straussianism is, ranging from the belief that it is "some kind of sinister cult replete with secret rites of initiation" to a "political movement, often allied with 'neo-conservatism'" (2). Smith makes a strong case for the notion that Strauss' "works do not endorse any political program or party, whether of the Left or of the Right, Democratic or Republican. He was a philosopher," and that "Strauss was fundamentally a skeptic for whom the ends of politics and philosophy were inherently irreconcilable." He further suggests that

---

[34] Cf. Tuplin (2004b) 13 n. 1: "Several participants in the 1999 conference quite rightly drew special attention to the great importance of Higgins 1977 in the development of Xenophontic scholarship."

[35] In addition to Higgins (1977), examples of works on Xenophon that might be called "Straussian" in their reading of his irony are Tuplin (1993), Pangle (1994), Stevens (1994), Bartlett (1996), Too (1998), Howland (2000), Nadon (2001), Ambler (2001), Too (2001) and Johnson (2003). For a recent debate on the extent of Xenophon's irony, see Gray (2004) and D. M. Johnson (2004).

[36] Nadon (2001) 2 n. 7 notes regarding Tuplin (1993) that despite his "Straussian" approach to reading Xenophon, "Not a single work by Strauss appears in Tuplin's otherwise extensive bibliography. His explanation of Xenophon's reticence [i.e. fear of persecution] might well account for his own."

[37] For instance, Pomeroy's (1996) negative review of Bartlett (1996) consists almost entirely of the revelation that the essays are written in "Straussian style" by scholars whose primary affiliation is "with Political Science, not Classics," and who cite Leo Strauss throughout the volume. Cf. also Griswold (2002a) xvi n. 6: "I would further recommend that the use of the term 'Straussian' be suspended from Platonic studies, on the grounds that it has come to function primarily as a distracting polemical label and that its meaning is almost always vague conceptually." For a fair-minded assessment of Strauss' Plato and of the strangely virulent reactions to it among scholars, see Ferrari (1997).

"Straussianism is characterized above all by what its practitioners often call the art of 'careful reading'."[38] Nevertheless, there are trends in Strauss' "careful reading" that might give a more specific meaning to Straussianism, such as his belief that philosophical texts can have both an exoteric and an esoteric meaning, the latter of which is revealed only to select readers, who are attentive to irony and capable of "reading between the lines."[39] This belief underlies his controversial interpretations of Plato and Xenophon, and while his specific analyses of these authors tend to be marginalized in both classical and philosophical circles, his general approach to finding subtext and irony in these Socratic works and to reading them as works of literature has taken hold with many ancient philosophers and classicists – and not just with political scientists already in the "cult."[40]

My own approach to Xenophon is "Straussian" in the sense that I believe his writings are often deeply ironic, with an underlying meaning that can only be teased out by carefully studying the contradictions within the text. I prefer, however, to see the "esoteric" aspects of his texts as motivated not by fear of persecution or a sense of social responsibility,[41] but by the

---

[38] All three quotations are from S. B. Smith (2006) 12, 13 and 6 respectively. Cf. also G. B. Smith's (1997) similar conclusions: "Strauss was not a political partisan. When one looks at his large and complicated corpus, one primarily sees a great number of novel thought experiments undertaken in the service of resurrecting the *possibility* of political philosophy" (187); "Beyond a shared hermeneutic commitment to taking texts seriously as they present themselves, or in putting forward the ongoing need for political philosophy, there is no such thing as Straussianism" (187–88).

[39] See, for example, Strauss (1952) 25: "Persecution, then, gives rise to a peculiar technique of writing, and therewith to a peculiar type of literature, in which the truth about all crucial things is presented exclusively between the lines. That literature is addressed, not to all readers, but to trustworthy and intelligent readers only."

[40] Platonic studies are roughly divided between those who read Plato's dialogues as literary works whose meaning is never identified with a "straight" interpretation of any of the voices in his dialogues, and those who take Socrates at his word and (usually) as representing Plato's views. For a statement of the differences between the "literary" or "dramatic" and "doctrinal," "analytic," or "dogmatic" readings of Plato, and for further subdivisions of scholars within each approach, see Press (1993) vii–ix, (1996), and (1997). For an attempt to forge a "third way" in Platonic studies, i.e. "an interpretation that, unlike the sceptical one, grants positive content to Plato's philosophy, and that, unlike the 'doctrinal' one, is able to show some necessary connection between this philosophy and the dialogue form," see Gonzalez (1995) (quotation from p. 13). Gonzalez's attempt to find middle ground between the two approaches seems to be a trend. Cf. Griswold (2002a) x: "The emerging consensus in Platonic scholarship should help motivate us to drop the tired contrast between 'literary' and 'philosophical' approaches to Plato, insofar as these terms are used to describe supposedly self-standing approaches that could represent genuine alternative interpretive stances" and Press (1996) 514 "In short, the state of the question about Plato has changed. The question is no longer *whether* to take literary and dramatic aspects into consideration, but *how*."

[41] Cf. S. B. Smith's (2006) 7 summary of Strauss' explanations for esoteric writing: "Strauss's discovery – actually, he called it a 'rediscovery' – of esoteric writing can be attributed to a number of causes, from the simple desire to avoid persecution for unpopular or heterodox opinions, to a sense of 'social responsibility' to uphold the dominant values of one's society, to the wish to tantalize potential readers with the promise of buried treasure."

Socratic desire to actively engage his listeners/readers in untangling the contradictions of the dialogue as part of the learning process and quest for knowledge. On this interpretation, the use of irony, satire, and parody in his works is meant not to exclude a group of readers from the "true" meaning of the text so much as to force all readers to figure out for themselves what is wrong with the various professions of knowledge in the dialogues. Thus, I see a serious, protreptic purpose to Xenophon's satires, and this purpose ultimately distinguishes them from the later genre of Menippean satire, which satirizes not just those who profess to have knowledge, but the philosophical quest itself.[42]

Varro and Xenophon have suffered a similar fate among modern readers: despite that fact that each was revered in antiquity as a great intellect, they have been less appreciated in recent times. Indeed, Varro is usually regarded today as a pedantic and uninspired scholar.[43] While the study of Xenophon is finally undergoing a renaissance, it is unlikely that Varronian studies will be similarly transformed for the simple fact that their texts have *not* suffered a similar fate: whereas all of Xenophon's works have been preserved, only one complete work of Varro has survived intact, namely the *De Re Rustica*, and this work has been relatively neglected, even in Varronian studies.[44]

---

[42] In this interpretation of the relationship between Socratic dialogue and later Menippean satire, I am close to Relihan (1993) 185, though he uses only Plato and not Xenophon as an example: "Menippean satire gradually turns from the parody of philosophers to the parody of philosophy, and in this we can see the history of the genre as one of the increasing influence of Plato . . . as Plato becomes through the ages the quintessential philosopher his works are increasingly subjected to Menippean scrutiny."

[43] See Norden [1898]/(1983) I.194, Laughton (1956) 39, and Tarver (1997) 161. As Stull (2002) notes, neglect of Varro is particularly strong in English-speaking countries. For the ancient appreciation of Varro, see Cardauns (2001) 82–84. While the ancients revered Varro's intellect, they are as critical of his style as the moderns. On this ancient critique, see Heurgon (1950) 57, Laughton (1960) 1, Skydsgaard (1968) 89–100, Flach (1996) 36–37, Green (1997) 427 n.1 and Diederich (2007) 172.

[44] In addition to the *De Re Rustica*, several books of the *De Lingua Latina* survive (5, 6 and parts of 7–10 out of 25 total), and 600 fragments from the *Menippean Satires*. Augustine gives polemical testimony about Varro's religious and philosophical works, and Cicero provides some further evidence, but neither is an unbiased or reliable source for reconstructing anything but the most basic information. See Jocelyn (1982) 205, who argues for caution in interpreting Varro's *Antiquitates Rerum Divinarum* through the lens of Augustine. On the catalog of Varro's works, see Cardauns (2001) 85–87, who lists further bibliography. Ritschl [1866]/(1978) III.485–88 estimates that Varro wrote a total of 74 works and 620 books. On the neglect of the *De Re Rustica*, even in Varronian studies, see Skydsgaard (1968) 7, White (1973) 463–65, Salvatore (1978) 12 n. 7 and Brandenburg (2006). Recent years have seen full commentaries appear in French and German on the *De Re Rustica* (see Heurgon [1978], Guiraud [1985] and [1997], Flach [1996], [1997], and [2002]), but only a partial commentary exists in English (Tilly [1973]). With the exception of Skydsgaard (1968), there have been no monographs dedicated entirely to the *De Re Rustica*, though substantial chapters on this work appear in Martin (1971), White (1973), Salvatore (1978), and Diederich (2007). In addition, several recent dissertations have focused on the *De Re Rustica*, including B. Reay (1998) *Cultivating Romans: Republican Agricultural Writing and the Invention of the Agricola* (Stanford University), J. McAlhany (2003) *Language, Truth*

Readers of Varro tend to take him very much at his word and over-arching "schools" of Varronian interpretation have not developed.[45] Indeed, most have interpreted the work simply as an urbane version of Cato's *De Agri Cultura*, with perhaps more of a focus on the ideological underpinnings of farming in elite Roman society.[46] Many have recognized Varro's use of humor and wit in the *De Re Rustica*, but not the sort of complex irony or subversive satire and parody that have been associated with the genres of Menippean satire and Socratic dialogue.[47]

Indeed, even interpretations of Varro's *Menippean Satires* tend to insist that Varro plays the part here not of a subversive and ironic Menippean figure but of an old-fashioned Roman moralist, familiar from interpretations of verse satire.[48] An exception is provided by Relihan, who argues that Varro's *Menippeans* are very much in the Greek tradition of subversive and

---

      and Illogic in the Writings of Varro (Columbia University) and G. Nelsestuen (2008) *Varro the Agronomist: Political Philosophy, Satire, and Agriculture in the De Re Rustica* (University of Texas at Austin). I became aware of the latter two dissertations after completing my manuscript and was pleased to see many similarities in our approaches to the *De Re Rustica*. Perhaps I spoke too soon in denying the likelihood of a renaissance in the modern study of Varro, and particularly of the *De Re Rustica*.

[45] On taking Varro too much at his word, see Tatum (1992) 190: "Still, a few authors have earned our unconscious credence, it would seem, merely by dint of their artlessness; we simply do not respect them enough to doubt them. A case in point: Varro's *De Re Rustica*, a remarkable ensemble of three dialogues, a highly literary work, yet one whose obvious inadequacies have distracted readers from its attempts at literariness and consequently have led them to take its veracity for granted."

[46] E.g. Miles (1980) 37: "Varro's treatise may be regarded as an effort to answer that question [i.e. "what is a villa?"] and thus, more generally, to arrive at a definition of what should be the proper relation of country and city, retired and public life"; Conte (1994) 219: "Thus, not intended (except superficially) for the practical instruction of the steward, but written rather to foster and gratify the ideology of the rich landowner, the *De Re Rustica* in a way estheticizes the farmer's life." Green (1997) reads the *De Re Rustica* as "a commentary (or even a satire, in its widest and most Menippean sense) on the social and political state of Rome . . . with farming as a Xenophontic, or Cincinnatan, metaphor for wise government" (431). She comes closest to my approach in her allegorical reading of book 3 (and, indeed, her article initially inspired my rereading of Varro), but overall she still sees Varro as a traditional Roman moralist, for whom "Rome . . . never could be separated from the farmers who were its true founders, or from the land, its true foundation" (447). I will engage closely with her interpretation in part II.

[47] On Varro's use of humor and wit, see Hirzel (1895) 1.556, Wedeck (1929) 12, Heurgon (1950) 58, Laughton (1978), Traglia (1985) 93–96, Linderski (1989) 114, Flach (1996) 41, Cardauns (2001) 25–29 and Diederich (2007) 197–203. As noted previously, some scholars have attributed superficial or formal Menippean features to the *De Re Rustica*, such as the use of word-play and "speaking names," though only Green has tentatively been willing to call it a satire (see quotation in previous note).

[48] See Relihan's (1993) 52–53 summary of the common assumptions made about Varro based on his *Menippeans*: "He is a true Roman satirist, and champions the cause of the old, patriotic, religious, rustic Roman life over the decadence, indulgence, and impiety of modern sensual Rome; his theme is the contrast of then and now, *tunc* and *nunc*." See also Relihan 236 n. 21 for a bibliography of "modern critics looking in Varro for the social criticism common in verse satire." Lehmann (1997) 263–98, Cardauns (2001) 40–49, and Weinbrot (2005) 29–39 should be added to the list of those who read Menippean Varro as a moralist who is operating in a tradition very different from the subversive, Greek version of Menippean satire.

ironic Menippean satire and, if anything, represent a *parody* of the moralizing present in Roman verse satire.[49] For Relihan, "Varro puts his own encyclopedic knowledge to self-parodic use in his *Menippeans*, frequently abusing the ideas that we know he held elsewhere, and depicting himself as a ridiculous reformer to whom no one pays any attention" (49). While ultimately, the *Menippeans* are too fragmentary to settle the debate on their interpretation, the *De Re Rustica* is fully intact and, I hope to show, has a satiric spirit like that of Varro's *Menippeans* as described by Relihan.[50] Even more than the *Oeconomicus*, the *De Re Rustica* is destructive of conventional politics, morality, and learning, and there is no Socratic figure in it to represent an alternative search for truth and meaning.[51]

Unlike Xenophon and Varro, it cannot be said that Virgil has been ignored by modern scholarship or his literary abilities underestimated; indeed, Dryden has called the *Georgics* "the best poem by the best poet,"[52] and many after him would agree. Despite the *Georgics'* popularity, however, there is no consensus about how the poem should be read, and it has been deemed "one of the most fundamentally intractable works of ancient literature."[53] Criticism in the past few decades has been particularly polarized by debates about its essential optimism or pessimism, and, more recently, by debates about this debate, with some arguing for more nuanced terms, others for an end to the debate altogether.[54] These debates

[49] Relihan (1993) 49–74. It is important to note that recent studies of Roman verse satire have emphasized the ironic and self-parodic aspects of its moralizing, as well. For example, Freudenburg (1993) 17–18 supports Relihan's depiction of Varro as a *parodist* of serious dogmatic moralists, instead of one himself, and he presents Horace as a similar sort of self-parodying satirist. Griffin (1994) 1–34 also sees similarities between the "complex ironies" and "dialogical parody" of Menippean satire and formal verse satire.

[50] In fact, I would even go further than Relihan and suggest that Varro, instead of "abusing the ideas that we know he held elsewhere" ([1993] 49) in his *Menippeans*, has a satiric mentality in many of his works usually classified as serious, as I will discuss further in chapter 3. In addition, Varro seems to have mixed philosophy and satire in dialogues called the *Logistorici*, known only by fragments and titles, and in certain dialogues written in the manner of the philosopher Heraclides, which are known only from a few mentions in Cicero's letters (*Att.* 15.13.3, 16.11.3 and 16.12). See Tilly (1973) 11 and Gottschalk (1980) 361. See also Diogenes Laertius' characterization of some of Heraclides' dialogues as being in the style of comedy (D.L. 5.88). While these two groups of dialogues remain mysterious, and perhaps even refer to the same work (on this controversy, see, most recently, Rösch-Binde [1998] 543–61 and Cardauns [2001] 72; their notes have further bibliography), they may in fact be similar to the philosophical satire I am claiming the *De Re Rustica* to be.

[51] Read in this manner, the *De Re Rustica* could be said to represent a later stage in Relihan's construction of the development of Menippean satire as discussed above, when the genre had moved fully beyond the Socratic quest for Truth and towards the satiric dismantling of that very concept.

[52] Dryden's quotation is from a dedicatory letter attached to his translation of the *Georgics*.

[53] Batstone (1997) 125. On the poem's difficulty, see also Thomas (1988) 1.16 and Nappa (2005) 2.

[54] For recent discussions of the general approaches to reading Virgil and, particularly, the *Georgics*, see Thomas (1990), Batstone (1997), Morgan (1999) esp. 1–14, Gale (2000) esp. 1–17, Thomas (2001a) esp. 1–24, and Nappa (2005) esp. 1–22.

are fueled by the dialogic and polyphonic nature of Virgil's text, which Batstone suggests is inspired by the dialogue format of Varro's *De Re Rustica*.[55] While, technically, the narrator of Virgil's didactic poem is the sole speaker of the poem, this speaker puts forth such schizophrenic attitudes, emotions, and ideologies in the course of the work that it is indeed easier to interpret them as belonging to many different personae instead of just one. Some of these voices evoke a view of the world that might reasonably be labeled "optimistic" and "pro-Augustan," despite the oft-noted shortcomings of these terms, while others express deep sadness or ambivalence about the human situation in the universe.

The question every reader of the *Georgics* has to grapple with, then, is how to reconcile or resolve these voices and contradictions. Purely "optimistic" readings tend to give little weight to the bleaker voices in the text, or find positive things to do with them, and discount the notion that voices which praise Augustus or express patriotic or optimistic views of life might be undermined or subverted in the course of the poem.[56] In contrast, "pessimistic" readings present a poem full of ambiguity, irony, and contradictions, and one whose optimistic visions are ultimately shown to be illusions.[57] With few exceptions, the definite critical trend in the past two decades has been towards readings that give serious weight to all the voices in the poem and which therefore might be labeled "ambivalent," though the line between "ambivalent" and "pessimistic" readings is often tenuous.[58] There is also much diversity within the "ambivalent" interpretations. Indeed, the two most recent examples of this approach have quite different positions on what the reader should do with opposing voices

---

[55] Batstone (1997) 134: "It is my suggestion that Virgil, beginning in some sense with the addressees, contexts and complex ambiguities of Hesiod, took the multiple perspectives of Varro's conversants as a model for his own multivalent voice in the *Georgics*."

[56] Recent "optimistic" readings include Cramer (1998), Jenkyns (1998), and Morgan (1999). Cramer (1998) takes a radical approach to the optimism/pessimism debate and cuts the Gordian knot, as it were, by athetizing many of the "pessimistic" passages. For critical discussions of this approach, see Volk (2000) and Thomas (2001b). Morgan (1999) looks at the "upside" of the pain and suffering emphasized in the *Georgics* and suggests that "Virgil's preoccupation with violent conflict has a highly optimistic import" (front summary) and that the *Georgics* demonstrates the "constructive potential of violence" (89).

[57] E.g. Ross (1987) and Thomas (1988). Cf. Ross (1987) 241: "Virgil's poem is profoundly pessimistic . . . It is, however, the pessimism of the grand vision, which, like that inherent in the tragic struggle, offers (if not a catharsis) something clarifying and supportable."

[58] One might argue that Ross (1987) and Thomas (1988) have been used somewhat as straw men in the recent debates about the *Georgics*, particularly since Thomas himself would label his reading not "pessimistic" but "ambivalent" (Thomas [1990]) and suggests that neither he nor Ross deny "that there are upbeat aspects" to the *Georgics* (Thomas [2004] 372). Recent studies that ally themselves with this "middle course" include Perkell (1989), Batstone (1997), Nelson (1998), Gale (2000), and Nappa (2005).

in the text: Gale (2000) argues for a "profoundly open text" (15) with "no strongly-marked authorial 'voice' in the *Georgics*, which might lead us to privilege one particular theological, ethical or epistemological position over another" (270–71). Nappa (2005) accepts many of Gale's premises, but resists the conclusion that the poem compels us "to surrender completely to aporia and ambiguity" (15). Instead, he argues that "the poem's chaotic vision is not a flaw but a strategy, a way of provoking the reader . . . to construct or reconstruct a view of the world and his place within it" (2) and that "the poem arouses and reflects our need to find one or more reliable meanings in the world around us. It also reflects the way the world has of thwarting us in our attempts to fix meaning" (3).

My own approach to the *Georgics* has much in common with Nappa's: like Nappa, I see the *Georgics* as a text that reflects upon the human need to create meaning, as well as the world's resistance to this need. Unlike Nappa, however, I do not see Virgil as playing the part of protreptic teacher, encouraging his readers to create these imperfect constructions of meaning, and nor do I read the work as particularly focused on teaching Octavian. Instead, I see Virgil as working very much within the tradition of destructive satire that begins with Socratic dialogue and continues through Menippean satire. The *Georgics* reveals the failures of systems of knowledge and forces the reader to grapple with and understand these failures through techniques of irony and parody. However, it also goes *beyond* these Socratic and Menippean strategies by additionally confronting the human need to constantly construct these systems of meaning. In that sense, I might label the *Georgics* a meta-Menippean satire since it enacts the techniques of that tradition while also commenting upon them and contemplating why the nihilistic attitude often associated with Menippean satire will never be a dominant one in human life.

My reading of the *Georgics* might be labeled "pessimistic" to the extent that I share with the "pessimistic" approaches the belief that the purely happy and optimistic voices of the poem are qualified as (at least partially) deluded responses to a chaotic world, but I share the resistance to this term that many others have noted.[59] I also would agree with Gale (2000) that "the darker sections of the poem (especially the plague in book 3) are just as exaggerated in their detail as the 'praises' of book 2" (216 n. 58). That is, I do not associate Virgil's own "voice" with any of the individual voices in the text, happy or sad, and instead find meaning in how the voices

---

[59] E.g. Nappa (2005) 17: "The darkness of the Vergilian worldview is only pessimistic if Vergil himself thought a brighter, easier universe was in some way possible or at least plausible."

interact with and undercut each other. I differ from Gale in my conclusion that these interactions suggest the equal *invalidity* of the world views they express instead of their equal validity.

Bakhtin has usefully analyzed different types of polyphony and created the term "passive double-voiced discourse" to describe parodic texts in which there is one main voice that is in control and discredits the other voices in the text.[60] I would argue that Xenophon's text, in which the strong figure of Socrates guides the dialogue, is of this "passive double-voiced" variety, but Varro's and, especially, Virgil's texts are more complicated. Morson's (1989) discussion of metaparody is useful for thinking about Virgil's polyphony:

> The audience of a parody – that is, the readers who identify a text as a parody – knows for sure with which voice they are expected to agree. We may now consider a class of texts that are designed so that readers do *not* know. In texts of this type, each voice may be taken to be parodic of the other; readers are invited to entertain each of the resulting contradictory interpretations in potentially endless succession. In this sense, such texts remain fundamentally open, and if readers should choose either interpretation as definitive, they are likely to discover that this choice has been anticipated and is itself the target of parody . . . We shall refer to texts that are designed to exploit this dialogue between parody and counterparody (or, as we shall see, between genre and anti-genre) as *metaparodies* . . . Generally speaking, metaparodies anticipate readers of varying degrees of sophistication and appreciation of ambiguity, and are constructed to sort out, and so to define implicitly a typology of, their own readers. (81–82)

I would suggest that the *Georgics* is similar to a metaparody; it engages already parodic texts, anticipates all of their conclusions, and goes beyond them.[61] I also agree with Morson that such a text anticipates vastly different interpretations of its meaning, a fact that well explains the interpretive

---

[60] See Bakhtin (1981) 364 and (1984) 189. Morson and Emerson (1990) 150 give a clear explanation of the kinds of double-voiced discourse: "Double-voiced discourse can be either passive or active. In the passive variety, the author or speaker is in control. He uses the other's discourse for his own purposes, and if he allows it to be heard and sensed, that is because his purposes require it to be. In short, the 'passivity' giving this class of double-voiced words its name belongs to the 'word of the other,' which remains a passive tool in the author's (or speaker's) hands. By contrast, in active double-voiced words, the word of the other does not submit so easily. It actively resists the author's purposes and disputes his intentions, thereby reshaping the meaning and stylistic profile of the utterance."

[61] It should be understood that there is no sense in which a parody need aim at humor. Cf. Morson (1989) 69: "[P]arody is not always comic. Parody recontextualizes its object so as to make it serve tasks contrary to its original tasks, but this functional shift need not be in the direction of humor. As negation can be on an indefinitely large number of grounds, parody can, in principle, adopt an indefinitely large number of tones." Cf. also Nightingale (1995) 7–8 and Edmunds (2001) 141–42.

history of the *Georgics*.[62] Thus, I do not fundamentally disagree with those who read a more "open" *Georgics*, one in which the voices of the text all have weight and participate in a true dialogue with each other, instead of simply undercutting and undermining themselves, and I do believe that the text is preprogrammed for readers to come up with drastically different responses to it. My response is just one of the many that are possible and that are anticipated by the text.

My general approach, then, to reading Xenophon, Varro, and Virgil as authors capable of complex and subversive irony is not without parallel, though certainly the dominant trend in each field has been to resist such readings, whether because the author is deemed incapable of irony (Xenophon, Varro) or so adept at portraying multiple points of views that the reader cannot be meant to discount some in favor of others (Virgil). Indeed, irony and the related concept of ambiguity are frequently emotional topics in literary debates. As Booth puts it, "The critic who asks us to ironize our straight readings may seem to be corrupting a beloved object and repudiating our very souls"; he notes, too, that "every reader will have greatest difficulty detecting irony that mocks his own beliefs or characteristics."[63] To suggest that a text means something other than what it seems to say, which is the basic rhetorical move of irony, opens up all sorts of interpretive problems,[64] and most modern theorists of irony accept

---

[62] Cf. Batstone (1997) 125: "I would like to argue that the diversity of compelling interpretations is part of the *Georgics*' larger value and meaning." Morson (1989) uses the example of *Don Quixote* and the *Amadis of Gaul*, one of the objects of *Don Quixote*'s parody, to show how a parodic text can lead to vastly different interpretations over the ages: "It is also possible for a parodied text to survive and function primarily as the object of a parody that was itself designed or discovered to be meaningful in other ways: for example, *Amadis of Gaul*, the life of which has been prolonged by *Don Quixote*. When this happens, an ironic consequence may be that the parody helps in the revival of its object at a time when readers react against the parodist's point of view and identify the target as their forerunner: for example, the romantic revival of medieval literature, a process that often involved 'amadizing' the *Quixote* itself" (67–68). Thomas (2001c) documents a similar phenomenon in connection with the reception of the *Georgics* and *Aeneid*: "The post-Virgilian georgic vernacular tradition has tended to engage only the surface of Virgil, and worse, only the received surface, the myth of idealized European pastoral and the pietistic surface of the *Aeneid*, filtered too often through the brilliant rewriting of Dante." (131–32).

[63] Booth (1974) 44 and 81, respectively. See also Thomas (2000) 382: "The identification of ambiguity has always evoked anger, particularly from those who see themselves as guardians of language and of the meaning that language conveys, and particularly in the areas of philosophy and rhetoric, as we saw above." Thomas' article has further bibliography on debates among classicists about ambiguity and irony, particularly as relates to the study of Virgil. On the "risky business" of irony and the discomfort it can cause, see also Hutcheon (1995) 9–36.

[64] At the same time, reading ironically has been called the essence of literary criticism. See Colebrook (2004) 5: "This process of ironic re-reading, where we dare to imagine a text as somehow meaning something other than what it explicitly says, characterises much of what counts as literary criticism. Indeed, one could argue – as many twentieth-century critics were to do – that literature is characterised by its potential for irony, its capacity to mean something other than a common-sense or everyday use of language."

the inherent difficulty of deciding when irony is or is not present in a text, especially in a text whose original context is far removed from our own.[65] While there are some critics, such as Wayne Booth, who are optimistic about the possibility of pinning down the presence of irony and the meaning of ironic texts, most are less so, and even Booth recognizes a type of irony which is "unstable" and ultimately difficult to interpret in any secure fashion.[66]

Thus, there is frequently no consensus on whether a work is ironic or not, and, as Colebrook (2004) notes, "even the most 'obvious' ironies bear the possibility of not being read, and they do so precisely *because* of the contextual nature of irony" (12). Ironic readings of works that are not universally agreed to be ironic will always be controversial, and they also raise the question of why authors bother to be ironic if they risk being misunderstood. There are many answers to the question "why irony?," ranging from practical ones, like a fear of censorship or persecution, to more philosophical or aesthetic ones, like the educational value of untangling irony or the pleasure of wit, and all of these answers are relevant to my analyses.[67] Still there is something inherently counterintuitive and discomforting about irony that will always bother some readers, as well as an inevitable whiff of

---

[65] Cf. Dentith's (2000) 39 related point on the difficulty of detecting parody whose context is far removed from our own: "One of the features of parody is that it depends for its effect upon recognition of the parodied original . . . The greater the historical distance which divides us from parodic literature, the harder it becomes to reconstruct with any confidence the discursive dispositions, or even the specific targets, from which parody emerges and towards which it is aimed."

[66] Cf. Booth (1974) 240: "At last we cross that formidable chasm that I have so long anticipated – the fundamental distinction between stable ironies and ironies in which the truth asserted or implied is that no stable reconstruction can be made out of the ruins revealed through the irony. The author – insofar as we can discover him, and he is often very remote indeed – refuses to declare himself, however subtly, *for* any stable proposition, even the opposite of whatever proposition his irony vigorously denies." Cf. also Colebrook (2004) 44: "For philosophers like Searle and literary critics like Booth and Muecke, all of whom were wary of the tendency for modern 'theory' to overemphasise linguistic instability, irony is evidence of the fundamental coherence of language and literature. By contrast, for philosophers more interested in literature and negativity like Sören Kierkegaard (1813–55) and Nehamas and twentieth century literary critics with an interest in the postmodern like Candace Lang and Linda Hutcheon, irony tends towards the multiplication of viewpoints and incoherence." Griffin (1994) 67 would categorize most of the irony used in literary satires as unstable: "[T]hough we assume an author in control of the irony, we cannot reconstruct that author's precise meaning with any confidence. In some cases we have reason to think that even satirists cannot contain the irony they have let loose."

[67] On the fear of persecution, see Strauss (1952). Cf. also Griffin (1994) 139: "If open challenge to orthodoxy is freely permitted, then writers will take the most direct route and debate the ideas and characters of political leaders openly in newspapers, protected by guarantees of free speech . . . But if open challenge is not permitted, writers will turn to irony, indirection, innuendo, allegory, fable – to the fictions of satire." On the educational motivation of Platonic irony, in particular, see Griswold (2002b). On the aesthetic value placed on subtle irony, see Hutcheon [1985]/(2000) 54 and (1995) 151–52.

elitism, since ironic texts have a tendency to sort out readers into different categories: "as most theories put it, there are those who 'get' it and those who do not."[68]

I approach my own ironic readings of Xenophon, Varro, and Virgil duly cautioned by these warnings about the shaky interpretive ground associated with trying to prove a text is ironic and accepting of the fact that not all readers will be convinced. I also present my reading of their works as only one possible way of making sense of the many voices in their texts – and not the only way. Booth (1974) wisely cautions that "[o]ur pride is more engaged in being right about irony than about many matters that might seem more important" (44), and at times my commitment to my own interpretation may seem to belie the more judicious statements I am making now; yet, that sort of emotional commitment to an ironic reading is also part of the power of irony. Reading ironically gives the reader a sense of unlocking secrets and discovering a truer, more important meaning – even if the reader understands and accepts that she may be completely "wrong." My risk of being completely "wrong" goes up further when I own up to the fact that my analyses imply some sort of authorial intention behind the ironies of the text. Indeed, when discussing the modes of irony, satire, and parody, it is difficult to get away from positing some sort of authorial intent, even if one admits that ultimately it is the reader's construction.[69]

My methods of detecting irony in the texts of Xenophon, Varro, and Virgil, are similar to those developed by theorists of ironic speech, such as Booth. In fact, Hutcheon notes that after a wide ranging investigation into the variously cited markers of irony, she realizes "there is, in fact, a limited number of examples of signals which are repeated often enough in most Western cultures that they get discussed in the abundant commentary on the subject." She lists the "five generally agreed-upon categories of signals

---

[68] Hutcheon (1995) 54 (see Hutcheon's full discussion on 53–56). On irony's potential elitism, see also Colebrook (2004) 19–20.

[69] For a recent defense of the concept of authorial intention in interpretation of literature, see Nappa (2005) 4–6. See also Farrell (1991) 21–23, Hinds (1998) 47–51, Gale (2000) 4–6 and Heath (2002) 59–97. For a critique of intentionalism, see Edmunds (2001) esp. 19–38 and 164–69. On the necessity of postulating some sort of authorial intention in the interpretation of irony, see Hutcheon [1985]/(2000) 52–53: "There is little disagreement among critics that the interpretation of irony does involve going beyond the text itself (the text as semantic or syntactic entity) to decoding the ironic intent of the encoding agent." Similarly, on parody: "Yet, when we call something a parody, we posit some encoding intent to cast a critical and differentiating eye on the artistic past, an intent that we, as readers, then *infer* from the text's (covert or overt) inscription of it" (Hutcheon [1985]/[2000] 84). See also Hutcheon (1995) 116–40, Booth (1974) 11–12, 120–34, and Dutton (1987) 200–01.

that function structurally" as "1) various changes of register; 2) exaggeration / understatement; 3) contradiction / incongruity; 4) literalization / simplification 5) repetition / echoic mention."[70] Booth also lists five main categories of "clues" to irony, which Hutcheon conveniently summarizes as: "1) straightforward hints or warnings presented in the authorial voice (titles, epigraphs, direct statements); 2) violations of shared knowledge (deliberate errors of fact, judgment); 3) contradictions within the work ('internal cancellations'); 4) clashes of style; 5) conflicts of belief (between our own and that which we might suspect the author of holding)."[71] I will make use of all of these "clues" in the course of my analyses, but I also acknowledge that there are always other ways of explaining these potential "markers of irony," and for this reason, detecting irony will always be more of an art than a science, despite the very "scientific" style of these lists.[72]

ALLEGORY IN XENOPHON, VARRO, AND VIRGIL

Allegory shares many features with irony:[73] both involve hidden or deeper meanings and might be defined as "saying one thing and meaning another,"[74] and both are difficult to detect with certainty.[75] While the Greek and Roman rhetorical handbooks treat allegory as an easily definable type of literary ornamentation, recent discussions of allegory make

---

[70] Hutcheon (1995) 156 (all quotations).

[71] Hutcheon (1995) 151. Booth's (1974) original discussion is on 53–86. Strauss discusses his "markers" for "reading between the lines" in Strauss (1952) 30. For a discussion of the markers of Socratic irony, see Hyland (1995) 105–06. The discussion of Socratic irony is a field unto itself, and a controversial one. See, most recently, the contributions of Vlastos (1991), Gordon (1996), Nehamas (1998), Vasiliou (1999), (2002), Griswold (2002b), and Edmunds (2004).

[72] O'Hara (2005), in a discussion of the importance of interpreting inconsistencies in Roman epic instead of simply explaining them away through emendation or the like, cites as a humorous caution against absolute certainty in such matters the work of Herschel Parker, who "presents some pretty funny examples of elaborate theories worked out to interpret inconsistencies in Twain, Melville, Crane, Fitzgerald, and others, where he can prove, using diaries and other documents, that the inconsistencies were introduced by lazy revisions, poor or puritanical editing, or even typesetting errors" (21). Still, O'Hara comes down firmly on the side of first considering whether inconsistencies "are being used with some skill to make certain suggestions" (24) before dismissing them as inconsequential mistakes.

[73] Innes (2003) 20 notes that irony is a standard subdivision of allegory in ancient rhetorical treatises.

[74] Indeed, an early Greek term for allegory was ὑπόνοια ("hidden thought," "underlying meaning") (e.g. Pl. *R.* 2.378d and X. *Smp.* 3.6). On ancient terms for and definitions of allegory, see Rollinson (1981) 3–28 and 111–15, Whitman (1987) 263–68, and Boys-Stones (2003b) 2–3. Allegory is defined both as an extended metaphor (e.g. Cic. *Orat.* 84, *de Orat.* 3.166 and Quint. *Inst.* 8.6.44) and as saying one thing but meaning another (e.g. Trypho *Trop.* 3.193.8–12 Spengel).

[75] Cf. Laird (2003) 153: "Examples of allegory are like Macavity the Mystery Cat: it is very hard to tell whether or not they were really there." See also Whitman (1987) 1–13 on the problems of interpreting allegory. He calls allegory the "preeminently oblique way of writing" (267).

it clear that ancient writers had a far more nuanced and sophisticated understanding of the concept than the handbooks suggest.[76] Certainly, the type of allegory that I read in the texts of Xenophon, Varro, and Virgil is *not* a simple literary trick that is clearly signaled in the text but is subtle, complex, and open to vastly different interpretations.

My basic approach to reading each work allegorically, with farming as an extended metaphor for various political and ethical approaches to life, is not without precedent, though it is only recently that this approach has been suggested for Varro.[77] For Xenophon and particularly Virgil, however, there is a tradition of reading these works as being about more than farming in the literal sense. Farming in the *Oeconomicus* belongs to the broader category of *oikonomia*, or household management, which has explicit connections in Greek thought to the art of political rule.[78] In addition, Greek economic literature in general might be classified as a branch of practical ethics rather than as a technical, economic science.[79] Thus, while some readers interpret Xenophon as writing nothing more than a technical treatise on household management,[80] many are comfortable attributing some sort of metaphorical layer to the economic and agricultural subject matter, particularly readers who interpret Xenophon as a serious Socratic philosopher.[81]

[76] In particular, the contributions to Boys-Stones (2003a) provide thoughtful testimony to the many complex ways in which ancient writers (and readers) utilized allegory.

[77] As noted previously, Green (1997) reads the *De Re Rustica* as a commentary "on the social and political state of Rome . . . with farming as a Xenophontic, or Cincinnatan, metaphor for wise government" (431).

[78] For analogies between household management and political rule, see X. *Oec.* 13–14, *Mem.* 3.4.12, 4.2.11; Pl. *Plt.* 258e–259d; *Prt.* 318e–319a; Ps.-Arist. *Oec.* 1.1343a, 2.1345b–1346a (Aristotle rejects such comparisons in *Pol.* 1.1252a). On the use of *oikonomia* in this broader sense, see Pomeroy (1984) 98, Descat (1988) 106–09, Kanelopoulos (1993), Faraguna (1994) 554–55, Johnstone (1994) 231–32, Natali (1995) 98, Tsouna McKirahan (1996) 701–02, and Nagle (2006). The related comparison between shepherding animals and ruling men is frequent, as well, in both Socratic (e.g. X. *Mem.* 3.2.1; Pl. *R.* 343a–345e, *Plt.* 275a–277c) and non-Socratic literature (cf. Homer's epithet ποιμὴν λαῶν "shepherd of the people"). It is also the analogy used in Xenophon's *Cyropaedia* for Cyrus' rule (*Cyr.* 1.1.1–3, 8.14.2). On the metaphor of the "shepherd of the people" in Greek epic and philosophy, see Haubold (2000) 14–46. On the herdsman in Plato, see Gutzwiller (1991) 66–79.

[79] On the genre of ancient economic literature, see Vegetti (1970), Descat (1988), Faraguna (1994), Natali (1995), and Figueira (forthcoming) (with their notes for further bibliography). Prose works on *oikonomia* form a continuum with wisdom literature like the *Works and Days*, and Too (2001) 69 even calls the *Oeconomicus* "in some sense a fourth-century Athenian 'works and days'."

[80] E.g. Marchant and Todd (1923) xxiv: "The thoughts and reflections, whether put into the mouth of Socrates or Ischomachus, are so entirely Xenophon's own that we may wonder why he did not frankly produce a treatise on the management of an estate instead of a Socratic dialogue."

[81] E.g. Stevens (1994) 235–36: "Socrates is using the topic of estate management to teach Critoboulus about friendship. . . . [T]he *Oeconomicus* is a Socratic dialogue, not a treatise expressing Xenophon's views on farming."

Readers of the *Georgics*, from its earliest documented reception to today, have swung to different extremes in how literally or symbolically they have interpreted the topic of farming.[82] While the dominant trend in the past few decades has been to interpret the agricultural subject matter as only the ostensible subject of the poem, some critics have called for a middle ground between the two approaches, one which ties together the "surface" and "deeper" meaning of the text by emphasizing the symbolic meanings of farming that already existed in Roman culture before Virgil made his farm a "laboratory for life."[83] Indeed, farming is intimately connected in Roman culture with the ethical and political world – both because of the moral connotations of farming and because of the traditional stories about early Roman heroes snatched from the farm to accomplish great military or political achievements.[84]

---

[82] For bibliography and summary of how farming has been interpreted in the *Georgics*, see Spurr (1986) 164–65, Nelson (1998) xi, 172–73 (n. 5 and n. 6), Volk (2002) 120–21, and Doody (2007) 180–83. Christmann (1982), Spurr (1986), and Doody (2007) emphasize that Virgil was considered an agricultural authority in the early reception of his work, especially by Pliny and Columella, and that agriculture in a literal sense was a real concern of Virgil. Not all early readers of Virgil thought his purpose was truly agricultural, however, and Seneca states that Virgil "wished not to teach farmers but to delight readers" (*nec agricolas docere voluit, sed legentes delectare*, *Ep.* 86.15). Seneca's basic approach has been influential on modern readers of the *Georgics*, and Burck (1929) began a trend of interpreting the *Georgics* as a unified poem, whose purpose is not really to teach farmers to farm. What the poem is "really" about is still debated, though the most recent readers have been influenced by the approaches of Parry (1972) and Putnam (1979), for whom the *Georgics* is "ultimately about the life of man in this world" (Parry [1972] 36) or "a grand trope for life itself" (Putnam [1979] 15).

[83] The phrase "laboratory for life" is found in Nappa (2005) 6. Spurr (1986) 182 argues that "'surface' and 'depth' must work (and be considered) together, if the poem is to succeed as a unified whole." Cf. also Ross (1987) 13–14: "The *Georgics* is a poem about life more thoroughly and intensely than any other I know, and is so precisely because it is not simply a metaphor or a trope for life . . . It was not Virgil's idea that agriculture could stand for, or be about, the forces of life, because for many centuries agriculture was the study of nature." Nelson (1998) exemplifies this "middle ground" approach to reading the subject matter of the *Georgics*. See also Gale (2000) x: "It is also misleading, I think, to describe Virgil's agricultural subject-matter as a metaphor or trope. Clearly, it makes no sense to treat the poem as a practical handbook; yet the poet seems to me to be no less (and no more) serious about his theme than Hesiod or Lucretius . . . For the Roman reader, the farmer embodied a very particular set of ideals: honest and unstinting toil, old-fashioned piety, the toughness and natural justice which made Rome great. Naturally, then, these themes too are central to Virgil's poem."

[84] As Cato writes in the preface to the *De Agri Cultura*: "But from farmers both the bravest men and the strongest soldiers are born" (*at ex agricolis et viri fortissimi et milites strenuissimi gignuntur*, pr. 4). Cicero's writings emphasize the central role that agriculture played in the development of the Roman state, in both a literal and figurative sense. In *Rep.* 2.5, he uses the metaphor of sowing in his description of Romulus' "planting" of the *res publica* and also emphasizes Romulus' agricultural upbringing (*Rep.* 2.4). In his *De Senectute*, Cicero's Cato runs through the traditional stories about early Roman farmer-heroes such as Manius Curius and Quinctius Cincinnatus (*Sen.* 16.55–56) and says, "At that time senators were in the fields" (*in agris erant tum senatores*, 16.56). On the moral connotations of farming, see also the initial section of this introduction.

My allegorical readings of Xenophon, Varro, and Virgil fit in with approaches which interpret farming (or household management) in a symbolic manner but which also draw on the symbolism that these activities already possessed in Greek and Roman culture. The main difference between my approach and most previous ones, then, is that I see the agricultural allegories present in these works as embodying *negative* ethical and political behavior, and not as the models of wise and virtuous activity they are traditionally set up to be. As mentioned at the beginning of the introduction, I interpret Xenophon, Varro, and Virgil as capturing the spirit of Mandeville's subversive beehive, which turns this traditional image of wise government on its head.

MORALITY AND ETHICS

To return briefly, then, to Mandeville's hive, I would like to examine further some of its ethical implications before comparing the ethical implications of the agricultural allegories in Xenophon, Varro, and Virgil. Allen (2004) suggests that it is not Mandeville's "mere inversion of the trope that inspires the hyperbolic reactions of Mandeville's contemporaries. It is his use of the inversion to undercut an age-old method of using nature to support constructions of moral and political authority" (78). She sees him as critiquing two different contemporary moral theories, each of which "inclined to naturalizing fallacies" (79) – that is, they derived moral values from natural facts: "on the one hand, the 'rigorist' argument that human beings, as rational creatures, should use reason in order to conquer their appetites and thereby achieve virtue in accordance with their rational natures; and on the other, the 'Shaftesburian' argument that human beings are virtuous by nature" (79–80). In contrast to both, Mandeville's hive revealed that this image of apparent virtue was in fact an amoral social structure guided by greed and other self-interested passions. Indeed, according to Mandeville, all of the supposed moral virtues which involve some sort of self-denial or concern for others are equally based upon self-interest, and moralists who believe otherwise are deluded and hypocritical.[85]

As suggested previously, Mandeville is not necessarily praising greed and the successful political and economic structures it creates so much as pointing out the hypocrisy of those who *do* appreciate the benefits of

---

[85] Cf. *The Fable of the Bees* 1:42 [28]: "[I]t is not likely that any Body could have persuaded them [human beings] to disapprove of their natural Inclinations, or prefer the good of others to their own, if at the same time he had not shew'd them an Equivalent to be enjoy'd as a Reward for the Violence, which by so doing they of necessity must commit upon themselves."

successful cities while at the same time decrying greed as the greatest of evils. On a philosophical level, this hypocrisy takes the form of advocating moral systems that unknowingly commit naturalistic fallacies and derive their virtues from the same sort of self-interested and materialistic desires that motivate greed. These sorts of hypocrisies seem to characterize well many of Mandeville's critics, and it is easy to see why his satire was so inflammatory. As Hundert (1994) notes, the Augustan moralists were fiercely opposed to "vices" like greed and luxury, and "[f]or the Augustans, the primary language of political opposition engaged a vocabulary that opposed virtue to corruption, the dignity of landed to mobile property, and public service to self-interest" (9). In addition, they found inspiration in the moral climate of Republican Rome and Lycurgan Sparta and, in particular, accepted Sallust's analysis that greed destroyed the Roman Republic.[86]

While there were many differences between the moral and political climates of Mandeville's England and the Greece and Rome of Xenophon, Varro, and Virgil, there were also some interesting similarities that provide further possible connections between these writers' political and moral allegories. In the Athens of Xenophon and the Roman Republic of Varro and Virgil, luxury and greed were also treated as chief vices; they were associated with materialistic and carnal pleasures and blamed for political unrest and moral decline.[87] In contrast to greed and narrow self-interest, classical Athens and Republican Rome both valued the virtues of frugality, self-control, and service to the state.[88] Indeed, Hundert's (1994) formulation

---

[86] Cf. Hundert (1994) 9: "They [the Grand Jurors] attacked Mandeville in the context of an intense and comprehensive critique of modernity, undertaken in the name of an ideal of virtue practiced in antique Mediterranean republics, particularly republican Rome and the quasi-mythical Sparta framed by Lycurgus' laws." See also Horne (1978) x: "In the early eighteenth century John Trenchard and Thomas Gordon carried on the tradition in their *Cato's Letters*, written in 1720–23, which held before their readers the glory of the Roman republic that 'conquered by its virtue more than its arms . . .' and the fall of that republic because of magnificence, luxury, and pride, which corrupted the manners of the people."

[87] On greed in classical Athens, see Balot (2001). He notes at the outset of his study: "Greed is central to ancient Athenian history, ideology, and political thought. It motivated political action and occupied the attention of contemporary analysts of civic conflict and imperialism" (1). He briefly touches upon greed in Roman culture and notes that "Roman political thinkers and historians embedded greed deeply within their analyses of social unrest, individual competition, and the wide framework of characteristically Roman desires to get more prestige and power" (16). For a more in-depth discussion of greed in Roman culture, see Edwards (1993), who treats greed in conjunction with other prodigal pleasures such as sexual immorality and luxury. She notes, "All the vices discussed here can be seen as manifestations of what Roman moralists sometimes termed *incontinentia*, 'self-indulgence', 'lack of self-control' (though they by no means exhaust this category)" (5). For examples of Roman attributions of political and moral decline to rampant greed and luxury, see Sal. *Cat.* 10, Liv. pr. 10–12 and Grat. 312–25.

[88] On the importance of serving the state in classical Athens, see most recently Christ (2006), which details all the ways in which "bad citizens" failed to do so. See also Seager (2001) 385: "The most

of Augustan morality, which "opposed virtue to corruption, the dignity of landed to mobile property, and public service to self-interest" (9), could well apply to classical Athens and Republican Rome, as well.[89] Accordingly, the citizen-farmers of Xenophon's, Varro's, and Virgil's text should represent ideal moral figures; instead, I argue that these authors used the iconic farmer, as well as the iconic beehive, to explore inconsistencies and tensions in the moral values of their cultures.

Indeed, modern scholars have noticed many tensions in the moral values of classical Greece and Republican Rome. For instance, Christ (2006), in discussing the way in which classical Athens "sought to harness individual self-interest for the common good" (9), suggests "there is something inherently risky in the city promoting good citizenship on the basis of mutual self-interest: to the extent that citizens viewed their relationship with the city in these pragmatic terms, this might lead some, through selfish calculation, to acts of bad rather than good citizenship" (32). Balot (2001) emphasizes a related tension between the Greeks' "agonistic 'virtues' of competition, the individual striving for more, and the promotion of the self as opposed to, and even at the expense of, the common good" and their need to "devise sophisticated mechanisms of social control whereby the communally sanctioned striving for more would also be sufficiently limited to permit the community as such to flourish" (12–13).[90] A similar tension in Roman values is emphasized by Long (1995), who focuses on the problematic function of glory in Roman ideology:

The glory a Roman noble could achieve, however *honestum* its sphere of action might be, was supremely *utile* to his competitive life-style. An ideology of this kind is radically unstable, and that for two reasons. First, it conflates what is socially desirable and therefore deserving of honour with what is personally advantageous. Secondly, it is always at risk of sliding from praiseworthy to praise conferred, and from honourable to honour given. Or, to put it another way, the ideology is always at risk of deriving ethical worth from material status, and of using the glory and wealth that accrue to the powerful as absolute standards of their actual merit. (216–27)

---

basic demand made by the city on the individual citizen is that he should at all times manifest his solidarity with the interests, preoccupations, and aspirations of the civic community as a whole" (his full discussion is on 385–91). On the fundamental connections between Roman *virtus* and military and political service to the state, see Earl (1967) and Myles (2006).

[89] On the distrust of "mobile property" and commercial enterprises in classical Athens, see Dover (1974) 173–74 and Balot (2001) 36–44. The classic statement of the aristocratic Roman belief in the superiority of land-based wealth is made in the prologue of Cato's *De Agri Cultura*, on which, see most recently Reay (2005).

[90] As Balot (2001) 13 notes, this tension was first extensively formulated and studied by Adkins (1960).

What all of these examples of tensions in Greek and Roman morality have in common are the difficulties that arise from reconciling competing interests when moral values are based not on intrinsic and firmly fixed notions of right and wrong, good and evil, but on socially constructed categories of actions and behavior that are praised or blamed according to how they help the group overall. Such categories are often inconsistent and unstable since the very same type of behavior that can help the group can also help destroy it. These moral difficulties are by no means unique to Greek and Roman culture, and some moral skeptics would argue that there are no such things as "objective" right and wrong anyway;[91] yet, many scholars have noted an especial tendency for traditional Greek and Roman morality to be guided more by external, communally determined standards of behavior, than by intrinsic concepts of right and wrong.[92] Further, many have questioned whether these traditional moralities have anything to do with "morality" at all, if morality implies the concepts of moral duty and absolute standards of right and wrong.[93] While the moral language of

---

[91] E.g. Mackie (1977).

[92] See Adkins (1960), Habinek (1998) 45–59, Roller (2001) 22 (further bibliography in n. 10) and Myles (2006) esp. 110–13 (further bibliography in 111 n. 21). Of course, this view can be taken too far: Cairns (1993) has rightly challenged the traditional notion that Greece was purely a "shame-culture" and questions whether such a thing can even exist: "All societies, surely, rely on both external and internal sanctions; to rely on the former alone would, in fact, imply that the society possessed no norms of culturally approved behaviour at all, for it would imply that both the initiators and the recipients of external sanctions saw no intrinsic value in any standard of behaviour whatever . . . I know of no convincing proof that such an unusual, unsocial society exists" (40).

[93] Williams' (1985) distinction between "ethics" and "morality" has been influential (on 6–14). He reserves the terms "moral" or "morality" for a narrower subset of ethics that is usually associated with Kant, and focuses on moral obligation or duty (see 174–96). Myles (2006) 110–13 makes a similar distinction between ethics and morality but reverses the terms and uses "moral" to indicate behavior that is right according to prevailing social standards and "ethical" to indicate behavior that is judged against absolute standards of right and wrong. Many modern philosophers would also not grant ancient philosophical ethics the status of true moral theory. Cf. White (2002) 62: "One often hears the historical claim that morality – whether the notion, or the institution, or both – was unknown to the Greeks and was discovered or created in the modern era, and that this fact marks a crucial difference between the two periods. It is also claimed that the modern sense of the term 'morality' is different from any ancient meaning of any term." Cf. also Williams (2006) 44 on Greek ethics: "[T]his system of ideas basically lacks the concept of *morality* altogether, in the sense of a class of reasons or demands which are vitally different from other kinds of reason or demand." Even so, Williams, is a proponent of Greek-style "virtue ethics," which he prefers to modern moral theories focused on obligation, and suggests that "the basic ethical ideas possessed by the Greeks were different from ours, and also in better condition" (Williams [1993] 4). He is also skeptical of "progressivist" views of Greek ethics which suggest that Greek ethics was somehow more primitive than modern moral systems and believes there is actually less difference than we think between ancient Greek morality and our own (Williams [1993] 1–20 and *passim*). Annas (1992) is supportive of the notion that ancient morality (and not just ancient "ethics") exists and also believes that modern philosophers have exaggerated the differences between ancient and modern moral theories. White (2002) provides further support for the view that paradigms which sharply differentiate ancient ethical theory from modern are distorted.

classical Athens might have pretensions to objectivity and stability,[94] both ancient and modern writers have noted the very fragmented state of the moral values it references, whether as a result of the imperfect mingling of Homeric and polis-centered value systems, the rationalist critique of religion and conventional morality, or the trauma of civil war.[95] Similar comments have been made about the state of moral language and values in Late Republican Rome, which was also a time of great political and cultural upheaval.[96]

Both classical Athens and Republican Rome had figures that fought against these moral dislocations and sought to re-anchor moral values in a rational fashion to secure notions of right and wrong, as well as figures that pushed in the opposite direction and emptied morality of any meaning that was not grounded in material self-interest.[97] These various attempts to explore the foundations of morality also form an important background to the ethical questions raised in the works of Xenophon, Varro, and Virgil. In particular, Socrates is often associated with the beginning of ethical philosophy and the attempt to ground Greek morality *not* in notions of material or physical success, but in notions of absolute goodness and virtue, which can only be approached through a life of philosophical investigation.[98] As

---

[94] Mackie (1977) 48 makes a persuasive case that ordinary moral language always includes this pretension: "Indeed, ordinary moral judgements involve a claim to objectivity which both non-cognitive and naturalist analyses fail to capture. Moral scepticism must, therefore, take the form of an error theory, admitting that a belief in objective values is built into ordinary moral thought and language, but holding that this ingrained belief is false." In my own discussions of moral and ethical issues, I will try to reserve the words "moral" and "morality" for the more narrow type of ethical thought that attributes objective reality and inherent value to moral concepts and does not (knowingly) reduce moral values to natural values (such as pleasure or survival), but I also tend towards the moral skepticism of Mackie. In addition, I recognize the difficulty of delimiting the concept of morality in any precise way, especially when such a range of meanings is attributed to it in philosophical and popular literature. Cf. White (2002) 62–64 on the "slippery term 'morality'."

[95] On the conflict between Homeric values and classical Athenian values, see Adkins (1960) and MacIntyre (1984) 131–45. On the sophists' rationalist critique of traditional morality and religion, see most recently de Romilly (1992), Bryant (1996) 168–200, Woodruff (1999), and Decleva Caizzi (1999). Thucydides provides one of the more explicit ancient testaments to the damaging effect of the Peloponnesian war on the stability of moral values (e.g. 2.53, 3.82–83).

[96] See Minyard (1985) and Wallace-Hadrill (1997). Like Thucydides, Sallust provides explicit testimony of the changing meaning of moral words (e.g. *Cat.* 52.11).

[97] In classical Greece, these opposing approaches to morality are perhaps best exemplified by the debates between Socrates and the sophists in Plato's dialogues; in Republican Rome, by Cicero's critique of the Epicureans, who derive moral virtues from *voluptas* (cf. Cicero's quotation of Epicurus in *Tusc.* 3.41–42 and also Cicero's critique of this material basis for morality in *Off.* 3.118).

[98] Cf. Bryant (1996) 191–92: "What, then, is the true nature of man? In providing his answer to this most fundamental of questions, Sokrates was to initiate a momentous transvaluation in the history of ethical discourse: for rather than locate the keys to human nature in our material or somatic dimensions, Sokrates chose to stress the primacy and uniqueness of the human *psychē*. . . . [T]he proper activity of the *psychē* is of necessity moral." It is not just modern scholars who view Socrates

scholars have noted, Socrates uses the same moral vocabulary as traditional Greek ethics, but he undermines traditional morality by revealing through elenchus the essentially non-moral foundation of conventional virtue.[99] Socrates' entire lifestyle epitomizes his revaluation of Greek virtue since he invests his conventionally shameful lifestyle, that of an ugly, impoverished philosopher, who pursues the contemplative life, with the language of virtue and presents himself as a true political figure, who helps his fellow men by way of philosophical dialogue.[100]

The Socrates I have just described is usually associated with Plato's rather than Xenophon's version of the philosopher, the latter of which is

as a "watershed" figure in ancient ethics, but ancient ones, as well. As Cicero famously notes in *Tusc.* 5.4.10: "On the other hand, Socrates was the first to call down philosophy from the sky and place it in the cities; he even introduced it into the home and compelled it to investigate life and morals, and good and bad things" (*Socrates autem primus philosophiam devocavit e caelo et in urbibus collocavit et in domus etiam introduxit et coëgit de vita et moribus rebusque bonis et malis quaerere*). For other ancient estimations of Socrates' pivotal role in the history of ethics, see Guthrie (1971) 97–105 and Vander Waerdt (1994b) 48–49. The exact nature of Socratic virtue and its connection to happiness is debated by scholars, who disagree about whether Socrates believed virtue to be instrumental to happiness, necessary and sufficient for happiness but only a component of it, or identical with happiness. See Brickhouse and Smith (2000) 123–55 for a good summary of the different positions scholars have taken on this question, as well as the relevant Socratic passages, to which could be added Annas (1999) and Reshotko (2006). I tend towards the identity thesis, though all of the versions can accommodate the revolutionary importance that Socrates accords moral virtue, and I also find it likely that Socrates would not care to formulate his view of virtue in such specific, theoretical terms. Even Irwin (1995), a proponent of the instrumental theory, suggests as much: "Still, it remains possible that Socrates does not see that he must choose between an instrumental and a non-instrumental account of the relation between virtue and happiness . . ." (77).

99 Cf. Bryant (1996) 191: "Sokrates acknowledges that a desire for personal well-being is a basic fact of human existence. But as to the true nature of *eudaimonia*, that is an altogether different matter, as Sokrates proceeds to demonstrate in a series of Platonic dialogues that pointedly assail both traditionalist and intellectualist misconceptions. Wealth, power, somatic pleasures, and all the other conventional 'goods' are shown to be insufficient to bring about happiness." See also Adkins (1960) 220–315 on Plato's transformation of ordinary Greek ethical vocabulary.

100 Nehamas (1998) and Edmunds (2004) emphasize the irony of Socrates' entire way of living, and not just of his rhetoric. Nehamas (1998) 68–69 calls it "[A] life of *aretē* that did not meet the conditions necessary for being such a life." Cf. also Adkins (1960) 259: "Nothing could be more *aischron* than Socrates' life and death; and yet this was the unpromising subject whom Plato, in the closing words of the *Phaedo*, chose to term 'the most *agathos*, *phronimos*, and *dikaios* of all the men of his time whom we have known.'" On Socrates as a true politician, see Pl. *Grg.* 521d–e. In many ways, the *Gorgias* is a good companion to the *Oeconomicus* in its use of the confrontation between the active and contemplative lives, borrowed from Euripides' *Antiope*, to structure the debate between Callicles and Socrates. Socrates dissolves the dichotomy between the active and contemplative life by taking on the Euripidean Amphion's defense of the contemplative life, while at the same time claiming to be the only true politician in Athens because he aims at "what is best, not at what is most pleasant" (πρὸς τὸ βέλτιστον, οὐ πρὸς τὸ ἥδιστον, *Grg.* 521d). On the use of the *Antiope* in the *Gorgias*, see Carter (1986) 163–79, Slings (1991), Arieti (1991) 79–93, and Nightingale (1992), (1995) 60–92.

said to present Socrates as a thoroughly conventional moralist.[101] Indeed, this perceived discrepancy between their two versions is at least partially responsible for the ongoing "Socratic problem" of disentangling the historical Socrates from the writers who memorialize him, though frequently scholars simply solve that part of the problem by discounting Xenophon's version as the less faithful of the two due to Xenophon's inability to comprehend philosophy.[102] While I make no claim to be discovering the "real" Socrates when I reference the Socrates of Xenophon or Plato, I do hope to show that there are ways of reading Xenophon's Socrates such that the differences between his and Plato's version are lessened.[103] In particular, I hope to convince that Xenophon's Socrates in the *Oeconomicus*, far from promoting the conventional Athenian virtues of the gentleman-farmer Ischomachus, instead deconstructs the traditional notion of *kalokagathia* ("nobleness, goodness") associated with Ischomachus' ethics and is as fully "anti-economic" as Plato's Socrates.[104] In the course of the dialogue, in

---

[101] E.g. Brickhouse and Smith (2000) 43: "Xenophon's 'Socrates' tends to accept uncritically conventional Athenian moral values and to preach to his friends about the importance of embracing those values. Raising questions about the relationship between morality and the good life or about what moral virtue consists in seems, for the most part, foreign to the man Xenophon commends to us." For a more even-handed assessment of the differences between Xenophon's and Plato's Socrates, see Dorion (2006), though Dorion still does not consider Xenophon's Socratic writings "especially critical or speculative" (94). Of course, there are many inconsistencies within Plato's depictions of Socrates, and not just between his and Xenophon's. Cf. Vlastos' (1991) division of Plato's dialogues into "early" (or "Socratic") Plato and "middle" Plato: "I have been speaking of *a* 'Socrates' in Plato. There are two of them. In different segments of Plato's corpus two philosophers bear that name. The individual remains the same. But in different sets of dialogues he pursues philosophies so different that they could not have been depicted as cohabiting the same brain throughout unless it had been the brain of a schizophrenic . . . Those two groups of dialogues fall arguably into the earlier and middle periods of Plato's literary production" (45–46). On the history of this paradigm, which dates to the nineteenth century, see Taylor (2002). For arguments against the chronological dating of the Platonic dialogues based on philosophical style or stylometric studies, see Howland (1991), Annas (1999) 9–30, Annas (2002), and Griswold (2002c), as well as the bibliography collected in Press (2000) 3 n. 13.

[102] E.g. Russell (1945) 83 (on Xenophon): "A stupid man's report of what a clever man says is never accurate, because he unconsciously translates what he hears into something he can understand." See also Vlastos (1991) 81–106. This was not always the view of Xenophon's testimony: Vander Waerdt (1994a) 9 n. 28 notes, "The present dismissive attitude toward Xenophon's testimony seems to have won out around the beginning of the present century." For further defense of Xenophon's testimony, see Morrison (1987) and Dorion (2006).

[103] Thus, I disagree with Dorion's (2006) claim that "there is no hope of harmonizing their [Xenophon's Socrates and Plato's Socrates] doctrines. Those who claim otherwise are contenting themselves with surface agreements that conceal deeper disagreements" (95).

[104] On Plato's "anti-economic" Socrates, see Vegetti (1970) 594–96 and Faraguna (1994) 558. The first attestation of the word *oikonomia* comes in Plato's *Apology* (36b), and it is in the context of a list of the things that Socrates, unlike most people, does *not* care about. For the belief that Xenophon's Socrates differs from Plato's in his appreciation of wealth and prosperity, see, most recently, Dorion (2006) 98–99.

which Ischomachus instructs how he runs his household like a beehive, Socrates reveals that Athenian ideology (and Persian and Spartan)[105] is essentially based on physical and material notions of success; in addition, he prods his young companion Critobulus towards a life focused on obtaining true moral virtue. While Socrates leaves the exact nature of moral virtue vague, it does seem to be intimately connected with the philosophical quest and to be of a different essential substance than the "natural" qualities that are moralized to form the foundation of traditional Athenian ethics.

As suggested previously, Xenophon's philosophical satire has a serious protreptic purpose, and its "destructive" tendencies ultimately lead towards a constructive impulse and a search for moral virtue. Thus, it differs from the more purely destructive tendencies of Mandeville's satire. Varro, however, writes very much in the spirit of Mandeville, even if he is more subtle and evasive in his irony.[106] Varro uses his farming dialogue, with its lengthy digression on beehives, to satirize not just traditional Roman morality, obsessed with blaming society's ills on greed and luxury while at the same time deriving its core values from materialistic notions, but also the intellectual and philosophical culture of the Late Republic. One of his major interlocutors for the latter aspect of his satire is the unnamed figure of Cicero.

Cicero is responsible for importing into Rome not only an unironic reading of Xenophon's *Oeconomicus*, but also his own interpretation of the major schools of Greek philosophy.[107] While Cicero aligns himself with the skeptical tradition of Academic philosophy, the normative content of

[105] Ischomachus most obviously represents Athenian values, but many have also noted connections between his household and Persian ideology, as described by Xenophon. See Pomeroy (1984), (1994) 240–42, 275–80, Roscalla (1990) 43–52, Gray (2000) 152, and Nadon (2001) 28. In addition, scholars have drawn connections between Xenophon's visions of Sparta and Persia, particularly in the *Cyropaedia* and *Constitution of the Lacedaemonians*. See Pomeroy (1994) 251 (*ad* 4.20), Tuplin (1994), and Nadon (2001) 30 and n. 12. Indeed, I would suggest that Xenophon subtly conflates vastly different political regimes in his works in order to underline the ultimately similar (and flawed) nature of political life. Cf. Nadon's (2001) 179 interpretation of the *Cyropaedia*: "By showing the necessities that limit the attainment of justice in all regimes, Xenophon prevents us from giving ourselves wholeheartedly to any one, or to political life altogether. Such is the subtle pedagogy of the *Cyropaedia*."

[106] Indeed, because of the bluntness of Mandeville's satire, Adolph (1975) would suggest that Mandeville is paradoxical more than ironic in his style: "Irony is always indirect. For the most part Mandeville, though too much the Augustan to resort to simple invective, presents himself in the *Fable* as the opposite of indirect, as the blunt, no-nonsense, clear-sighted middle-normal satirist. Where ironists delight in first 'caressing the object they wish to demolish', his procedure is usually the opposite" (163).

[107] Unfortunately, Cicero's three-book treatment of the *Oeconomicus* is lost, but Cicero references it in *Off.* 2.87, and it also presumably influenced "Cato's" discussion of farming in Cic. *Sen.* 51–60. From this evidence, it seems that Cicero interpreted the *Oeconomicus* as straight praise of farming and a practical manual on household management. On Cicero's translation, see Alfonsi (1961–64).

his moral thought frequently sounds Stoic and participates in the moralization of the natural world that all the Hellenistic schools of philosophy encouraged.[108] Unlike a figure such as Socrates, Cicero does not seek to transform conventional Roman morality; on the contrary, Cicero's philosophizing efforts seek to give a rational foundation to conventional Roman virtues and to fully preserve the traditional value that the Romans placed on political activity.[109] Cicero also engages Varro in a strained friendship, depicted in Cicero's letters (*Fam.* 9.1–8), in which Cicero alternately seeks Varro's approval and chastises him for no longer being actively involved in politics. In one of the letters, he urges him to read and write *Republics* (*Fam.* 9.2.5); I would suggest that Varro responds with the *De Re Rustica*. He uses it not to celebrate the active life or to support the *mos maiorum*, but to reveal the inconsistencies and problems with traditional morality, politics, and intellectual culture in the Late Republic and to celebrate the "less virtuous" contemplative life.

Virgil goes a step beyond Varro: he takes as a given the self-interested passions of human beings and the materialistic foundations of morality and political life, but instead of just working in the destructive mode of satire, the *Georgics* examines the forces that lead to the beliefs and systems that Varro tore down. Virgil draws the reader into the emotional highs and lows of human life and shows an interest in the type of moral psychology that had so preoccupied Mandeville. He reveals the confusion and depression that result from the inevitable collapse of moral, religious, and political systems and shows how these same emotions lead to their rebuilding. The voices in Virgil's text participate not just in a dialogue with each other but in a dramatic narrative: the pessimistic voices, which reflect the fear of an amoral and chaotic world, are shown to generate the optimistic ones, which resist moral chaos by forcing order and meaning on the world. To put it another way, Virgil's focus is on how human beings try to cope with the absurd life that Varro depicted in his satire, and in the process, Virgil creates a more complicated psychology for humankind in the *Georgics*.

---

[108] On Cicero's philosophical allegiances, see Glucker (1988) and Powell (1995) esp. the introduction and chs. 1 and 3. On the naturalism of Hellenistic ethics, and the difference between ancient and modern naturalism, see Annas (1993) esp. 135–41. For further discussion of Aristotelian and Hellenistic appeals to nature, see Schofield and Striker (1986) esp. 113–263.

[109] Cf. Minyard (1985) 29: "[Cicero's] goal was the demonstration that not only could the *mos maiorum* accommodate Greek thought but that it could arbitrate between the competing Greek philosophical systems. His position was that the Roman categories, when properly understood, were flexible and potentially rich enough to comprehend the wider knowledge consequent upon Roman expansion into the Hellenistic world, and these categories and their concomitant values could provide a standard of truth for testing the validity of Greek assertion."

While Varro had presented people as motivated by material needs and profit, Virgil identifies a more basic impulse in human beings: the need to make sense of the world and believe there is meaning in life. Virgil's farmers, then, are characterized not just by a materialistic ethics, but by a ceaseless effort to create order in the world – both on a physical and metaphysical level.

GENRE AND INFLUENCE

My analyses of the *Oeconomicus*, the *De Re Rustica*, and the *Georgics* do not depend upon the notion that each author after Xenophon found direct inspiration in the previous one or read the previous works as I do (nor do I claim that Mandeville read these works ironically). Varro was certainly familiar with the *Oeconomicus* since he cites Xenophon in his preface and displays his influence in various passages that I will discuss later, but it is difficult to sort out whether Varro was influenced by an "ironic" *Oeconomicus*, or whether Varro read it unironically and uses it as a target of his parody. The missing link of Cicero's lost *Oeconomicus* complicates the intertextual relationship between Varro and Xenophon further.[110] The close, intertextual connection between Varro and Virgil is easier to demonstrate, and scholars have acknowledged the pervasive influence of Varro's agricultural dialogue on the *Georgics*, though this influence has been characterized primarily as technical and structural.[111] Farrell (1991) notes the heavy influence of Varro on the *Georgics*, particularly on book

---

[110] Thus, it is possible to interpret Varro's work either as correcting Cicero's interpretation of the *Oeconomicus* or as parodying both his *and* Xenophon's praise of the farming life, and I ultimately leave this an open question. Philodemus' fragmentary work Περὶ οἰκονομίας is another interesting document in the reception of Xenophon's *Oeconomicus* at Rome, and presumably Varro was familiar with it, as well. Like Cicero, Philodemus seems to have read the *Oeconomicus* unironically, but unlike Cicero, he is critical of what he perceives to be Xenophon's materialism, his inappropriate use of a philosopher like Socrates to discuss economics, Socrates' use of ambiguous language and Xenophon's presentation of an unphilosophical man like Ischomachus as a man of virtue. On Philodemus' critique of Xenophon, see Laurenti (1973) 21–53, Angeli (1990), and Tsouna (2007) 169–76. As Tsouna (2007) 166 puts it, "[I]t is difficult to see how *oikonomia* can coincide with a virtuous disposition, when the property manager gives preponderance to financial objectives above all others. This tension constitutes the main focus of Philodemus' criticisms of both Xenophon and Theophrastus." So, while Philodemus does not read deliberate irony in the text, he does perceive potential tensions and ambiguities in the text, which another reader might resolve by reading ironically.

[111] Cf. Thomas (1988) 1.11: "[T]he *Georgics* would have looked very different had Varro not published his treatise shortly before Virgil began work on his poem." See also Salvatore (1978) (see 55 nn. 1–4 for a bibliography on the subject through 1978), Leach (1981), Ross (1987) 32–33, 28–39, 235–37, Thomas (1987), Thomas (1988) *passim*, Farrell (1991) 155–57, and Baier (1997) 147–64. While there have been naysayers in the past regarding Varro's influence on Virgil (e.g. Schultz [1911] and Engelke [1912]), there is a general consensus today that the *De Re Rustica* left a deep imprint on the *Georgics*,

1 (155–57), but concludes, "in the *Georgics*, the Varronian material, to say nothing yet of the Aratean, occurs in what is manifestly an overarching contextual allusion to *Works and Days*" (156). However, he also throws down the gauntlet to those who would like to argue otherwise:

> While the importance of Vergil's Hesiodic program is (I hope) manifest, the influence of Varro, though different perhaps in kind, is hardly less great. It is ultimately pointless to argue that one of these authors preceded the other in shaping Vergil's conception of the *Georgics*. At the same time, I am trying to illuminate Vergil's use of the epic tradition; and this effort inevitably involves an implicit assumption of Hesiod's priority with respect to Varro and other prose authors as a Vergilian source. I must therefore leave the study of Varronian influence, with its attendant biases, to other scholars. (156 n. 35)

My own inclination is to read Virgil's *Georgics* as a reaction to an ironic *De Re Rustica* and not simply as a beneficiary of its technical, agricultural knowledge, though I acknowledge that this claim is ultimately impossible to prove and is not essential to my interpretation of the *Georgics*.

I am also not trying to claim that any of the authors would use the term "Menippean satire" to describe his work. Xenophon predates the introduction of the genre; Varro's *Menippeans* were presumably distinct in their formal features from his *De Re Rustica* (though we do not know much about their features); and Virgil's poem is clearly allied with the genre of didactic poetry. Yet, Xenophon's and Varro's works do share the genre of philosophical dialogue, which most scholars agree is intimately connected to Menippean satire, and Virgil's selection of the didactic genre seems a perfect "ironic" choice for incorporating elements of a genre whose core focus might be called the parody of didacticism. So, I do believe it is fair to suggest that the "spirit" of Menippean satire pervades each of their works, if this genre is defined as a type of intellectual satire that focuses on undermining philosophies and systems of knowledge, instead of as a set of formal features.

Another way to look at the genre issue is to see these works as all connected to Socratic dialogue, which, like Menippean satire, is full of irony, parody and self-parody, allegory, encomia, polyphony, and the display of faulty erudition.[112] Indeed, Weiss' (2006) recent formulation of Socrates'

---

though some would exclude *Georgics* book 1 from that influence (e.g. Bayet [1967] 200–07), or even books 1 and 2 (Baier [1997] 161–64). A few readers of Virgil have seen more than structural or technical connections between the *De Re Rustica* and the *Georgics* (e.g. Salvatore [1978] and Leach [1981]), but their interpretations of these connections differ dramatically from mine since they do not read Varro's work as satire.

[112] On Plato's use of these literary devices, see Nightingale (1995) esp. 93–132.

therapeutic goal sounds very Menippean in spirit ("his overarching aim is to eradicate the false beliefs and puncture the bloated self-image of others," 4), and the long-standing connections scholars have drawn between the two genres seem warranted.[113] Xenophon's, Varro's, and Virgil's works also share with Socratic dialogue the theme of the contrast between the active and contemplative life, as well as a reinterpretation of conventional morality.[114] However, because a strong Socratic figure is missing from the works of Varro and Virgil, I prefer to see them as Menippean in spirit as opposed to Socratic and as belonging to that part of the tradition that turned "from the parody of philosophers to the parody of philosophy" (Relihan [1993] 185).

However one characterizes the genre of each work or their relation to each other, I hope to convince that these literary works also do serious philosophy, even if their most challenging ideas are found not in the voice of any one character but in the ways in which the voices all fit together (or fail to do so). Indeed, it is one of the fundamental ironies of Socratic dialogue that the genre which so perfectly blurs the line between literature and philosophy is also associated with raising a barrier between the two disciplines, one which persists in modern universities.[115] Presumably the irony of this rhetorical move of distinguishing between literature and philosophy within a highly literary philosophical genre was not lost on Plato and should serve as an important reminder to the reader to appreciate both the form and the content of the dialogues, if not to read between the lines.[116] As the next seven chapters will try to show, Xenophon, Varro, and Virgil

---

[113] Cf. also Hyland's (1995) interpretation of the comic element of Platonic dialogue: "In one way or another, then, the central comic dimension of the dialogues revolves either around the claim to *be* wise which gets unmasked, or the foolishly optimistic belief that wisdom can be *attained* (if only we can succeed in properly defining this or that virtue), a pretense, that is, to wisdom either attained or easily attainable" (134). On the relationship between Menippean dialogue and Socratic dialogue, see discussion in the above section, "Menippean satire, ancient and modern."

[114] While these themes were embraced by Socratic writers, they are not, of course, unique to them. On the theme of "genres of life" and the contrast between the active and contemplative one in Greek and Roman literature, see Grilli (1953), Joly (1956), and Carter (1986).

[115] Cf. Nussbaum (2003) 211–12: "The modern university, in Europe and North America, sharply segments philosophy from literature . . . In Athens of the fifth century BC . . . there was no general category of 'literature'; there was no general category of 'philosophy', and thus, obviously, no understanding of philosophy as a field of inquiry or expression distinct from literature. Plato began to forge that understanding, in conflict with the poets; what he describes as a 'contest of long standing between the poets and the philosophers' is one to the forging of whose conceptual categories he contributed in a major way. But Plato himself understood his own art to involve a literary, even a mimetic, dimension."

[116] Cf. Williams (1993) 13–14: "With [Plato], moreover, we meet the special problem that he was the first to offer the categories in which we discuss these questions, the categories of 'literature' and 'philosophy'. It is hardly likely that the works in which he developed these categories should

all wrote works whose style is characterized fundamentally by competing voices that make vastly different claims about moral and political knowledge and whose dialogic form is not simply ornamental but "expressive of a view of life."[117]

themselves respect them. We should not expect this even if we could suppose him to be straightforward: if we could assume, for instance, that he did not seek to qualify or undermine the doctrines professed by authoritative speakers in the dialogue, above all by Socrates. Moreover, we do not always have reason to assume it." Nussbaum (1990) 3–53 attests to the tendency in "contemporary Anglo-American philosophy . . . either to ignore the relation between form and content altogether, or, when not ignoring it, to deny the first of our two claims [i.e. that 'style makes, itself, a statement' 7], treating style as largely decorative" (8).

[117] The quotation is from Nussbaum (1990) 6: "The first claim [i.e. that there is a connection between form and content] directs us to look for a close fit between form and content, seeing form as expressive of a view of life."

PART I

Xenophon's Oeconomicus

The *Oeconomicus* begins with a discussion between Socrates and his young friend Critobulus on the meaning of estate management (*oikonomia*) and the value of farming (chs. 1–6). Most of the work, however, is dominated by a third figure, the Athenian gentleman-farmer Ischomachus, whose reputation for being *kalos kagathos* (roughly, "noble and good") led Socrates to desire to learn from him how he runs his household and estate. The second part of the dialogue (chs. 7–21) consists of Socrates' recounting of this discussion with Ischomachus to Critobulus. Interpretations of the work turn on how the reader interprets the character of Ischomachus and unites the past discussion between Ischomachus and Socrates with the present one between Socrates and Critobulus.[1] Ischomachus, as a typical Athenian gentleman with a reputation for *kalokagathia*, represents the conventional virtues of the polis, and for many his teachings represent the ideological core of the dialogue.[2] Yet, he may also be identified with a historical Ischomachus, who eventually lost much of his wealth and whose wife was involved in a notorious scandal after his death, which involved bearing

---

[1] The bifurcated nature of the work has led some scholars to theorize that they were composed at different times. On the different compositional theories of the work, see Taragna Novo (1968) 1–8 and Pomeroy (1994) 5–8.

[2] Readers often assimilate Ischomachus' lifestyle and values with Xenophon's and see his Socrates as an empty mouthpiece for Ischomachus' ideology. For a list of those who would identify Ischomachus with Xenophon, see Stevens (1994) 210 n. 5, to which could be added Field (1967) 138, Pomeroy (1994) 259–64 (*ad* 6.17), Martin (1995) 85, and Brickhouse and Smith (2000) 39. Danzig (2003) 74–75 offers a more nuanced assessment of Xenophon's character and his similarities to Ischomachus: "Xenophon did not lead the life of an impoverished philosopher, but that of a successful soldier and commander, and later a wealthy estate-owner and writer-apologist. His own life resembled that of Ischomachus much more than that of Socrates . . . In his own writings, Xenophon represents himself as at best an imperfect follower of the great master . . . But it would certainly be wrong to conclude that they also indicate that Xenophon rejects Socrates' way of life, preferring the life of an Ischomachus. Although Xenophon did not live as Socrates, this does not mean that he did not recognize his superiority . . . If he is an Ischomachus, he is an apologetic one." On Xenophon's presentation of himself as an imperfect student of Socrates, see *Mem.* 1.3.11–13 and *An.* 3.1.4–8.

a son to her daughter's husband.[3] Whether or nor this identification is correct, I will argue that within the course of the dialogue, Socrates undermines the values that structure Ischomachus' moral and political views and shows them to be based entirely on material notions of success.[4]

On this reading, the figure of Socrates, and not Ischomachus, is the ideological core of the work and unifies both parts of the dialogue: in the opening discussion with Critobulus, he redefines the meaning of *oikonomia* to be equivalent to Socratic philosophy. In the second part of the work, he presents Critobulus with the teaching of Ischomachus so that he might understand what sort of household and state is built upon the "virtues" of conventional *oikonomia*. Through his dialectic, Socrates reveals Ischomachus to be only an apparent image of *kalokagathia*, and not the real thing. He tries to turn Critobulus away from his preoccupations with material success and pleasure and toward a life of philosophy, which is the true art of ruling, whether the state, one's household, or oneself.

---

[3] See Strauss (1970) 157–58, Davies (1971) 264–68, Harvey (1984), Stevens (1994) 212–13, 217–23, Too (2001) 72 and n. 21, and Danzig (2003) 72–73. See also Andocides, *On the Mysteries* 124–27, which describes the scandal. Pomeroy (1994) 259–64 (*ad* 6.17) examines the evidence but concludes: "[I]f Xenophon intended to undermine his entire treatise by introducing as a successful businessman an Ischomachus who later lost the bulk of his property and as Ischomachus' wife an unnamed woman who became depraved and notorious when widowed, there would have been little point in his writing the *Oeconomicus*" (263). One could argue, however, that the Socratic method of doing philosophy is based on undermining seemingly successful people and institutions and the "unmasking of impostors" (Hyland [1995] 130).

[4] Others who interpret the *Oeconomicus* as a critique of Ischomachus include Strauss (1970), Stevens (1994), Pangle (1994), Ambler (1996), Too (2001), and Danzig (2003).

CHAPTER I

*Socrates and Critobulus (*Oec. *1–6)*

Socrates presents his radical redefinition of farming and estate management in the *Oeconomicus*' opening dialogue with Critobulus (*Oec.* 1–6). He does so not by using any radically new words or terms to define it, but by expanding or contracting the meaning of ordinary nouns like "estate" or "property" and evaluative adjectives like "beneficial" or "harmful." He begins by asking Critobulus what the function of *oikonomia* is, and Critobulus' naïve answer turns out to be essentially correct: "the [function] of a good household manager is to manage his own household well" (οἰκονόμου ἀγαθοῦ εἶναι εὖ οἰκεῖν τὸν ἑαυτοῦ οἶκον, 1.2). However, Socrates redefines the meaning of each term in Critobulus' answer in typical Socratic fashion so that the *oikos* ("house") comes to mean all property that is "beneficial for one's life" (ὠφέλιμον εἰς τὸν βίον, 6.4) and for something to be beneficial, one has to know how to use it (6.4). Thus, before becoming a good *oikonomos* ("household manager"), one first must figure out what is truly good and beneficial in life – that is, one must become a Socratic philosopher. In the context of the *Oeconomicus*, becoming a Socratic philosopher involves figuring out that the virtues of farming and household management, as described from both a conventional Persian and Greek perspective, are derived entirely from the material benefits it provides its practitioners, and that there are more important things in life than material wealth or physical success. Socrates lays the groundwork for this reconfiguration of morality in the first six chapters of the dialogue.

Critobulus is a challenging student for Socrates and does not immediately understand Socrates' desire to add a moral and metaphorical dimension to household management and to separate it from material wealth. As Xenophon makes clear in the *Symposium* and *Memorabilia*, as well as in the *Oeconomicus*, Critobulus is a young man who, despite his longing to be noble, is enslaved to external beauty and material goods and confuses the false pleasures of the body with the true pleasures of the soul.[1] Thus, Socrates' strategy in teaching Critobulus to be a good *oikonomos* must take into account this stage of Critobulus' ethical development. In order to lead Critobulus to desire what is truly good, he is willing to appeal to Critobulus' false desires and conceptions, though at the same time he provides him with the information he needs to question and refine his conventional beliefs.[2]

After the initial exchanges between Socrates and Critobulus, in which they define what property, wealth, and the function of a good *oikonomos* are, Critobulus asks a question which allows Socrates to further direct the conversation towards an identification between true *oikonomia* and philosophy: Critobulus wonders why some men who have the knowledge and means to increase their estates do not do so (1.16). In response, Socrates launches into an attack on conventional moral vices such as laziness, greed, and ambition, the "mistresses" (δέσποιναι) that keep men enslaved to their bodily desires and harm their bodies, souls, and households (1.19–23). In the process of diagnosing the "enemy" as these kinds of desires, Socrates introduces a crucial distinction between real pleasures and deceptive pleasures, which in the long run turn out to be pains (1.20). The good *oikonomos* must take care of his soul before he can begin to care for anything else, and to do so, he must learn to distinguish false pleasure from the truly good.

Socrates' attempt to raise the philosophical level of the conversation with Critobulus fails, however, and Critobulus responds that he has no need to worry about these vices since he is "in control of such things" (τῶν τοιούτων ἐγκρατῆ, 2.1). He immediately belies this claim, however and shows his inability to distinguish true from false pleasures by next asking Socrates to help him get rich (2.1). Socrates once more tries to transfer Critobulus' concept of wealth from the material to the philosophical realm by telling Critobulus that despite his (Socrates') poverty, he's richer than Critobulus because he has all he needs; in contrast, Critobulus lives in a materialistic city that requires constant monetary contributions from its citizens, and his friendships further drain his material resources instead of adding to them (2.2–9). Critobulus *still*, however, perceives Socrates' wisdom in a monetary way and decides he can learn from Socrates' ability to

---

[1] See *Smp.* 4.10–28 and 5.1–6.1; *Mem.* 2.6; *Oec.* 2.5–8. On the character of Critobulus in both Xenophon's and Plato's dialogues, see Stevens (1994) 214–17.

[2] Cf. Danzig (2003) 60: "Socrates is clearly not interested in providing Critobulus with the information he seeks. He exploits Critobulus' interest in finance in order to turn him towards higher things." On Socrates' teaching techniques in Xenophon, and particularly on how he adapts his methods to the different nature of each pupil, see Morrison (1994). On Socrates' similar tailoring of his teaching to a particular interlocutor in Plato, see most recently Weiss (2006).

make "a great surplus" (πολλὴν περιουσίαν, 2.10). Socrates denies knowledge of the sort of household management that Critobulus is interested in, but he does agree to show Critobulus experts in money-making, who in turn could make Critobulus a "clever money-maker" (δεινὸν χρηματιστήν, 2.18). In addition, despite not having first-hand experience with this kind of chrematistic *oikonomia*, Socrates teaches Critobulus the basic principles of this art, since they are easy to learn and depend on common sense notions of order and diligence (2.18–3.6).

Before Socrates introduces the expert money-makers to Critobulus,[3] he makes an important demand: he tells Critobulus that he must pay attention to the show Socrates puts on for him with a view to becoming an expert in the field; he should not simply watch Socrates' production in the way he watches tragedies and comedies, with a view to the pleasure of the senses (3.9). This request makes an important demand on the reader, as well, and signals that the rest of the dialogue will require the active participation of the audience to interpret its meaning.[4] Socrates will create a drama of his own to replace the civic comedies and tragedies that Critobulus loves to attend, but its subject matter will be philosophical and not just poetic because it will appeal to the soul and not just the senses.[5]

Critobulus shows signs that he is still not ready to be a perceptive audience for Socrates' drama, as he next asks Socrates to show him what branches of economic knowledge "*seem* to be the most noble" (δοκοῦσι κάλλισται, 4.1) – wording that suggests Critobulus is still moving in the world of appearances and not reality. Instead of berating him, however,

---

[3] Socrates' lack of interest in helping Critobulus become a good money-maker is indicated by his failure to bring any of these experts into the dialogue, with the exception of Ischomachus (and he is not truly present but is remembered by Socrates). Ambler (1996) 112–13 notes that in Socrates' recap (*Oec.* 6) of his points of agreement with Critobulus in the discussion thus far, he conveniently leaves out his earlier promise to take Critobulus to see experts on household management.

[4] Cf. Stevens (1994) 227: "This passage [3.7–10] is a guide to the interpretation of the *Oeconomicus*. What we are about to see is a comedy, but not one that is designed to delight. It is a comedy of education and an educating comedy. Socrates will speak in a way that Critobulus will misunderstand unless he 'puts himself to the test,' 'acts as his own dialectical opponent' (*sautou apopeirasthai*, *Oec.* 3.7)."

[5] On reading the *Oeconomicus* as a philosophical comedy, and particularly as one that counters the comedic portrayal of Socrates in the *Clouds*, see Strauss (1970) and Stevens (1994) esp. 223–29. Much work has been done on the dramatic roots of Socratic dialogue and on interpreting Plato's works as dramatic rivals to Athenian tragedy and comedy. See, among others, the works of Arieti (1991), Press (1993), Clay (1994), Hyland (1995) 111–37, Nightingale (1995), and Blondell (2002). Less attention has been paid to Xenophon's own contribution to Socratic drama, and it has even been denied that there is one. Cf. Nightingale (1995) 4: "But it should be noted that Xenophon's Socrates bears little or no relation to either comic or tragic heroes; nor does Xenophon borrow or imitate structural, stylistic, or thematic elements of the genres of comedy and tragedy. It is only in Plato that we find the imprint of comedy and tragedy."

Socrates responds on his level: he begins by mentioning the branches of knowledge that are *not* deemed noble by cities, namely the banausic arts. He suggests the reason that they are held in low esteem is because they physically weaken the body and, when that happens, "the souls become much weaker" (αἱ ψυχαὶ πολὺ ἀρρωστότεραι γίγνονται, 4.2). In addition, such artisans seem to be bad friends and citizens because they have no time to spend on helping friends or defending their city. Thus, warlike cities in particular forbid the banausic arts (4.3). While Critobulus has no problem with this blanket condemnation of these sorts of craftsmen, Socrates makes clear that he is only reporting the opinion of cities, and particularly of warlike cities. That Socrates himself might have different criteria with which to judge which arts are good and bad is still possible.[6]

PERSIAN FARMING

Critobulus' assent to the importance of physical strength and health in determining what is noble leads Socrates to an assessment of farming itself; however, as with the banausic arts, he describes its worth not from his own perspective but from someone else's, namely that of Cyrus the Great. Socrates relates that people say Cyrus considered farming and the art of war to be among the "most noble" (καλλίστοις) and "most necessary" (ἀναγκαιοτάτοις) concerns (4.4). While the mention of Cyrus impresses Critobulus, Socrates' pairing of farming with war implies that once again, the criteria for nobility have more to do with the physical needs of the state than inherent moral worth.

   This impression is confirmed in Socrates' further description of the role of farming in Cyrus' empire. First, Socrates emphasizes Cyrus' concern for military matters, both domestic and foreign, and explains his system of rewards and punishments for keeping his military subordinates in line and dedicated to making a profit for him (4.5–8). Cyrus also hands out rewards to his governors who keep the land well cultivated and punishes those who do not (4.8) because cultivated land enables garrisons to be nourished and

---

[6] While these arts are said to enfeeble the soul, it is not clear that they make the soul "worse" in a Socratic, moral sense, and when Socrates recaps this portion of his dialogue in 6.5, he adds that these arts *seem* to weaken the body and soul. In fact, in the *Memorabilia* (2.7), Socrates goes out of his way to defend the work of artisans (τεχνῖται) and chastises his friend Aristarchus for not letting his female relatives do such work, despite their desperate need for income. Cf. Strauss' (1970) 115 interpretation of Socrates' rejection of the banausic arts: "As we see, Socrates adapts himself to the needs, or the tastes, of Kritoboulos, i.e., to the pomp he has assumed and his reputation by rejecting the arts which he rejects, with a view to their reputation and to how they are called; for it is hard to see why the practice of smithing, for instance, should make the body soft."

tribute to be paid (4.11). Finally, Socrates describes Cyrus' penchant for gardens that are "full of all the beautiful and fine things that the earth is accustomed to produce" (πάντων καλῶν τε κἀγαθῶν μεστοὶ ὅσα ἡ γῆ φύειν θέλει, 4.13). The important moral words that Socrates spends his life trying to investigate (*kalos* and *agathos*) are reduced to lawn ornaments in Cyrus' garden, and farming is portrayed as a mercenary and militaristic activity that aims at the health and physical well-being of Cyrus and his subjects, but not at their moral improvement.

In addition to showing what kind of agricultural *oikonomos* Cyrus is, Socrates also reveals something about his political *oikonomia*. Just as Cyrus or his subordinates work the land to get material profit or pleasure, so Cyrus manages his people with a view to his own profit or pleasure. His system of rewards and punishments encourages his subordinates to desire political honors and material goods and also inspires competition and mistrust among his men (4.10–11). Cyrus, too, is revealed to be competitive and desirous of praise when he pronounces to his workers, while handing out rewards, that in fact he (Cyrus) deserves all the rewards since he is the "best" (ἄριστος) farmer and military defender (4.16).[7] He simultaneously tries to flatter the workers, however, by telling them that they make the lives of "the brave" (ἄλκιμοι) possible (4.15). This comment is both a reminder of the lack of equality in the Persian empire and a demonstration of how Cyrus uses rhetoric and praise to conceal that inequality.[8]

Yet, by Socrates' logic in *Oec.* 1.19–23, Cyrus is as much a slave as his workers since he is equally bound to material desires, and his positive assessment of farming and war is motivated by ambition and greed. Thus, the conventional virtues that Cyrus values conceal unvirtuous motivations and goals.[9] While, physically, his regime appears to be run in an orderly

---

[7] Cyrus' ambitions and desire for praise are an important theme in the *Cyropaedia*, where they are not necessarily placed in a positive light. Cf. Nadon (2001) 42: "The example of Cyrus, 'who was said to be the greatest lover of honor and who risked all danger for the sake of praise,' will demonstrate how this love of honor, once liberated from the narrow perspective of the republican citizen, can undermine the very regime that fosters it (1.2.1)."

[8] Cyrus' clever and manipulative use of rhetoric is also a prominent feature of the *Cyropaedia*; for examples of this rhetoric, see Nadon (2001) 55–60, 64–66, 77–86, 94–100, and *passim*. Cf. also Too (1998) 295: "Cyrus requires the leaders of his empire to be able to 'charm (*katagoēteuein*)' their subjects. The verb *katagoēteuein* suggests deception and it identifies Cyrus' rulers with the stereotype of the fifth- and fourth-century sorcerer-rhetorician, the figure who charms, deceives and overpowers his audience through his skill at deploying a cultural language, above all words."

[9] Nadon (2001) 56 emphasizes this feature of Cyrus' new order in the *Cyropaedia*, i.e. the eradication of virtue practiced for virtue's sake: "Whereas the Persians have held that virtue is to be practiced for its own sake, Cyrus now declares that 'no virtue is practiced by human beings so that those who become upright (ἐσθλοί) should not get more than the wicked' (1.5.7–9)." Cf. also Bruell (1987) 99. Nadon (2001) 60 also notes that this sort of virtue, the sort "practiced for the sake of external goods,"

and successful fashion, even on this level there are signs of defects. For instance, Socrates is sure to point out that Cyrus requires a military not just to fight the enemy but also to control his own subjects (4.5). This fact, along with the atmosphere of mutual accusations described in 4.10, shows that potential instability and *stasis* bubble beneath the surface of his regime, which is controlled by force and the manipulation of material desires.[10] Cyrus is thus a failed *oikonomos* by the rigorous moral standards Socrates set out in the beginning of the dialogue because he does not know what true wealth is and so cannot possibly know how to use it.

Socrates is not done with the model of Persia yet and imperceptibly slips into talking about the younger, lesser Cyrus (4.18–25). While Pomeroy and others have suggested that "Xenophon deliberately blurs the distinction between the older and the younger Cyrus in order to endow the ill-fated pretender with the traditional virtues of his great predecessor,"[11] this conflation seems a dubious compliment in light of the virtues Socrates has just described. Socrates connects the younger Cyrus to the older by his similar ambition to be "the best" and differentiates him only in the extent to which he was less successful in his quest since he died before becoming king: "Cyrus, if he had lived, *it seems* would have been the best ruler" (Κῦρός γε, εἰ ἐβίωσεν, ἄριστος ἂν δοκεῖ ἄρχων γενέσθαι, 4.18). He follows up his introduction of the younger Cyrus with apparent "proof" (τεκμήρια) of his ruling abilities: when Cyrus was fighting his brother for the kingship, none of his men deserted him; instead, they died fighting around his body when he died, with the exception of Ariaeus, who was stationed on the left wing (4.18–19). The image of brother rebelling against brother and fighting over political power is hardly a positive one. In addition, the mention of

---

is said by Aristotle to be "'possessed by the Spartans and others like them'" (quoting *Eudemian Ethics* 1248b38–1249a17). Fittingly, it is Lysander the Spartan who admires Cyrus (the younger) in the *Oeconomicus* (4.18–25). See the "Morality and ethics" section of my introduction for bibliography on the similarities between the Persians and Spartans in Xenophon.

[10] It is also important to consider that after Cyrus the Great's death, instability erupts and destroys the empire. On the notorious ending of the *Cyropaedia*, which recounts this collapse, and the various critical responses to it, see Nadon (2001) 139–46. He quotes Walter Miller, the translator of the 1914 Loeb edition, as an example of the extreme lengths to which modern critics have gone to preserve a fully positive interpretation of Xenophon's Persia: "'Chapter VIII can be considered only as a later addition to Xenophon's work . . . It spoils the perfect unity of the work up to this chapter . . . Some violent opponent of Medic influence in Athens could not leave all this glorification of Persian institutions unchallenged, and so in this appendix he has supplied an account of the degeneracy of the descendants of the virtuous Persians of the earlier day. The chapter is included here in accord with all the manuscripts and editions. But the reader is recommended to close the book at this point and read no further'" (140; Miller's quotation is from the preface to chapter 8 of the *Cyropaedia*).

[11] Pomeroy (1984) 98. For further authors in agreement with this interpretation, see Too (1998) 287 n. 25.

Ariaeus, Cyrus' lieutenant and the commander of a large portion of Cyrus' non-Greek troops,[12] calls attention to the fact that he deserted along with all of his own men after Cyrus' death.[13]

As with Cyrus the Great, Socrates makes a transition from the younger Cyrus' military activities to his agricultural ones. He relates a vignette of Lysander the Spartan coming to visit Cyrus in his garden (4.20–25). Lysander is taken with the beauty of the garden and particularly with the orderly rows of trees and the pleasant smells (4.21). He tells Cyrus that he is amazed at their beauty and especially admires the person who measured them out and arranged them (4.21). Cyrus is pleased by this flattery and proudly says he arranged them all and even planted some of them himself (4.21–22). Lysander is astounded to hear this because he sees that Cyrus is luxuriously attired with robes, perfume, and jewelry (4.23). Cyrus explains that he uses agricultural work as a form of exercise, and that he never dines before engaging in some sort of agricultural or military activity, or exercising his ambition in some way (4.24). Lysander responds with praise of Cyrus as both a fortunate and good man ("Justly you seem to me, Cyrus, to be fortunate; for you are fortunate by being a good man," δικαίως μοι δοκεῖς, ὦ Κῦρε, εὐδαίμων εἶναι· ἀγαθὸς γὰρ ὢν ἀνὴρ εὐδαιμονεῖς, 4.25).

The story about Lysander and Cyrus is complex since it contains two different juxtapositions of appearance and reality for two different audiences. Lysander is the first "audience." He begins his encounter overwhelmed by the sensual beauty of Cyrus' garden and of Cyrus himself, but he clearly does not locate virtue in these aesthetic qualities, and he is only truly impressed by the utilitarian order of the trees, which are described as if they were rows of soldiers. His real interest in Cyrus begins when he finds out that Cyrus planted them himself and that he uses farming as a form of exercise, like military training. Thus, for Lysander, the apparent beauty of Cyrus' external appearance reveals true beauty and virtue underneath in the form of physical training and military strength. The second audience, however, consisting of Critobulus, the witnesses of the dialogue,[14] and the readers, have a further layer of "apparent" virtue to work through and do not have to be satisfied with Lysander's praise of Cyrus as a "good man."[15]

---

[12] See *An.* 1.8.5.

[13] His desertion is recounted by Xenophon in *An.* 1.9.31. Another attempted desertion from Cyrus by Orontas is described in *An.* 1.6, and it ends in Orontas' execution by Cyrus' men – a hint that loyalty to Cyrus was enforced by the threat of death and was not always "willing."

[14] Xenophon states that he witnessed the dialogue himself (1.1).

[15] Strauss (1970) 119 makes an interesting comparison: "His [Lysander's] praising Cyrus as happy while he saw him in Sardis reminds us of Solon's refusal to praise Croesus as happy when he saw that very wealthy king in the same city; Solon seems to have been wiser than Lysander."

At the core of the younger Cyrus' ambitions is a type of success that is measured in physical and material terms, and while he is willing to work hard in order to increase that success, his "virtues" always have an ulterior motive. Thus, the second audience of this story is prodded to see that not only can apparent pleasures turn out to be real pains, but apparent virtues can conceal hidden vices.

PRAISE OF FARMING

Socrates next praises farming from the point of view not of barbarian kings, but of Greek city-states (5.1–17). This praise has been called "the earliest extensive eulogy of rural life in Greek prose,"[16] and Socrates does give voice to encomiastic topoi about farming that presumably reflect the conventional morality of the city-state. Yet, I would suggest that this praise stops short of giving farming the full stamp of Socratic approval, and that it ultimately reflects a morality based on material self-interest and in conflict with the teaching of Socrates in chapters 1 and 2 of the *Oeconomicus*.[17] Socrates' praise has four main sections, though the themes in each overlap: section one praises farming primarily for its sensual pleasures (5.1–3); section two concentrates on the utility of farming in terms of physical strength and health (5.4–7); section three consists of a series of rhetorical questions which recap the points made in sections one and two (5.8–11); and section four praises farming as a moral teacher (5.12–17). Yet, throughout all these sections, the criteria used to determine what is pleasant, useful, or moral, are ultimately material criteria.

 Section one begins with a statement of the necessity of farming even for the blessed (μακάριοι, 5.1) and then states the three main benefits of farming: it seems to be pleasant, it increases the wealth of the household, and it provides exercise for the body so that all the activities which befit a free man may be done (5.1). However, that this sort of farming would befit the kind of free man that Socrates values, i.e. the man who is free from the slavery of sensual pleasures (cf. again *Oec.* 1.19–23), is in doubt, and the following description raises further potential problems:

---

[16] Pomeroy (1994) 254 (*ad* 5.1). Pomeroy notes the many formal, rhetorical features of Socrates' praise, and, once again, it should be noted that Xenophon shows as much literary skill as Plato in manipulating genres for philosophical purposes. On Plato's ironic use of the genre of eulogy, see Nightingale (1993) and Nightingale (1995) 93–132.

[17] Cf. Ambler (1996) 111–12: "After having experimented with Critoboulus' attitude toward the barbarian monarchs, Socrates turns us to a defense of farming that is more compatible with republican principles... There remain multiple reasons to doubt that this chapter is either a candid or an adequate defense of farming, however."

πρῶτον μὲν γὰρ ἀφ' ὧν ζῶσιν οἱ ἄνθρωποι, ταῦτα ἡ γῆ φέρει ἐργαζομένοις, καὶ
ἀφ' ὧν τοίνυν ἡδυπαθοῦσι, προσεπιφέρει· ἔπειτα δὲ ὅσοις κοσμοῦσι βωμοὺς
καὶ ἀγάλματα καὶ οἷς αὐτοὶ κοσμοῦνται, καὶ ταῦτα μετὰ ἡδίστων ὀσμῶν
καὶ θεαμάτων παρέχει· ἔπειτα δὲ ὄψα πολλὰ τὰ μὲν φύει, τὰ δὲ τρέφει· καὶ
γὰρ ἡ προβατευτικὴ τέχνη συνῆπται τῇ γεωργίᾳ, ὥστε ἔχειν καὶ θεοὺς
ἐξαρέσκεσθαι θύοντας καὶ αὐτοὺς χρῆσθαι. (5.2–3)

For first of all, the earth bears, for those working it, the things from which men
live, and she provides in addition the things from which they live pleasantly; next,
she provides the things with which they adorn altars and statues and by which they
themselves are adorned, and these are accompanied by the most pleasant smells
and sights; next, she provides much food, some she grows, some she nourishes;
for the art of animal breeding is connected to farming, so that [farmers] are in a
position to propitiate the gods by sacrificing, and so that they may use the animals
themselves.

This description presents farming, in its appeal to the eyes and the ears, as
akin to the theatrical productions that delighted Critobulus' senses (3.9).
It also recalls the garden of Cyrus the Younger, whose adornment, sights,
and smells merged with Cyrus' own adornment. Thus, while Socrates has
supposedly turned from talking about farming in monarchies, in which
the citizens are not free, to talking about city-states, in which the citizens are, it is clear that a tyranny of desire still keeps these farmers
enslaved, as they strive to live, and live pleasantly, but not necessarily to live
well.

Just as Cyrus' luxurious and sensual exterior concealed an inner work
ethic, which aimed at ultimately physical goals, so too does farming, and
the second section of the praise is dedicated to these aspects. Socrates relates
that the earth does not permit her goods to be taken "with softness" (μετὰ
μαλακίας, 5.4) but instead trains the ψυχή ("soul") to endure extremes
of heat and cold (5.4); she exercises the bodies of those working the land
themselves and strengthens them (5.4); she makes those who farm by
supervising others manly by waking them up early and compelling them
to move about vigorously (5.4). This physical conditioning is all ultimately
useful for the military and mercenary activities of the city: farming provides
food for horses in the cavalry and prepares the body for the infantry (5.5).
The earth feeds hounds and prey, which men can then enjoy hunting, and
horses and hounds also benefit from farming (5.5–6). In return, the horses
carry their masters to and from work, and the hounds protect the crops
and livestock from wild beasts (5.6). Finally, the farmers are motivated to
defend their land with weapons since their crops are out in the open and
thus liable to attack by the enemy (5.7).

Pomeroy (1994) notes that "Xenophon intrudes references to war (5, 7, 13–16) that shatter the idyll" (255), and this last detail about the liability to attack by the enemy is a reminder of the vulnerability of lives whose success depends on material circumstances. Yet, if cities encourage the kind of ethics of farming laid out here, that is, an ethics based on the goodness of physical and material benefit, then it is inevitable that in a world of limited resources, there will be war and fighting. Thus, agriculture and agricultural ethics are closely tied to military activity in both Persia and the polis because they are part of a vicious cycle of life driven by material needs. While Socrates had warned against a "softness of spirit" (μαλακίαν ψυχῆς) in 1.20 and suggested that it, and related vices, can prevent men from engaging in "useful deeds" (ὠφελίμων ἔργων, 1.21), there is no indication that his version of useful deeds would match that of Cyrus or the city-states. In addition, the fact that Socrates suggests hounds and horses get benefits from farming just as men do (5.6) is a further clue that he believes the morality of this type of farming is appropriate for animals – but that perhaps humans can do better.

The final "moral" section of Socrates' praise is the most potentially ironic of all, for in it, Socrates makes the bold claim that the earth "teaches justice" (δικαιοσύνην διδάσκει, 5.12). As becomes clear, the type of "justice" that the earth teaches is thoroughly conventional and derived from the material benefits it gives. The first part of the explanation for how the earth does so is a topos and is reminiscent of the traditional "helping friends" conception of justice: "For she gives to those who cultivate her best the most goods in return" (τοὺς γὰρ ἄριστα θεραπεύοντας αὐτὴν πλεῖστα ἀγαθὰ ἀντιποιεῖ, 5.12).[18] The second part of the explanation completes the "harming enemies" part of the equation and, if not as much of a topos, is equally rhetorical and full of Gorgianic jingles (underlined in the text):

ἐὰν δ᾽ ἄρα καὶ ὑπὸ πλήθους ποτὲ στρατευμάτων <u>τῶν ἔργων</u> στερηθῶσιν οἱ ἐν τῇ γεωργίᾳ <u>ἀναστρεφόμενοι καὶ σφοδρῶς καὶ ἀνδρικῶς παιδευόμενοι</u>, οὗτοι εὖ <u>παρεσκευασμένοι</u> καὶ τὰς ψυχὰς καὶ τὰ σώματα, ἂν μὴ θεὸς ἀποκωλύῃ, δύνανται ἰόντες εἰς τὰς τῶν ἀποκωλυόντων λαμβάνειν ἀφ᾽ ὧν θρέψονται. (5.13)

And if those who are engaged in farming and educated both in a vigorous and virile way should be deprived of their works by a multitude of armies, these men, being well prepared both in their souls and bodies, are able, if a god should not prevent them, to go into the country of those hindering them and take the things which will nourish them.

---

[18] Cf. the similar praise of earth's justice in *Cyr.* 8.3.38, Ps.-Arist. *Oec.* 1.1343a.26, and Verg. *G.* 2.460. See also Thomas (1988) 1.246 (*ad* 2.459–60), who compares Philemon fr. 105 Kock.

So, the second "lesson" in justice taught by farming is that if an army takes a farmer's crops, he is well prepared to attack them in return and steal their crops; this lesson, however, is qualified by the cautionary phrase, "if a god should not prevent them," (ἂν μὴ θεὸς ἀποκωλύη), a warning that underscores the uncontrollability of agricultural and military affairs.[19] These lines are followed up by an equally ominous maxim: "And often in war it even is safer to search for food with weapons than with farming tools" (πολλάκις δ᾽ ἐν τῷ πολέμῳ καὶ ἀσφαλέστερόν ἐστι σὺν τοῖς ὅπλοις τὴν τροφὴν μαστεύειν ἢ σὺν τοῖς γεωργικοῖς ὀργάνοις, 5.13). The justice of farming, then, is reduced to its ability to feed those who work the land and to prepare men for war. It seems unlikely that this is the justice of Socrates, who earlier in the dialogue makes clear that he does not value material wealth or the pleasures of the body.

In addition to connecting farming to a conventional conception of justice, Socrates also connects it to the political arts of ruling and cooperation. He praises the cooperative skills taught by farming and suggests these are equally beneficial in war (5.14). He says that both the good farmer and the good general must learn to make his subordinates obedient, and the general must "contrive" (μηχανᾶσθαι) a system of punishments and rewards (5.14–15). The farmer, too, needs to learn how to encourage his workers and give them something good to hope for, especially the slaves, so that they remain willingly (5.16). These are all elements of ruling that preoccupied Cyrus, as well (4.6–11), a fact that further conflates the values of city-states and barbarian empires. Indeed, what both types of political systems have in common is an ethical code based on a self-interest that is defined by material goods and physical needs.

Now that Socrates' encomium is done, Critobulus has a chance to show whether he has understood what is at the foundation of the ethics of farming and the conventional morality of the polis. Critobulus responds:

ἀλλὰ ταῦτα μὲν ἔμοιγε, ὦ Σώκρατες, καλῶς δοκεῖς λέγειν· ὅτι δὲ τῆς γεωργικῆς τὰ πλεῖστά ἐστιν ἀνθρώπῳ ἀδύνατα προνοῆσαι, <δῆλον·> καὶ γὰρ χάλαζαι καὶ πάχναι ἐνίοτε καὶ αὐχμοὶ καὶ ὄμβροι ἐξαίσιοι καὶ ἐρυσῖβαι καὶ ἄλλα πολλάκις τὰ καλῶς ἐγνωσμένα καὶ πεποιημένα ἀφαιροῦνται· καὶ πρόβατα δ᾽ ἐνίοτε κάλλιστα τεθραμμένα νόσος ἐλθοῦσα κάκιστα ἀπώλεσεν. (5.18)

Certainly in these things you seem to me to speak well, Socrates: but it is impossible for a man to foresee most things in farming; for sometimes hail and frosts and droughts and excessive rain storms and blights and other things often destroy what

---

[19] Marchant even takes this disruptive phrase out of his translation of *Oec.* 5.13, though he leaves it in the Greek (Marchant and Todd [1923] 404–05).

has been well devised and well done; and sometimes plague attacks and terribly destroys cattle raised very well.

What makes farming a less attractive lifestyle in Critobulus' eyes is the fact that physical destruction periodically occurs; thus, on a superficial level, at least, Critobulus recognizes the problems that come from relying on external goods for happiness even if he does not perceive any deeper moral issues in doing so. Socrates is ready for Critobulus' objection and responds that the gods control agricultural matters, just as they do military ones; for this reason, men perform sacrifices and use divination to propitiate the gods, and prudent men tend to the gods on behalf of their crops, livestock, and possessions (5.19–20). This interconnectedness between farming and religion recalls the opening line of the encomium ("because not even the very blessed are able to abstain from farming," ὅτι τῆς γεωργίας οὐδ᾽ οἱ πάνυ μακάριοι δύνανται ἀπέχεσθαι, 5.1); it also has the effect of presenting traditional state religion as a means of exerting control over external goods and circumstances.

   Does Socrates approve of the farmer's and soldier's use of religion, or is this statement, too, ironic? Without getting too entangled in the question of Socrates' religious beliefs and relation to polis religion, suffice it to say that while Socrates is described as pious and in support of the religious laws of the city in the apologetic literature,[20] his version of the divine and what it means to honor the gods seems different from the farmer's and soldier's.[21] Even in a work like the *Memorabilia*, which strives to present as conventionally acceptable an image of Socrates as possible,[22] the difference between Socrates' religion and the religion of ordinary Athenians is clear. For instance, in *Mem.* 1.1.6–9, Xenophon outlines the crucial but restricted role that Socrates gives to religion in human life: human beings should use human skills to figure out their problems, except when it is impossible to do so; when the outcome of something is unclear, a person should go to the oracle to ask whether something should be done (1.1.6). While the crafts, such as carpentry, farming, ruling, and household management, might be grasped by human understanding, the most important part of this knowledge is reserved only for the gods and is not clear to human beings (1.1.7–8). Xenophon goes on to clarify further what Socrates means:

---

[20] E.g. *Mem.* 1.1.2, in which Xenophon states that Socrates openly sacrificed and consulted the gods at home and in the city.
[21] For recent treatments of Socrates' religion, see McPherran (1996), Gray (1998) esp. 26–40, and Destrée and Smith (2005).
[22] On Xenophon's portrayal of Socrates as a typical sage from wisdom literature in the *Memorabilia*, see Gray (1998).

οὔτε γὰρ τῷ καλῶς ἀγρὸν φυτευσαμένῳ δῆλον, ὅστις καρπώσεται, οὔτε τῷ καλῶς οἰκίαν οἰκοδομησαμένῳ δῆλον, ὅστις ἐνοικήσει, οὔτε τῷ στρατηγικῷ δῆλον, εἰ συμφέρει στρατηγεῖν, οὔτε τῷ πολιτικῷ δῆλον, εἰ συμφέρει τῆς πόλεως προστατεῖν . . . (1.1.8)

For it is not clear to the person who planted his field well who will harvest it, nor is it clear to the person building a house well who will live in it, nor to the one expert in generalship if it is beneficial to be a general, nor to the one skilled in statesmanship if it is beneficial to rule a city . . .

While in some sense, Socrates' advice is conventional in that he suggests using the gods to help explore issues that are unclear to human beings, in another sense, it is not. These "issues," though couched in typical Socratic ambiguity in the examples above, raise moral questions. Socrates suggests that people consult the gods on the very same questions that he uses moral philosophy and his *daimonion* for, i.e. questions that ultimately lead to the most important question: "is it good?" Religion, for Socrates, cannot be separated from questions of morality.

Some of these differences between Socratic piety and conventional piety are made clear in *Mem.* 1.3.2–3, when Xenophon relates that Socrates only ever prayed for "good things" (τἀγαθά), since the gods know best what the good things are, and that praying for gold, silver, or tyranny was like praying to win a game of dice or a battle or anything else whose outcome is unclear (1.3.2). Thus, Socrates implies that he does not approve of what most Athenians pray for, since they do not first investigate the moral nature of their requests from the gods but just assume they are good.[23] In addition, Xenophon notes that Socrates' sacrifices were humble and that he believed the gods did not care if sacrifices were great or small; if they did, that would mean rich wicked people could receive more benefits from the gods than the good (1.3.3), and for Socrates, this would constitute truly impious belief. Once again, the implications of this statement are radical and undermine the whole system of sacrificial religion as practiced by the Athenians, since its underlying assumption is that gods *can* be influenced by material things. Though Socrates seems to believe in the existence and beneficence of the gods and in the importance of honoring them,[24] his support for polis religion is also a reinterpretation of it along moral, Socratic lines.

With this background from the *Memorabilia*, we can return to the *Oeconomicus* and the question of Socrates' tone in his statement that "prudent

---

[23] Xenophon relates his own experience in asking the "wrong" question of the oracle and being chided by Socrates in *An.* 3.1.4–7.

[24] See *Mem.* 1.4, in which Socrates tries to convey the importance of honoring the gods and to prove the existence of divine providence to Aristodemus.

men" (οἱ σώφρονες) cultivate the gods on behalf of their crops and live-stock and possessions (5.19–20). As usual, Socrates loads his statement with words that can be interpreted in different ways. In one sense, he could simply be describing conventional Athenian uses of religion, and while he deems men "prudent" who are concerned for the health of their posses-sions, he does not deem them wise or good. On the other hand, perhaps they are also wise and good if their "possessions" are defined in the Socratic sense – namely, as truly beneficial things that their owner knows how to use. Thus, farmers who simply pray for more crops or less rain, or generals who pray to win a battle are sidestepping the most important questions: is it good to plant or to have more possessions? Is it good to fight this battle?

Critobulus now has another chance to show if he has understood what Socrates has been saying about the only apparent virtue of conventional farming (and military activity); however, despite his profession of increased knowledge about how to live (6.1), he still wants Socrates to teach him how he can make money through *oikonomia* (6.11). He even compares his conversation with Socrates to business partners going through their accounts without argument (6.3). It is clear that Critobulus is still moving in a world of appearances, material profit, and pleasure.[25] Socrates responds to Critobulus' request to be taught how to be a profitable *oikonomos* by again redirecting the topic in a moral direction. He replies that he will tell him a story about meeting a man "who really seemed" (ὃς ἐμοὶ ἐδόκει εἶναι τῷ ὄντι) to be worthy of the "title" (τὸ ὄνομα) of a "beautiful and good man" (καλός τε κἀγαθὸς ἀνήρ, 6.12). Before introducing his dialogue with Ischomachus, however, he backtracks a bit in his story. He tells Critobulus that initially he was misled by the word καλός into thinking that a beautiful appearance might be the key to virtue (6.15). However, he learned the all-important lesson that appearances can be deceiving and that, in fact, a beautiful exterior can conceal a wretched soul (6.16). Thus, he decided to investigate one "of those who are called beautiful *and* good" (τῶν καλουμένων καλῶν τε κἀγαθῶν, 6.16).

With this back-story, Socrates gives Critobulus the key to decoding his dialogue with Ischomachus, for it too will be about distinguishing between appearance and reality. In addition, just as the vignette about Lysander and Cyrus the Younger contained two levels of apparent virtue to work through, so too does Socrates' quest to find the meaning of the καλός τε κἀγαθὸς ἀνήρ. The first level he has already decoded: virtue does not

---

[25] Note that in Critobulus' two short responses in this section, there are three uses of words for pleasure (ἡδύ, 6.3; ἥδιστον, 6.11; ἡδέως, 6.11).

consist of physical beauty. The second level is a challenge for Critobulus and Xenophon's readers to decode, and it requires figuring out that the virtues of political regimes, and of conventional morality, are fundamentally directed towards material needs. Socrates has already given large hints to this effect in his Praise of Farming, but he will elaborate extensively on this theme in his dialogue with the reputed gentleman, Ischomachus. Critobulus, who desires to be worthy of the *name* of gentleman, will instead be taught to understand the reality behind the name.[26]

---

[26] Cf. Critobulus' desire in 6.12 "to be worthy of the *name*" (τούτου τοῦ ὀνόματος ἄξιος γενέσθαι) of a beautiful and good man with Socrates' desire in 6.14 to understand what makes one worthy to be called that.

CHAPTER 2

A philosopher and a gentleman (Oec. 7–21)

Socrates begins his dialogue with Ischomachus when he finds him "at leisure" (σχολάζειν, 7.1) in the Stoa of Zeus Eleutherius waiting for some guests in the agora (7.1–2). This setting sets out the key themes of the ensuing dialogue, and they are themes that for the most part recapitulate those in the dialogue with Critobulus:[1] Ischomachus' state of leisure, which elicits surprise from Socrates (7.1), activates the contrast between the active and contemplative life since Ischomachus, the "active man," is now at leisure, while Socrates, the "contemplative man," is actively seeking knowledge. Ischomachus' placement in the Stoa of Zeus Eleutherius, in the heart of the agora, connects him to conventional Athenian life and values.[2] The epithet of Zeus "Eleutherius" introduces the concept of freedom and its opposition to slavery, while the circumstances of his gaining the epithet, i.e. Athens' victory over Persia, emphasizes the opposition between the barbarian empire and the Athenian democracy. Finally, the Stoa was also a picture gallery and, as Pausanias relates (1.3–4), contained paintings of the twelve gods, Theseus, Democracy, Demos, the Battle of Mantinea, and a cavalry battle with Xenophon's son Gryllus. Thus, as a venue for beautiful paintings of noble deeds and concepts, the Stoa also connects to the dichotomy of appearance and reality.[3] All of these dichotomies are explored and reconceptualized in the course of the dialogue as Socrates probes beneath the surface of conventional virtue and the art of ruling.

---

[1] On the importance of the setting of Platonic dialogues, see Hyland (1995) 13–33, who argues: "[W]hat the dialogues capture, and what most philosophical essays ignore, is that most of our philosophic discussions are, in a non-pejorative sense of the terms, *ad hominem* and *ad locum*. They take place in given contexts and with given people, and these factors are often determinative both of the content and the manner of our discussion" (23).

[2] Cf. Pomeroy (1994) 265 (*ad* 7.1): "The location of the stoa may have inspired some of the material of the dialogue. Statues of great generals, such as Conon, Timotheus, and Evagoras of Cyprus stood outside of it . . . It faced the agora . . . Athenian courts and perhaps inscriptions of laws were to be found in the vicinity of the stoa . . . In it, Ischomachus was in the centre of Athenian political life."

[3] Cf. Socrates' comment later on, that he would rather learn about the virtue of a real woman than look at a beautiful painting of one (10.1).

Socrates initiates the dialogue by asking Ischomachus what he does to be called καλὸς κἀγαθός (7.2). Ischomachus replies by explaining in the next twenty-one chapters how he runs his household. Of course, by now *oikonomia* has come to mean a lot more than household management; so, in effect, what Ischomachus does is explain how he runs his mini-kingdom, and in the process, he reveals the foundations for the moral values and laws that support his rule. Since Ischomachus is *the* conventionally noble man of Athens, his values are also the values of Athens, and, just as in the discussion between Critobulus and Socrates, his Athenian values become conflated with Persian ones. Like Cyrus, Ischomachus values physical order and material wealth, and his art of ruling appeals to the self-interested instincts of those he governs.

Throughout this examination of Ischomachus' world, there is an implicit comparison and contrast with that of Socrates. Indeed, as many critics have noted, Xenophon explicitly gives Ischomachus the role of the anti-Socrates.[4] It is not just in his precisely opposed value system that Ischomachus becomes Socrates' "evil twin," but it is also in his method of teaching. For instance, like Socrates, Ischomachus is concerned with the distinction between appearance and reality (e.g. ch. 10). He is obsessed with dividing items into their proper categories (e.g. 9).[5] He teaches dialectically through question and answer, reaches points of agreement, and recovers forgotten knowledge (e.g. 15–19).[6] He is a teacher of the art of ruling and of justice (e.g. 13–14). He uses animal analogies and analogies from other *technai* to get his points across (e.g. 13.2, 17.5). He seeks out uncultivated land so that he can make it better (20.22), just as Socrates seeks to improve souls,[7] and also like Socrates, he spends his life practicing his defense

---

[4] E.g. Danzig (2003) 73: "In his concern for wealth, reputation, and household matters, and in his willingness to devote his time to pursuing these, while displaying no interest in philosophy, Ischomachus is the anti-Socrates."

[5] Cf. Strauss (1970) 147–48: "Ischomachos' separating his indoor things according to tribes in order to establish order within his house reminds us of Socrates' separating the beings according to races or kinds in order to discover the order of the whole . . . He asserted that the activity is called *dialegesthai* with a view to the fact that men coming together for joint deliberation pick or select (*dialegein*) things according to races or kinds." He further notes (148 n. 3) that "Ischomachos speaks of *dialegein* in *Oec.* VIII.9."

[6] On *anamnesis*, or recollection, in the *Oeconomicus*, see Wellman (1976), who concludes: "It therefore seems a fair surmise that anamnesis is Socratic in origin rather than Platonic" (315). Cf. also Pomeroy (1994) 336–37 (*ad* 19.15): "Here Socrates is subjected to the Socratic method of teaching, but of course since he is actually the narrator of the conversation with Ischomachus he is playing the active role. Implicit in the elenctic process enacted here is the theory that the soul is immortal. Knowledge is recollection and teaching is actually an attempt to regain latent knowledge (see also XV.10 λεληθέναι and Pl. *Meno* 80 D)."

[7] Cf. Stevens (1994) 234: "They first discuss the nature of the soil (16.1–2). As a teacher, Socrates had first to consider the nature of his students (*Mem.* 4.1.3)."

(11.21–24).[8] Yet, these superficial similarities only underscore the very different ways in which they understand morality.

Ischomachus begins his account of how he runs his household by relating a discussion with his wife, one which effectively reveals what he understands the foundations of religion, morality, and law to be. For instance, when his wife asks him what her duties are and what it means to practice self-control (σωφρονεῖν, 7.15), he replies:

ἀλλὰ σωφρόνων τοί ἐστι καὶ ἀνδρὸς καὶ γυναικὸς οὕτω ποιεῖν, ὅπως τά τε ὄντα ὡς βέλτιστα ἕξει καὶ ἄλλα ὅτι πλεῖστα ἐκ τοῦ καλοῦ τε καὶ δικαίου προσγενήσεται. (7.15)

But it is the duty of both self-controlled men and women to make it so that their property will be in the best condition possible and that as much as possible will be added to it by noble and just means.

According to Ischomachus, the goal of a moral quality like σωφροσύνη ("self-control, moderation") is to make as much material profit as possible. When his wife further questions how she should go about increasing their estate (7.16), he responds with a reference to religion and law:

ναὶ μὰ Δῖ, ἔφην ἐγώ, ἅ τε οἱ θεοὶ ἔφυσάν σε δύνασθαι καὶ ὁ νόμος συνεπαινεῖ, ταῦτα πειρῶ ὡς βέλτιστα ποιεῖν. (7.16)

By Zeus, I said, try to do as well as possible those things which the gods made you naturally capable of doing and which the law praises, as well.

While it might seem that religion and law are the twin foundations of Ischomachus' morals, his elaboration of what these commandments and laws are has the effect of assimilating both sources of morality to the dictates of nature, whose goal is the physical thriving of the species.

For instance, when his wife asks for more specifics, Ischomachus responds with a comparison of his wife's duties to those of a "Queen Bee in the hive" (ἡ ἐν τῷ σμήνει ἡγεμὼν μέλιττα, 7.17) and then launches into a discussion of the purpose of marriage and procreation. He says the gods have yoked together the man and the woman so that their union will be beneficial to each other (7.18); in addition, so that the various species will not become extinct, males and females produce children, who in turn support them in old age (7.19). Human beings are different from cattle in needing

---

[8] Cf. Pangle (1994) 131: "As E. C. Marchant notes, there is an evident parallel between this passage and the passage we earlier cited from the *Memorabilia* (4.8.4), in which Socrates describes his own lifelong preoccupation with defending or giving an account of himself." Cf. also X. *Ap.* 3.

shelter (7.19–20), and a division of labor develops so that all the provisions are provided for and obtained. The women control the indoor work and care for the children (7.22–25) since they are naturally more suited to it, and the men control the outdoor work. They both, however, have equal capacity for "memory and diligence" (τὴν μνήμην καὶ τὴν ἐπιμέλειαν, 7.26) and "being self-controlled" (τὸ ἐγκρατεῖς δὲ εἶναι, 7.27), and the gods also allow that the person who is more self-controlled benefits more from this virtue (7.27). Men and women need each other and benefit one another since they complement each other's weaknesses (7.28). Thus, Ischomachus' gods command precisely what natural instincts command to preserve the species, and "law" (ὁ νόμος) supports what the gods support by praising and declaring honorable the natural order of things (7.30). Accordingly, morality, law, and religion are all directly connected to the material benefits they allow and do not seem to be valued for their inherent goodness.

In addition, as Ischomachus' language explicitly reveals, his conception of the human good makes it hard to differentiate from the good of other species. In addition to comparing his wife to a Queen Bee, he discusses human "yoking" and procreation in the context of the preservation of all "animal species" (ζῴων γένη, 7.19). He even talks of taming and domesticating his wife ("she was tamed and domesticated," χειροήθης ἦν καὶ ἐτετιθάσευτο, 7.10) and explicitly uses "teaching methods appropriate for wild animals" (ἡ δοκοῦσα θηριώδης παιδεία, 13.9) for training his slaves. Ischomachus not only treats his subordinates like animals but also treats himself like one. In chapter 11, which is the chapter dedicated to detailing his own activities, he describes how he trains himself for war by doing maneuvers on his horse (11.17). The specific exercises he practices (going up hills and across ditches and streams) are precisely the ones Xenophon recommends that horsemen should have their *horses* practice in *The Art of Horsemanship* (3.7).

Prior to Ischomachus' description of his practice in horsemanship, Socrates introduces a crucial vignette, which shows the difference between Socrates' and Ischomachus' value systems. It begins with Ischomachus' suggestion that Socrates can correct him if he notices anything wrong with his (Ischomachus') description of his own activities (11.2). Socrates responds with a humorous portrait of himself as someone who seems "to be an idle chatterer" (ἀδολεσχεῖν), "to measure the air" (ἀερομετρεῖν) and is "poor" (πένης), and who is thus an unlikely candidate to correct a perfect gentleman (11.3).[9] However, Socrates goes on to say, this charge of

---

[9] As Strauss (1970) 164 and others have noted, "The *Oeconomicus* is then in a properly subdued manner a comical reply to Aristophanes' comical attack on Socrates." For further bibliography, see my introductory section of chapter 1.

being poor would have depressed him had he not come upon a crowd of admirers looking at a horse belonging to Nicias; Socrates asked him if the horse had many possessions, and Nicias replied that he of course did not (11.4–5). Socrates draws the moral that because it is permitted for a poor horse to be good if he has a good soul by nature, it is also permitted for Socrates to become a good man since being good has nothing to do with material possessions (11.5–6) – a lesson that recalls Socrates' downgrading of material wealth to Critobulus in *Oec.* 2.2. A further lesson that the reader might draw from this vignette, is that unlike Ischomachus, Socrates does not strive to approximate the good of a horse by training himself in horsemanship; instead, he strives for the good of the human soul by engaging in philosophical dialogue.

Ischomachus' conception of morality and his art of ruling is essentially different from Socrates', then, and similar to that of political entities, whether the polis of Athens or the empire of Persia. Religion and morality, as Ischomachus presents them, train citizens to desire what is ultimately beneficial for the city in terms of its physical and material strength. In addition, just as political entities use praise and blame, rewards and punishments, to provide a self-interested motivation for actions that ultimately benefit the political group as a whole, Ischomachus uses similar methods to train his wife and his steward to be obedient. In turn, he teaches his wife and steward these methods in order for them to make the slaves loyal and diligent. Finally, just as the city attaches the language of morality to actions that are beneficial or harmful to it, so Ischomachus deems "good" and "just" those who are loyal and obedient to him and "bad" those who are not. Yet, he never investigates what these terms mean in a Socratic fashion and conceives of his benefit in a purely material way. This non-Socratic method of teaching and ruling is revealed to be a flawed method for organizing human interests in the course of the *Oeconomicus*.

Chapter 14, in which Ischomachus tells Socrates how he teaches justice to his steward, provides an excellent example of the failings of Ischomachus' system. Ischomachus' conception of justice is a concrete and materialistic one. It consists of teaching his steward not to steal from him, and he combines laws from Draco, Solon, and the kings of Persia (14.4–6) in order "to put his slaves on the path to justice" (ἐμβιβάζειν εἰς τὴν δικαιοσύνην τοὺς οἰκέτας, 14.4).[10] The laws of Draco and Solon work by punishing those who

---

[10] It is interesting to note that throughout this chapter, Pomeroy (1994) 179 translates *dikaiosunē* as "honesty." While "honesty" may be a more accurate translation of Ischomachus' conception of

get caught with imprisonment or death (14.5). As Ischomachus explains, "They wrote these wishing to make shameful profit unprofitable for the unjust" (ἔγραφον αὐτὰ βουλόμενοι ἀλυσιτελῆ ποιῆσαι τοῖς ἀδίκοις τὴν αἰσχροκέρδειαν, 14.5). Ischomachus' explanation of the mechanism of these laws reveals that the moral language attached to them is nothing more than external ornamentation, for what these laws really teach is how to calculate a materially based self-interest.

Ischomachus says he combines those laws with laws from Persia because the latter, in addition to penalizing the dishonest, reward the honest (14.6–7). He distinguishes two different motivations for being just: a desire for "having more" (τῷ πλέον ἔχειν, 14.9) and a desire for "being praised" by Ischomachus (τοῦ ἐπαινεῖσθαι, 14.9). He treats the latter group "like free men" (ὥσπερ ἐλευθέροις, 14.9) "not only by enriching them but also by honoring them as noble and good" (οὐ μόνον πλουτίζων ἀλλὰ καὶ τιμῶν ὡς καλούς τε κἀγαθούς, 14.9). He further explains:

τούτῳ γάρ μοι δοκεῖ, ἔφη, ὦ Σώκρατες, διαφέρειν ἀνὴρ φιλότιμος ἀνδρὸς φιλοκερδοῦς, τῷ ἐθέλειν ἐπαίνου καὶ τιμῆς ἕνεκα καὶ πονεῖν ὅπου δεῖ καὶ κινδυνεύειν καὶ αἰσχρῶν κερδῶν ἀπέχεσθαι. (14.10)

For it seems to me, Socrates, that the honor-loving man differs from the profit-loving man in this way, that for the sake of praise and honor he is willing to work whenever it is necessary and to run risks and abstain from shameful profit.

Ischomachus' distinction between the honor-loving and profit-loving man gets to the core of his conception of what it means to be noble, good, and free. As the above quotation makes clear, the difference between these two moral types lies entirely in the external results of their behavior. Ischomachus prefers the honor- and praise-lover because he sees him as more willing to run risks on Ischomachus' behalf and less likely to steal from him. The honor-lover, however, runs the risks and abstains from shameful profit because he wants honor and does not want to be punished. Thus, neither honor-lover nor profit-lover is concerned with the inherent goodness of his actions. This similarity between honor-lovers and profit-lovers is even more explicit in the previous chapter. In chapter 13, Ischomachus makes a distinction between slaves who are motivated "by the belly" (τῇ . . . γαστρί, 13.9) and those who are motivated "by praise" (τῷ ἐπαίνῳ, 13.9). However, he then points to the underlying similarity between these groups of slaves by saying that "some natures hunger after

---

dikaiosunē than "justice," it is not the usual meaning of the word and so conceals the discrepancy between Ischomachus' concrete ideas about justice and Socrates' ongoing quest to discover its moral meaning.

praise no less than other natures hunger after food and drink" (πεινῶσι γὰρ τοῦ ἐπαίνου οὐχ ἧττον ἔνιαι τῶν φύσεων ἢ ἄλλαι τῶν σίτων τε καὶ ποτῶν, 13.9).[11]

In the same chapter, Ischomachus makes a distinction between training animals and training people: "It is possible to make human beings more persuadable with speech by showing them that it is advantageous to obey" (ἀνθρώπους δ᾽ ἔστι πιθανωτέρους ποιεῖν καὶ λόγῳ, ἐπιδεικνύοντα ὡς συμφέρει αὐτοῖς πείθεσθαι, 13.9). Yet, Ischomachus' conception of what it means to persuade with speech makes him seem more like a sophist than a philosopher – at least as described by Socrates in Plato's *Republic*, when he compares the teaching methods of a sophist to the taming of a beast (493a–c). Like Socrates' sophist, Ischomachus does not actually try to investigate what moral goodness is as a quality apart from material or physical benefit, nor does he help others to discover it; instead, he manipulates the desires of those he wants to persuade and makes them more obedient by using praise and blame, rewards and punishments. In fact, Ischomachus immediately reverts to the idea that slaves can be trained exactly like beasts (13.9), a clue that he fails to take advantage of the human capacity for reason, and that his version of "speech" creates an enticement no different from that provided by food or material profit.

Ischomachus also has no conception of what it means to be truly free or willing. He thinks that he knows the secrets of ruling men and creating obedience, but in fact he has simply learned how to "tame the beast." The coercive nature of his control is indicated by his constant need to inspect his workers' performance (e.g. 12.19–20) and his belief that "the eye of the master produces especially noble and good work" (δεσπότου ὀφθαλμὸς τὰ καλά τε κἀγαθὰ μάλιστα ἐργάζεσθαι, 12.20).[12] Even though his coercion is not always physical, it is always based on the use of external motivation for good behavior; thus, it does not instill true willingness. As final proof of this, just as Cyrus' empire fell apart as soon as he died, it seems that Ischomachus' did too, if the identification of the historical Ischomachus is correct. Indeed, what all political regimes (and households arranged according to political principles) have in common in Xenophon is inevitable collapse or decline, a point which is underscored at the end

---

[11] Note, too, that Socrates had included a love of honor or ambition (φιλοτιμία) among the many vices that turn people into slaves in 1.22. Cf. Ambler (1996) 128: "Socrates' only words about ambition, on the other hand, refer to 'foolish and expensive ambitions,' and he sees them as a sign of servitude, not freedom (1.22)."

[12] Cf. Cyrus the Great's personal inspections in *Oec.* 4.8 and his extensive spy network, called the "eyes" and "ears" of the king, described in *Cyr.* 8.2.10–11.

of the *Cyropaedia* and the *Constitution of the Lacedaemonians*, as well as in the *Oeconomicus*.[13]

Ischomachus himself is as much a slave to praise and profit as any of his slaves, and although he controls the kingdom of his *oikos*, he is not truly free according to the Socratic principles laid out in the *Oeconomicus*. At the beginning of chapter 12, Socrates notes how hard Ischomachus works not to lose the title of καλὸς κἀγαθός (12.2). This comment is in response to Ischomachus' not wanting to depart until the market closes in case his guests arrive; in addition, Ischomachus has just finished telling Socrates how hard he works practicing his defense since he is constantly being accused of things (11.22–25). This fact, combined with his previous surprise that anyone would call him καλὸς κἀγαθός (7.3), is evidence that Ischomachus is not only striving after a potentially empty goal in life, but is striving after an elusive one. Socrates has already hinted to Critobulus that his own lifestyle will not bring him happiness (2.5–8), and he says he pities him lest Critobulus suffers irreparable damage and finds himself in a state of much difficulty (2.7). Through Ischomachus, Socrates shows Critobulus more clearly the grim specter of his future life if he does not change his desires and orient them in a more philosophical direction.

Ischomachus' desires all lead in a materialistic direction, and his ideal consists of perfect order in the physical world. As he tells his wife in 8.3, "there is nothing as useful or noble for human beings as order" (ἔστι δ᾽ οὐδὲν οὕτως, ὦ γύναι, οὔτ᾽ εὔχρηστον οὔτε καλὸν ἀνθρώποις ὡς τάξις), and he defines poverty as not being able to find something when you need it (8.2) – a definition that contrasts with Socrates' own definition of wealth as not needing more than you have (2.2). The physical nature of Ischomachus' ideal of order is underscored by the many instantiations of

---

[13] On the historical identification of Ischomachus, see my discussion in the introductory section of Part I. On the ending of the *Cyropaedia*, see my discussion in chapter 1, "Persian farming." At the end of the *Constitution of the Lacedaemonians* (*Lac.* 14), Xenophon bemoans the ways in which contemporary Spartans have lapsed in their virtue. On this controversial ending, see most recently Humble (2004), who supports the view that "Chapter 14 is not a disillusioned addendum, in opposition to the rest of the work but, rather, provides an insightful summary of the flaws of the Spartan system, to which Xenophon had been carefully drawing attention in Chapters 1–13" (225). I agree with her analysis, and while it is not without precedent (cf. Higgins [1977] 65–75), it is certainly not the most common way of reading the work, which is usually read as straight praise and admiration for Sparta (see her summary of approaches to the work on 215–17 and 220–21). Gray (2007) 217–21 also reads chapter 14 as being in harmony with the rest of the work but does not think it takes away from the praise of Lycurgus' laws: "The fourteenth chapter does challenge the perfection of the system that Lycurgus devised, since it leaves him open to the objection that he did not secure it against the corruption of empire overseas, but this does not diminish the excellence of the paradigm."

it in visual images that Ischomachus provides, such as the sight of a well-ordered chorus (8.3), or an army (8.6), or a ship (8.11–16). In a symbolic sense, the Phoenician merchant ship that Ischomachus describes at such length in chapter 8 might as well be Ischomachus' ship of state, and it is full of cargo "for the sake of profit" (κέρδους ἕνεκα, 8.13).[14] The profit is ultimately all for the owner of the ship, whether a king, a tyrant, or collectivity; yet, even at the top of the pecking order, the rulers themselves are enslaved to their desires and ambitions. Thus, according to Socratic values, there is no one who truly benefits in political regimes arranged according to unphilosophical values.

THE ART OF FARMING

The last seven chapters of the *Oeconomicus* turn to the art of farming itself. However, just as Ischomachus' lessons in household management were also a display of his art of ruling, so his art of farming might be interpreted metaphorically as a display of his approach to improving the soul or teaching virtue. One clue that Ischomachus' art of farming has a metaphorical aspect is that he utilizes many Socratic methods in this last part of the dialogue, such as the use of question and answer, *technē* analogies, and analogies from the plant and animal world. In addition, it was common in fifth-century literature and philosophy to use plant and soil metaphors to discuss human nature, and the analogy between crops and human nature played a role in the different educational theories and debates of the fifth century.[15] According to Plato, the sophists made their names by purporting to teach virtue, and they profited monetarily by doing so. It was crucial for them to highlight the malleable quality of human nature because their livelihood depended on their ability to shape it.[16] Thus, when Socrates has Ischomachus talk about how he likes to improve uncultivated land and make it more productive in order to make a profit (e.g. *Oec.* 20.22), Socrates is presenting him as a typical sophist,

---

[14] Roscalla (1990) 52 also points out that as a Phoenician ship, it has Persian connotations.

[15] E.g. Pi. *N.* 8.40–42, E. *Hec.* 592–602, Antipho Soph. F60 Pendrick (= Stob. 2.31.39). See also Pendrick's (2002) discussion *ad* F60 (409–12), with further examples from Hippocrates, Protagoras, and Democritus. The following maxim, ascribed to Antisthenes and discussed in Henrichs (1967) 45–53, nicely captures the metaphor at work in the *Oeconomicus*: "The farmer tames the land, the philosopher [human] nature" (ὁ μὲν γεωργὸς τὴν γῆν, ὁ δὲ φιλόσοφος τὴν φύσιν ἐξημεροῖ). Finally, Plato also uses the metaphor of the farmer in *R.* 589b to describe the rational part of the soul's taming of the desirous part. Cf. also the brief agricultural metaphor in Pl. *Tht.* 149e.

[16] Cf. Kerferd (1981) 132: "Indeed we can well understand that the sophistic profession as a whole simply could not accept the doctrine that virtue cannot be taught, and Protagoras was quite forthright on the point, as represented to us in Plato's *Theaetetus*."

preaching a *technē*.[17] It seems that now more than ever, Socrates is hoping Critobulus will make a comparison between himself and Ischomachus as a teacher.

Ischomachus' art of farming displays the basic differences between Socrates' conception of virtue and Ischomachus' and thus underscores for a final time the differences between real virtue and apparent virtue. Throughout his lessons on farming, Ischomachus emphasizes how easy an art it is to learn: there is no need for a detailed theoretical investigation into the nature of the soil because everything you need to know you can get through empirical learning (16.1–3). For Ischomachus, the senses are the route through which one learns farming, and when personal experience is lacking, you can rely on the experience of previous generations (17.1–2). We have already seen that for Ischomachus, morality and virtue are based in the physical world and defined by the satisfaction of physical needs and desires, and his theory of farming further underscores the physical nature of his conception of virtue. He explicitly makes nature herself his teacher when he presents the example of the vine, which teaches the farmer to care for it by setting an example through its own natural movements and processes (19.17–19). Success is defined by physical well-being, and nature teaches man all he needs to know to clear away the weeds and obtain it.

Yet, Ischomachus must now answer Socrates' all-important question, reminiscent of Critobulus' question to Socrates in 1.16: if farming is so easy, why do some not farm well (20.1)? This question might be interpreted as an allusion to another popular topic of debate in fifth-century Athens: if virtue can be taught why are all men not virtuous?[18] Ischomachus replies that the entire difference between success and failure lies in the amount of diligence or concern that the farmer shows, and he once again connects farming with war by suggesting that it is the same with generals: they are better or worse only in their "diligence" (ἐπιμέλεια) (20.6).[19] Thus,

---

[17] Socrates relishes the opportunity to emphasize the monetary aspect of Ischomachus' farming and points out to him that his father, who taught Ischomachus how to make a profit in farming, loved farming as much as merchants love grain (20.27).

[18] Cf. the *Protagoras*, in which Socrates wants Protagoras to explain why, if virtue can be taught, some good fathers have bad sons. Protagoras does not back down from the teachability of virtue, but does suggest some have more of a natural aptitude for it than others (326e–328c). However, as Ischomachus does with farming, Protagoras distinguishes the political virtues that he teaches from expert skills like flute playing, which some people have no aptitude for at all (*Prt.* 327a–c; cf. *Oec.* 19.16–17). Cf. also Pl. *Men.* 95c–96b.

[19] Cf. Protag. DK 80.10: "[Protagoras said,] 'Skill without practice and practice without skill are nothing.'" (Π. ἔλεγε <μηδὲν εἶναι μήτε τέχνην ἄνευ μελέτης μήτε μελέτην ἄνευ τέχνης.>). Shorey (1909) 200 calls ἐπιμέλεια a "frequent virtual synonym" of μελέτη "in the earlier rhetorical

Ischomachus believes that order based on physical success and material self-interest is easy to attain and completely controllable. That he is deluded in this belief, however, was underscored earlier by Socrates in his Praise of Farming. There Socrates made the point that men need the gods in farming and war because there are many elements that are *not* controllable. Disaster *does* strike the material world, and there is nothing particularly ordered about it.

Socrates also makes a more subtle point about why mere diligence is not enough to bring order to the world of farming. The issue of why some farmers fail and why some are successful comes back several times in the opening dialogue with Critobulus (1.16, 1.21, 3.5, and 6.11), and it was Critobulus' repeated desire to learn to be one of the successful farmers that generated the entire dialogue with Ischomachus in the first place. Thus, Socrates' answer to Critobulus' query develops in several stages. His initial answer is quite similar to Ischomachus': laziness and a "lack of diligence" (ἀμέλειαν) prevent men from doing what is useful (1.19–21). Even Critobulus can pick out some flaws in this facile explanation for failure, and so he asks Socrates to explain why even those who are industrious and diligent sometimes lose their estates and find themselves in difficult circumstances (1.21). This question prompts Socrates to further elucidate the harsh masters that can rule people's minds and prevent them from being successful, such as gluttony, drunkenness, and *foolish and costly ambitions* (1.22).

I have mentioned this passage many times, because it is so crucial for understanding the deeper lesson Socrates is trying to convey: part of the reason the industrious farmer will never be successful is because his very conception of what constitutes success is faulty. His ambition to be a rich farmer is one of the evil mistresses enslaving his mind: diligence in the service of material profit enslaves the soul as much as gluttony and laziness. Thus, Socrates follows up this diagnosis of the unsuccessful farmer's problems with his lament for Critobulus' lifestyle and his fear that he will suffer some misfortune (2.5–8). Socrates' goal is not to teach Critobulus to be a successful farmer in Ischomachus' meaning of the word, but to get him to change entirely what it means to be happy and successful.

Ischomachus' art of farming is symbolic of his entire approach to life. He likes farming because it is profitable and easy to learn. He uses nature

and ethical literature of the subject and especially in Isocrates and Plato." While I am not suggesting that Ischomachus is arguing for a particularly Protagorean conception of *technē*, I would suggest that Socrates portrays him as thinking within a particular sophistic, intellectual tradition of defining the powers of *technē*.

as his teacher and so identifies what is good and bad with what enables physical survival and material profit. He thinks he already knows all there is to know about farming successfully and has nothing more to learn; thus, he is the exact opposite of a philosopher, who, as Socrates reminds him, is characterized by a love of learning (16.9). Ischomachus praises the earth for being undeceptive and suggests it is easier to test the earth than a horse or a man (20.13); yet, this analogy emphasizes once again how Ischomachus conflates human beings with animals and plants. For Ischomachus, they differ only in the extent to which the dumber creatures can be controlled more easily.

Indeed, the art that Ischomachus does admit is difficult and requires more than *epimeleia* is the art of ruling other men. He calls those who have willing followers "high-minded" (μεγαλογνώμονας, 21.8). Such men also possess a "kingly nature" (ἤθους βασιλικοῦ, 21.10) and are "divine" (θεῖον, 21.11). He concludes:

<ὃ> σαφῶς δίδοται τοῖς ἀληθινῶς σωφροσύνη τετελεσμένοις· τὸ δὲ ἀκόντων τυραννεῖν διδόασιν, ὡς ἐμοὶ δοκεῖ, οὓς ἂν ἡγῶνται ἀξίους εἶναι βιοτεύειν ὥσπερ ὁ Τάνταλος ἐν Ἅιδου λέγεται τὸν ἀεὶ χρόνον διατρίβειν φοβούμενος μὴ δὶς ἀποθάνῃ. (21.12)

[The art of ruling] is clearly given to those truly initiated into self-control: but they give the art of ruling unwilling people, it seems to me, to those whom they consider worthy of living just as Tantalus in Hades is said to do, spending all eternity fearing that he'll die a second death.

Ischomachus finds the art of ruling a divine task because it involves the essentially impossible goal of organizing competing self-interests into an ordered whole. As Ischomachus' experience with ruling his household shows, in order for the ruled to sacrifice "willingly" their own self-interest for that of the ruler, they have to be deceived into thinking it is in their interest to do so through a system of punishments and rewards. The material world is a zero sum game, and there will always be conflict if self-interest is interpreted in a narrow, materialistic way.

Socrates' teaching method, which is essentially *his* art of ruling, seeks the active, willing participation of his students and requires them to join him in a quest for knowledge that will never find its complete fulfillment; thus, it is not exactly an easy art either – nor is it a typical *technē*. While there is a large amount of secondary literature dedicated to unraveling Socrates' *technē* analogies and to the question of whether or not Socrates thought moral knowledge could be a *technē*, I find Roochnik's contribution to the debate the most persuasive.[20] Roochnik emphasizes the *non*-technical aspect of Socratic knowledge and argues against those who believe "that in the early dialogues Socrates' use of the techne analogy represents Plato's assertion of a serious theoretical model of moral knowledge as a guide and telos of his philosophizing" (4), a model which is then replaced in later dialogues by "doctrines such as recollection and the separability of the forms" (8). Instead, Roochnik suggests that "[m]oral knowledge for Plato is far more precarious and difficult to recognize, far less systematic and professorial, than this" (15). *Technē* ("art, skill") is "the paradigmatic form of teachable, marketable knowledge" (193), but it is value-neutral and thus inherently not *moral* knowledge.

Roochnik does not focus on Socrates' use of *technē* analogies in Xenophon, but I would argue that the same conclusion applies to the *Oeconomicus*. Socrates begins the dialogue with a question about whether or not *oikonomia* is a *technē*. The labeling of farming as a *technē* returns in the discussion of the art of farming at the end, so there is an obvious comparison set up between Socrates' use of *technē* and Ischomachus'. Ischomachus thinks he has mastered a specific field of knowledge that brings profit, and thus his conception of farming is technical, even if it is easy to learn (18.10). Socratic farming, however, does not produce material profit and does not even produce perfect moral knowledge; it simply strives for it and strives to help others seek it. Still, the end result of Socratic farming, even if it is non-technical, is a progression towards true knowledge and away from ignorance.

XENOPHON'S *REPUBLIC*?

Roscalla (1990) has called the *Oeconomicus* a polemical response to Plato's *Republic* (39), and from antiquity till today, it has been assumed that Xenophon and Plato were rivals in their differing presentations of Socratic philosophy and in their attitudes towards politics and economics.[21] I hope to have shown that Xenophon's Socrates has much in common with Plato's in his "anti-economic" stance, and that Xenophon's *Oeconomicus* is not a

---

[20] Roochnik (1996). His bibliography covers the relevant works on *technē* and Plato, though the following have appeared since his publication: Parry (1996), Löbl (1997), Hemmenway (1999), and Balansard (2001). For *technē* in Xenophon, see Schaerer (1930) 39–56, Kanelopoulos (1993), and Wilms (1995).

[21] Aulus Gellius gives a summary of the various theories of polemical rivalry in their works but ultimately decides that such contention was beneath these philosophers, whom he deems the "two luminaries of Socratic charm" (*Socraticae amoenitatis duo lumina*, 14.3.11). Instead, he believes the stories about rivalry between them grew from rivalries between their supporters.

standard tract on ancient household management. Instead, through the metaphorical employment of *oikonomia*, Xenophon examines the ethics and politics of Athens (and beyond) to show that Socrates was the only true teacher of virtue and to cast doubt on the virtue of conventional political life, whether in city-states like Athens or in empires like Persia. In addition, I would suggest that Xenophon's *Oeconomicus* is not a polemical response to the *Republic* of Plato but instead a complementary work that emphasizes many of the same themes and that ultimately questions the possibility of finding justice in political regimes.[22] I will briefly lay out some of the similarities I see between the two works in order to provide further potential evidence for common ground between Plato's and Xenophon's Socratic teachings.

Like the *Oeconomicus*, the *Republic* is a bifurcated work: it begins with a familiar type of Socratic dialogue on the nature of justice (book 1), which, just like the opening dialogue of the *Oeconomicus*, some scholars have argued was composed separately (and earlier). This introduction or προοίμιον (357a) is then followed by an unfamiliar type of Socratic exposition, often called "middle Plato" in its philosophical style, in which Socrates seems to set forth concrete suggestions for an ideal state (*kallipolis*). Also like the *Oeconomicus*, the *Republic* has been interpreted in drastically different ways depending on how literally the "second" part is read. The traditional approach has been to read books 2–10 as if Socrates is putting forth seriously intended, positive doctrine, just as the orthodox approach to the *Oeconomicus* has been to take Socrates-as-Ischomachus at his word. I find more persuasive those readings of the *Republic* which treat it as a philosophical drama, whose teaching resides less in how the ideal city is put together, than in how it eventually falls apart.[23]

On this reading, the Socrates of the second part of the *Republic* essentially takes on the dual role of Socrates and Ischomachus and puts forth positive doctrine that collapses upon itself. Just as Socrates in the *Oeconomicus*

---

[22] Howland (2000) gives a persuasive account of Xenophon's *Anabasis* as a similarly complementary work to Plato's *Republic*: "Xenophon's *Anabasis*, a military adventure interwoven with a story of philosophical self-discovery, is a companion piece to Plato's *Republic*. The *Anabasis* takes up in deed the two great political problems treated in speech in the *Republic*, namely, how a just community can come into being and how philosophy and political power may be brought to coincide. In addressing the first of these problems, Xenophon makes explicit a lesson about the limits of politics that is implicit in the *Republic*" (875).

[23] Though there is great variety within these broad categories of approaches to the *Republic*, some examples of this latter approach include: Strauss (1964) 50–138, Bloom (1968) 307–436, Saxonhouse (1978), Arieti (1991) 231–46, Hyland (1995), Clay (2002), and Roochnik (2003). My brief interpretation of the *Republic* that follows has been influenced by all of them, though most profoundly by Saxonhouse (1978) and Roochnik (2003).

lets Critobulus' misguided ambitions shape their dialogue and teaches Critobulus what not to value by creating an extreme image, in the figure of Ischomachus, of Critobulus' mistaken ideals, so in the *Republic*, Socrates is guided by the faulty ambitions of Plato's brothers, Adeimantus and, particularly, Glaucon. Like Critobulus, they are trapped in the material world of conventional values, and they readily agree to Socrates' suggestion that justice might be more clearly understood if they examine a "big" version of it in the city and then apply their findings to the soul (368e–369b). Thus, they assent to a proposal that treats justice as if it were a physical quality that can be magnified and reduced, but whether this is the appropriate method for seeking justice is left in doubt.

Socrates first discusses the origin of the city (369b–372c) in a way that is reminiscent of Ischomachus' discussion of the origin of the household (*Oec.* 7.17–28). Just as Ischomachus' household was organized by a division of labor to compensate for the fact that every individual is not self-sufficient, so the origin of the city is based on physical need and a lack of self-sufficiency; thus, a division of labor develops to meet these needs (369b). Like Ischomachus' ideal *oikos*, this first city, which Socrates calls the "true" (ἀληθινή) and "healthy" (ὑγιής) city (372e), is essentially like a beehive in its careful organization and economic structure.[24] Glaucon, however, calls it a city of pigs and rejects it because it does not cater to the human desires for luxurious living (372d–e). Because of Glaucon's objection, the "luxurious city" (τρυφῶσαν πόλιν, 372e) is born, and, with it, the need for war to fight with neighbors for resources (373d–e). *This* is the city that becomes Kallipolis (named in 527c); thus, as Clay has noted, "Kallipolis has its foundation in an act of injustice. It is this act of aggrandizement and the warfare it provokes that makes the guardian caste necessary to Socrates' fully evolved city, and it is with this caste that Kallipolis is so naturally identified."[25] Just as farming was closely linked to war in the *Oeconomicus*, so is the "ideal" city of the *Republic*. Indeed, the entire structure of the city is generated by the need to control the desires for material gain and pleasure

---

[24] Though Socrates does not use the language of the hive in the first discussion of the city, bee imagery frequently appears later in Kallipolis. Cf. Saxonhouse (1978) 898 n. 30: "When Socrates describes the deterioration of the best city into the tyranny in Book 8, the animal images continue; here, though, the primary image is that of the bee to which the philosopher had previously been equated: 552c–d; 559d; 564b; 564c; 564d; 564e; 565a; 567d." See also 520b, in which Socrates compares the philosopher-kings to "leaders and kings in the hive" (ἐν σμήνεσιν ἡγεμόνας τε καὶ βασιλέας). Roscalla (1990) 42 takes Xenophon's use of bee imagery as further evidence of his allusions to the *Republic*.

[25] Clay (2002) 27. Cf. Saxonhouse (1978) 888: "Socrates' city is founded on a series of injustices, according to his own definition as it occurs in the *Republic*. He demands injustice to the city's rulers, injustice to its women, and injustice to its neighbors." See also Hyland (1995) 56.

unleashed by Glaucon and to get back to the "healthy" equilibrium of the city of pigs.[26] Kallipolis' ideal is Ischomachus', namely perfect physical order, and the language of morality is applied to whatever is conducive to this order.

Socrates' definition of justice, which is the purpose of this whole exercise in founding a city, comes as something of an anti-climax:

ὃ γὰρ ἐξ ἀρχῆς ἐθέμεθα δεῖν ποιεῖν διὰ παντός, ὅτε τὴν πόλιν κατῳκίζομεν, τοῦτό ἐστιν, ὡς ἐμοὶ δοκεῖ, ἤτοι τούτου τι εἶδος ἡ δικαιοσύνη. ἐθέμεθα δὲ δήπου καὶ πολλάκις ἐλέγομεν, εἰ μέμνησαι, ὅτι ἕνα ἕκαστον ἕν δέοι ἐπιτηδεύειν τῶν περὶ τὴν πόλιν, εἰς ὃ αὐτοῦ ἡ φύσις ἐπιτηδειοτάτη πεφυκυῖα εἴη.

ἐλέγομεν γάρ.

καὶ μὴν ὅτι γε τὸ τὰ αὑτοῦ πράττειν καὶ μὴ πολυπραγμονεῖν δικαιοσύνη ἐστί, καὶ τοῦτο ἄλλων τε πολλῶν ἀκηκόαμεν καὶ αὐτοὶ πολλάκις εἰρήκαμεν

εἰρήκαμεν γάρ.

τοῦτο τοίνυν, ἦν δ' ἐγώ, ὦ φίλε, κινδυνεύει τρόπον τινὰ γιγνόμενον ἡ δικαιοσύνη εἶναι, τὸ τὰ αὑτοῦ πράττειν. (433a–b)

For what we were legislating from the beginning about what always must be done, when we were founding the city, this, it seems to me, or some form of this, is justice. Surely we were laying down and often said, if you remember, that it is necessary for each individual to take care of one of the needs of the city, whatever his nature was most suited to do.

Yes, we said that.

And furthermore that to do one's own work and to not be a busybody is justice, and this we have heard from many other people and we ourselves have often said.

Yes, we have said that.

This, therefore, I said, dear friend, is probably justice, when it exists in a certain way, to do one's own work.

Socrates' proposed definition, when interpreted literally and in the context of the city he has just described, is thoroughly Ischomachean and conventional,[27] a fact that is underscored by his admission that this definition has been "heard from many other people." Yet, as always, Socrates adds further possible dimensions to his words via qualifications of his definition (e.g. "it seems to me, or some form of this," ὡς ἐμοὶ δοκεῖ, ἤτοι τούτου τι εἶδος, 433a) and the use of vague words that can be interpreted in vastly different ways. For now, however, he sticks with the conventional understanding of this definition and represents it with an image of the

---

[26] Cf. Roochnik (2003) 48: "Kallipolean legislation is meant to cure the fever and to restore the stability found in the city of pigs."

[27] Cf. Ischomachus' instruction to his wife that they should "each accomplish their proper duties as well as possible" (ὡς βέλτιστα τὰ προσήκοντα ἑκάτερον ἡμῶν διαπράττεσθαι, 7.29).

three classes of their proposed city, namely the money-making, warrior, and guardian class, each doing its job (434c).

Socrates increases the strangeness of equating justice with this mundane description of doing one's own job by now trying to apply that model to the soul. The city-soul analogy in book 4 is notorious for its difficulties, which have been pointed out even by those who read Plato doctrinally.[28] More importantly, however, they are pointed out by Socrates himself when he says it is unlikely they will understand the makeup of the soul with these methods and that there is another longer road to understanding the soul (435d).[29] Glaucon, however, is quite content to continue with the present methods, and so Socrates carries on to give an account of the tripartite soul, with justice consisting of each part of the soul, i.e. the calculating, spirited, and desiring part, performing its own task (435e–443b). Without giving an exhaustive list of the noted problems with the city-soul analogy, I will mention some of the main problematic implications of the tripartite scheme, as summarized by Roochnik (2003): "Either (1) there are totally irrational, and hence nonhuman, beings in the city and a totally irrational or nonhuman part in the soul, as well . . . or (2) the scheme suffers Bobonich's 'deep problem' and Williams's 'absurdity' that is, it generates an infinite expansion of 'parts' within the soul" (22). In addition, Roochnik notes the further correlation that "if reason and desire are counted as distinct parts, then it becomes impossible to account for the passionate desire for wisdom – that is, for philosophy itself" (20).[30] As if to acknowledge these flaws, Socrates finishes his discussion of the tripartite city and soul by calling it a "dream" (τὸ ἐνύπνιον, 443b) and "an *image* of justice" (εἴδωλόν τι τῆς δικαιοσύνης, 443c). Real justice is still not in their grasp, and the quarry they thought they had trapped has escaped.[31]

[28] For recent discussions of the difficulties, see Roochnik (2003) esp. 10–50 and Blössner (2007).

[29] Cf. Roochnik (2003) 10–11 on Socrates' introduction of the city-soul analogy: "It is crucial to note, however, that at the very moment he proposes the analogy, Socrates also calls it into question . . . When describing how useful it will be for reading the smaller set of letters first to read them written large, he says, 'I suppose it would be a godsend to be able to consider the littler ones after having read these first, if of course, they do happen to be the same' (368d). His 'if clause should force the reader to wonder whether the isomorphism holds or not. In fact, his 'if should raise the more basic question of whether either city or soul is actually composed of letterlike entities to begin with." See also Blössner (2007) 347: "That city and soul are similar is put forward as a hypothesis, as a supposition that must be put to the test." Roochnik further emphasizes the importance of Socrates' questions in 436a–b, in which Socrates raises the possibility that our soul in fact operates as a whole and not as three distinct parts.

[30] The references are to Bobonich (1994) and Williams (1997). Roochnik details the various attempts made by scholars to get around this problem but concludes that this arithmetic psychology is meant to be faulty and provisional and is corrected and replaced in books 8–9 of the *Republic* by a more unified and psychologically realistic conception of the soul.

[31] Cf. Socrates' humorous warning to Glaucon that they had better keep a close watch on justice, like hunters, so that it does not escape (432b).

It seems, then, that justice is not as simple a matter as physical harmony, and, even if it were, physical order is always liable to degeneration, a point which the *Republic* also underscores. For instance, despite all of the city's extreme legislation that is designed to prevent factionalism and increase stability, including the infamous "noble lie," rigid education programs, the complete restructuring of family life, and the institution of philosopher-kings, Socrates indicates the extreme fragility of this political order when he attributes its demise to a small mistake in the calculation of the proper season for breeding (546a–d). He puts this collapse in the context of the natural order: everything that comes to be also passes way (546a), and Kallipolis will be no different, no matter how hard it struggles to control *eros*. This was also the lesson that Xenophon taught in his studies of the eventual declines of Persia, Sparta, and the Persian-Spartan household of Ischomachus.

More important than the physical flaws in Kallipolis are the moral ones. Already in books 2–4, the citizens of Kallipolis have been reduced to animals. As Saxonhouse (1978) notes, "Socrates' city parallels comedy as it transforms the members of its guardian class from individuals with the potential for private virtue into the inhabitants of a barnyard" (888); "[w]ithin the educational scheme proper, the guardians are trained like animals and encouraged to become animals" (895). Book 5 increases this animalization of the city by basing the entire defense of the equal treatment of men and women, the abolition of family life, and the institution of eugenic breeding on the model of animals.[32] Socrates thus creates his own version of the *Birds* and the *Ecclesiazusae* in Kallipolis,[33] but with ultimately serious intent. I would argue that that intent is *not* to seriously advocate these proposals as either a practicable or ideal model, as many scholars have assumed, but to undermine them and to point to the inevitable dehumanization of human beings in political life. Kallipolis, even if ruled by philosopher-kings, is ruled by physical needs and desires, and so everyone is enslaved. True philosophers would never willingly enter into a contract with such a city, and Socrates drives this point home by telling Glaucon that the philosopher-kings will have to be forced to be the king bees of

---

[32] Saxonhouse (1978) notes too that even when Socrates talks specifically about human beings, he uses language that applies to animals: "The term used for 'mount' or 'cover' by Socrates is again one that applies in Greek only to animals" (896); "[w]hile the adults breed as if they were animals, the offspring are treated as if they were lambs or kids" (897).

[33] While the parallel with the *Ecclesiazusae* is more frequently made, Saxonhouse (1978) 891 points also to the similarities with the *Birds*: "Here, two Athenians leave Athens to find a commodious and pleasant place in which to live ... What they seek, it turns out, is the natural city ... These men find their natural city, devoted to the pursuit of pleasure, among the birds ... Socrates tries in the *Republic* to create the natural city in which natural justice will be found. As the city is founded in book 2, nature [*physis*] is the criterion (369a–b; 370c)."

this hive.[34] He further explains that the law is concerned only with the harmonious condition of the whole city and not with the individual well-being of each part. Thus, compulsion and persuasion must be utilized to bind the citizens together and force them to benefit each other (519e–520a). Again, there are strong echoes of Ischomachus' binding together of his household through persuasion and compulsion for the supposed common good of them all.

The lesson of the *Republic* seems to be that true politics, just like true *oikonomia*, can only exist in the context of philosophy and philosophical community. Thus, Socrates' ideal city might really be constituted by the dialogue itself – not by the specific content of books 2–10, but by the community of speakers in book 1 who help Socrates construct a city in speech. *This* city of participants in dialogue is a city in which free expression of opinion and conflicting views are valued over repression, poetry is utilized as a learning tool, and *eros* is allowed to roam free. It is, thus, the exact opposite of the repressive, Sparta-like regime that is supposedly idealized in the rest of the work.[35] It is appropriate, then, that the *Republic* ends with the Myth of Er, which culminates in the decision of Odysseus to choose the life of the "private, apolitical man" (ἀνδρὸς ἰδιώτου ἀπράγμονος, 620c) over any other kind of life (620c–d). Xenophon's *Oeconomicus*, far from being a polemical response to the *Republic*, presents a similar critique of political life and a corresponding defense of the life of philosophy.

---

[34] Cf. Saxonhouse (1978) 900: "The philosopher king organizing and governing the regime of the *Republic* cannot make people better if its subjects are soulless animals." Hyland (1995) 127 makes the important point that it is unlikely the philosopher-kings trained in Kallipolis would be real philosophers, anyway: "Indeed, part of the implausibility of such a regime is the necessity of hypostacized philosopher-rulers, who are portrayed not as philosophers in the literal sense elsewhere insisted upon and exhibited by Socrates – that is, as people who lack wisdom, recognize that lack, and strive for wisdom (and so are exemplars of our erotic nature) – but who are portrayed instead as wise people, with a comprehensive knowledge of the forms and how such forms are to be applied in governing."

[35] Cf. Roochnik (2003) 76: "Quite simply, despite requiring philosophy in order to come into being, Kallipolis is not itself philosophical, for its essential thrust is to constrain and repress the erotic impulse from which philosophy necessarily originates"; "Kallipolis, with its rigid class system and fierce restraint of speech, action, and Eros, is infamously antidemocratic. And yet, as has been implied by all the examples cited above, the very context from which Kallipolis emerges is democratic. For this reason, then Plato's *Republic*, far from being the condemnation of democracy it is typically thought to be, is in fact a qualified (and dialectical) supporter of it."

PART II

Varro's De Re Rustica

Varro begins the *De Re Rustica* by apologizing to his wife, conveniently named Fundania,[1] for writing so hastily and not as elegantly as he could if he had the "leisure" (*otium*) (1.1.1). The reason, he explains, is that "as the saying goes, if man is a bubble, the old man is more so. Indeed, my eightieth year warns me to pack up my things before departing from life" (*ut dicitur, si est homo bulla, eo magis senex. Annus enim octogesimus admonet me ut sarcinas conligam, antequam proficiscar e vita*, 1.1.1). In other words, he could die any time and thus must write fast! Traditionally, Varro's professed haste at the outset of his work has been used to explain away all the "peculiarities in the treatise" that I would argue are instead clues to the satiric nature of his work.[2] Varro's characters, including the persona of Varro himself, might commit blunders and produce flagrant inconsistencies in the course of the dialogue, but Varro the author crafts a subtle, satiric drama for his readers to untangle, and the satirical tone begins in the preface.[3]

In the next three chapters, I will present a reading of the *De Re Rustica* that is quite different from previous interpretations of the work. Instead

---

[1] As Henderson (2002) 131 aptly dubs her, "Mrs. Farmery."

[2] Most scholars follow Skydsgaard's (1968) 90 view: "Moreover in his introduction, Varro, now an octogenarian, makes no secret of his sense of urgency. Consequently, the interpretation that tries to see many pecularities [*sic*] in the treatise as the result of haste is borne out by Varro's own words." Martin (1971) 226–35 prefers to see Varro's haste as manifested in how he put together the three books of the dialogue and argues that they were written at three different time periods. His compositional theory has won wide assent, but, again, it is motivated purely by a perceived need to solve some of the "peculiarities" of the treatise, such as why Varro changes his position on the morality of pastoral activity in comparison to agriculture. I hope to convince that the *De Re Rustica* is a carefully written and unified work and that it was written and published approximately when Varro says it was (i.e. 37 BC).

[3] The proverbial expressions in the opening lines quoted above are typical of satire. For example, commentaries compare Varro's *si est homo bulla* to expressions in the satires of Lucian (*Char.* 19), Petronius (42.4), and Persius (2.9–10) (see Flach [1996] 221 and Heurgon [1978] 92). Heurgon (1978) 93 compares *sarcinas colligere* to Juv. 6.146. On the general associations of proverbs and maxims with satire, see Freudenburg (1993) 16. Another satirical aspect of the preface is Varro's parody of divine invocations: he invents and invokes a group of twelve gods particularly suited to farmers (1.1.4–7). On the parodic nature of Varro's list of twelve, see Heurgon (1978) 94 and Heisterhagen (1952) 72–74.

of reading the *De Re Rustica* as representative of elite Roman ideology, I argue that it is a subversive work, which uses farming as a vehicle to expose the hypocrisy and pretensions of Roman morality, intellectual culture, and politics in the Late Republic. It does this primarily by debunking the cultural myth of the virtuous farmer. While a satirist like Horace revealed the hypocrisy of urban fantasies about rustic life in *Epode* 2,[4] Varro goes further: he reveals that farming is valued by the Romans because of the material benefits it brings them and thereby deconstructs the notion of moral value by showing how it collapses with material value in Roman culture.[5] Varro reveals the moralizers in his text, who decry luxury and greed while praising the materialistic frugality of farmers and the prosperous nation of Italy, to show the same sort of hypocrisy as those whom Mandeville critiques in the *Fable of the Bees*. In addition, by metaphorically connecting the art of farming with the art of ruling, Varro exposes the selfish and greedy motivations of those involved in the "active life"; he then sets forth his own version of the contemplative life as a potential alternative to the life of the politician-farmer. The *De Re Rustica* is more than just a moral or political satire, however; it is a work that attacks pretensions to many different forms of knowledge, including the intellectual culture of the Late Republic of which Varro was very much a part. Book I of the work presents a parody of the Late Republican penchant for transforming various realms of knowledge into over-intellectualized art forms and of the rational optimism that accompanies it.[6] As I indicated in the introduction, I would classify its wide-ranging, parodic, and self-parodic satire as Menippean in spirit, if not in its exact form or genre.

This vision of the *De Re Rustica* is unfamiliar partly because Varro himself is usually thought to be the very type of Roman moralizer and over-intellectualizing pedant that I am suggesting he satirizes in his dialogue,

---

[4] Horace's second epode presents a long praise of the country life but ends with the revelation that the speaker, Alfius, is a money-lender who has no real intention of leaving the city. On the ironic moralizing in Epode 2, see Clayman (1980) 76: "The effect of Epode 2, then, is not to make one long for the country. Horace's purpose is to expose the superficiality of the 'back-to-nature' fad that had seized upon the Roman intelligentsia of his day and of the poetry which expressed these stylish sentiments." Cf. also Hor. *Ep.* 1.7, in which Volteius Mena unsuccessfully transfers from the city to the country.

[5] Perhaps it is not just in the *De Re Rustica* that Varro pursues this theme. Della Corte has hypothesized that an Alfius type of figure is a speaker in Varro's *Menippean Satire* subtitled Περὶ φιλαργυρίας ("concerning the love of money"; frs. 21–24 Cèbe), and in the same satire, Heinze has suggested that Varro critiques agriculture as a business obsessed with making money. For references and discussion of these views, see Cèbe (1972) 105–06, who is critical of these interpretations and prefers to read straight praise of agricultural life in this satire.

[6] On this intellectual climate in the Late Republic, see Rawson (1985) esp. 132–42, Martin (1995) esp. 89, and Wallace-Hadrill (1997) esp. 21–22.

and he has suffered from Xenophon's problem of being over-identified with the participants in his dialogue.[7] Like Xenophon, Varro was obviously an elite, political man, but also like Xenophon, he lived through a civil war that threatened to destroy his country and his life, and he wrote the *De Re Rustica* during one of the darkest periods in Roman history.[8] Cicero's letters to Varro give clear hints of Varro's eventual disaffection with public, political life and his preference for a private, contemplative one. I hope to show that this disaffection pervades the *De Re Rustica* and that Varro uses the *De Re Rustica* not to celebrate Roman elite ideology or to evoke some lost Republican ideal but to reveal the self-interest that is at the core of political life in general.

---

[7] E.g. Brunt (1972) 308 and Martin (1995) 86.
[8] On Varro's life and political career, which included being tribune of the plebs and praetor, fighting pirates with Pompey in 67 BC, fighting with Pompey in the civil war, being proscribed by Antony and saved by Fufius Calenus (though his library was not), and living in retirement until 27 BC, see Dahlmann (1935) 1172–81, Della Corte (1970), and Osgood (2006) 208–12.

CHAPTER 3

The art of farming

Though Varro began the *De Re Rustica* with an invocation to twelve agricultural gods, the star of book 1 is *ratio* ("reason") and not *religio* ("religion"). In this book, agriculture is presented as a rational art form by the modern-sounding farming expert Cn. Tremelius Scrofa, who engages in debate with the old-fashioned agronomist C. Licinius Stolo. Scholars have generally interpreted Scrofa's agricultural theories with utmost seriousness and present him as a great innovator, who contributed much to the advancement of agricultural science in the Late Republic.[1] Instead, I would argue that Scrofa is a semi-fictional, satiric character and that Varro creates this hyper-intellectual discussion of agriculture in book 1 as a parody of academic debates in the Late Republic, debates which are best represented in serious guise by those in Ciceronian dialogue.[2] In the end, both Scrofa and Stolo come off as incompetent intellectuals and farmers, and the world of *ratio*, with its optimistic attitude towards controlling nature, is cut down to size.

---

[1] Cf. the footnote to Scrofa's theory of agriculture (1.18.7–8) in the Loeb edition of *De Re Rustica* (Hooper and Ash [1934] 232 n. 1): "'Here, in a few words,' remarks Mr. Fairfax Harrison, 'is the whole doctrine of intelligent agriculture.' The neglect of this injunction is what has retarded the advance of science." Cf. also Martin (1971) 237–55, White (1973) 461–63, and Maggiulli (1994) 490. Heurgon (1978) xxxix–xlv is more cautious about estimating Scrofa's contributions to agriculture on the basis of book 1 and finds in him more Varro than Scrofa.

[2] Skydsgaard (1968), who provides an excellent analysis of Scrofa's many failings as a theorist and agriculturist (see 10–37), raises the possibility that his character is meant as a parody, but ultimately resists it: "[N]othing about Scrofa indicates that he is represented as being parodied. He is introduced into the dialogue with much reverence, and in later literature he is mentioned with respect as an agricultural theorist . . . [T]here is no apparent reason for Varro to make his immediate predecessor a main character in order to parody him. Consequently, we have to leave this interpretation out of consideration, ingenious though it may seem" (37). Martin (1971) 244 n. 4 leaves the question open, but would interpret any parody as a good humored satire of a respected elder. White (1973) 460 is willing to entertain Martin's suggestion, but Flach (1996) 28 follows Heurgon (1978) xl in rejecting it because he thinks Scrofa sounds too Varronian to be a parody.

SCROFA

Before analyzing the debate between Scrofa and Stolo, I would like to say a brief word about the historical Scrofa. No doubt one of the reasons readers have taken Scrofa seriously as a character is that he is attested by other ancient authors as a respected agronomist. Yet, closer inspection of these references reveals that Varro's version of Scrofa is hard to square with them and that he took some creative liberties in his portrayal. Our two main sources for Scrofa the agronomist, Pliny the Elder and Columella, present him not as a modern innovator, but as an old, and old-fashioned, practitioner. Pliny mentions Scrofa once in the text of his *Natural History*, in the context of Scrofa's commendation of growing vines on trees, and refers to him, along with the two Sasernas, as "the most ancient agriculturalists next to Cato and most skilled" (*vetustissimis post Catonem peritissismisque*, 17.199). Thus, Pliny seems to regard him as a very old authority on a level with the Sasernas and not as the modern agronomist of Varro's text, who routinely scoffs at the antiquated notions of the Sasernas (e.g. Var. *R.* 1.2.25).

When Scrofa is first mentioned by Columella, it is again in company with the Sasernas, as well as with Stolo (1.pr. 32–33). In addition, Columella begins his first chapter by citing an adage of Scrofa's that sounds old-fashioned and Catonian in its simple style: "For certainly, as Tremelius said, that person will have the best cultivated land who knows how to cultivate, is able to, and is willing to" (*nam is demum cultissimum rus habebit, ut ait Tremelius, qui et colere sciet et poterit et volet*, 1.1.1).[3] Finally, Columella critiques Scrofa's belief that the earth is declining in fertility and attributes Scrofa's error to his over-reliance on ancient authorities (2.1.2). Again, this Scrofa looks very unlike the one who praises the increased fertility of the earth due to modern methods in Varro (*R.* 1.7.2).[4] While Columella's nine other brief references to Scrofa's opinions present no glaring contradictions with Varro,[5] they also provide no confirmation that Varro's portrait of Scrofa has any accuracy.[6] In addition, it has bothered

---

[3] Cf. the similar tricolon of verbs connected by *et* in Cato *Agr.* 5.5: *si hoc faciet, minus libebit ambulare et valebit rectius et dormibit libentius* ("if he does this, he will be less likely to walk about, he will be healthier, and he will sleep more peacefully").

[4] For acknowledgment and discussion of this discrepancy, see Martin (1971) 242 and Heurgon (1978) xlii–xliv.

[5] Col. 1.1.6, 2.1.5, 2.8.4, 2.10.8, 2.13.3, 3.3.2, 3.11.8, 3.12.5, and 5.6.2, collected in Speranza (1974) 50–55.

[6] Cf. Speranza (1974) 50, who notes the lack of correspondence between the fragments of Scrofa and the remarks of Scrofa in Varro's text. Heurgon (1978) xli notes that Var. *R.* 1.44.1 matches up with Scrofa's prescription in Col. 2.10.8 about how many *modii* of beans are required by a *iugerum* of land, but he also notes that in Varro, it is Stolo who is speaking and not Scrofa.

critics that Varro never mentions any of Scrofa's written works in the *De Re Rustica*. Many theories have been proposed to explain this silence, and most scholars suggest that Scrofa had simply not yet published his work when Varro composed book 1 or at book 1's fictional date.[7] Even if this explanation is accepted, it is still difficult to reconcile the old, traditional-sounding Scrofa of Columella's and Pliny's texts with the scientific expert and contemporary of Varro.

Not only are the various images of Scrofa *qua* agronomist hard to reconcile with each other, but the various dates of Scrofa's political achievements given in Varro's text and elsewhere suggest that there was more than one Scrofa making a name for himself in Rome at the time. For instance, the Scrofa who is described as *praetorius* (Var. *R.* 2.4.2) in 67 BC, the fictional date of book 2, is unlikely to be the same Scrofa who Plutarch (*Crass.* 11.4) says was quaestor during the war against Spartacus (i.e. 71 BC). Martin suggests there were two different Scrofas, a father and son; Brunt agrees but would make the second Scrofa collateral with the first; Perl distinguishes even more Scrofas.[8] Münzer finds chronological contradictions even within Varro's work that cannot be solved by distinguishing more Scrofas, not only because he identifies Varro's agronomist with the other contemporary references to Scrofas, who seem to be younger than our praetorian, but also because he interprets Scrofa's allusions to leading an army in Gaul (*R.* 1.7.8) as referring to a period after Caesar's first campaigns there (i.e. after 55 BC), and thus after the fictional date of book 1.[9] In an attempt to save Varro's accuracy and consistency, scholars have attacked Münzer's interpretation of the Rhine passage (*R.* 1.7.8), as well as his conflation of the Scrofas.[10]

Thus, Varro's Scrofa is a problematic character if interpreted as a serious historical portrait. Interpreted as a semi-fictional character, however, he is a brilliant addition to Varro's parodic dialogue. I would argue that Varro conflates two different Scrofas in his depiction: the respected agronomist of the older generation, who wrote on agriculture in an old-fashioned manner, and a younger Scrofa who served with Varro on Caesar's agrarian

---

[7] Skydsgaard (1968) 66 is not happy with the suggestion that Scrofa's work was simply published after the dramatic date of the dialogue because "we have found other anachronisms in Book 1, so this will not explain either, with any degree of certainty, why Varro does not somehow mention Scrofa's work. Considering that Scrofa was a close friend of Varro's and a prominent member of Roman society, it is in fact inexplicable that Varro does not pay him the compliment of mentioning his work." On this problem, see further Martin (1971) 241–43, Brunt (1972) 307, Noè (1977) 120–22, and Flach (1996) 25–27.

[8] See Martin (1971) 238–41, Brunt (1972), and Perl (1980).   [9] Münzer (1937).

[10] See Martin (1971) 238–41, Brunt (1972), Perl (1980), and Badian (1996). Flach (1996) 252 defends Münzer's dating and interpretation of the Rhine activity.

commission (*R.* 1.2.10) and had wealthy estates, but no particular expertise in agriculture.[11] The humor of this depiction, then, comes not just from the mistakes in Scrofa's hyper-intellectual discourse, but from the misrepresentation of his character, a misrepresentation that I suggest parodies the Ciceronian practice of imposing unrealistic views and conversations on his dialogue participants.

Indeed, in the *De Oratore*, which Martin (1995) has shown provides a model for the debate between Scrofa and Stolo in book 1,[12] Cicero transforms Crassus and Antonius into Late Republican intellectuals who debate whether or not oratory has the status of an art form. That the discourses which come out of their mouths (especially Crassus') sound more like Cicero's views than those of either historical character is recognized by modern critics, as well as by ancient (cf. Quint. 10.3.1). Even Cicero acknowledges (*de Orat.* 2.7) that neither man had a reputation for a learned intellect (though he hopes his dialogue will change that impression) and implies that Antonius' surviving writing looks nothing like the *De Oratore* (*de Orat.* 1.94, 2.8).[13]

It is not just in the *De Oratore* that Cicero ignores historical accuracy in favor of creating Ciceronian-sounding experts. In the *De Senectute*, he turns the money-oriented and plain-speaking Cato the Elder of the *De Agri Cultura* into a Greek-inspired philosopher-farmer focused on the pleasures of farming.[14] Jones (1939) has suggested that perhaps Cicero was criticized

---

[11] After all, when Varro explains why Scrofa was "a man polished in all the virtues and considered to be the Roman most skilled in agriculture" (*virum omnibus virtutibus politum, qui de agri cultura Romanus peritissimus existimatur*, 1.2.10), his explanation has nothing to do with theoretical expertise but simply adduces Scrofa's fertile estates as evidence (1.2.10). Of course, Scrofa himself has nothing to do with the actual farming of his estates, an activity which is left to hired hands or slaves, as he points out in 1.17.2: "all fields are cultivated by slaves or freemen or both" (*omnes agri coluntur hominibus servis aut liberis aut utrisque*).

[12] In particular, Martin (1995) 86–87 notes an allusion in Scrofa's reply to Agrasius' question about whether agriculture is an art ("he, not reluctant . . ." *ille non gravatus . . .* , *R.* 1.3.1) to the beginning of Crassus' speech in *de Orat.* 1.107 ("nor will I be reluctant . . . ," *neque gravabor . . .*), in which Crassus characterizes oratory loosely as an art, albeit one that does not aim at precise knowledge and certainty.

[13] Cf. Brunt (1972) 308: "[I]n that very dialogue [i.e. *De Oratore*] Cicero makes Antonius refer to the *libellum* in disparaging terms (i.94; cf. 206), no doubt that the reader may be reassured if the views ascribed to him in the dialogue are not identical with those in his published work." See also Rawson (1985) 146 on the presumably "primitive" nature of Antonius' tract and Jones (1939) 317–18 on Antonius' unlikely development from book 1 into a more intellectual figure in book 2: "There is a strong contrast to this attitude in Book II, in which Antonius is portrayed with a knowledge of, and appreciation for, Greek writers, especially orators and historians (*De Or.*, II, 55–58, 59, 60, 61, 93–95, 160). Cicero's arguments to refute the charge that Antonius was unlearned are weak and are contradicted by a specific statement in the *Brutus* (214)."

[14] On some of the discrepancies between these two versions of Cato, see Cossarini (1976–77) 80–81, Novara (1980), and Maggiulli (1995).

for attributing Greek learning to Cato and so "to avoid similar criticism in the *De Amicitia . . .* he made Laelius refer but seldom to Greek literature and philosophy, feign an ignorance of Greek learning, and avoid all mention of Diogenes and Panaetius" (316). Whether or not that particular criticism was made, we know from a letter to Quintus that a similar criticism was made about the participants in the *De Re Publica* (*Q. Fr.* 3.6): Cicero relates that after hearing a draft of the *De Re Publica* read aloud to him in the presence of Sallustius, the latter suggested that Cicero transfer the dialogue to the present era with Cicero as one of the speakers since otherwise it would sound as if he had imposed unrealistic views on his speakers (3.6.1).[15]

Cicero notes further criticisms of himself in the first edition of the *Academica*: "There are also those who deny that the people who talk in my books have knowledge about the things they discuss; these people seem to me to envy not only the living but also the dead" (*sunt etiam, qui negent in iis qui <in> nostris libris disputent fuisse earum rerum de quibus disputatur scientiam. qui mihi videntur non solum vivis sed etiam mortuis invidere*, 2.7). Despite his criticism of his critics here, Cicero himself expresses relief in several letters to Atticus (*Att.* 13.12.3, 13.16.1, and 13.19.3) that he could transfer the conversation of the *Academica* to Varro since he admits it was a bit of a stretch to superimpose the sophisticated academic discussion on Catulus, Lucullus, and Hortensius. Of course, even the conversations with Varro were never actually held, as Cicero explains in a letter to Varro (*Fam.* 9.8): "I think that when you read it, you will be surprised that we had a conversation which we never actually had, but you know the convention of dialogues" (*puto fore ut, cum legeris, mirere nos id locutos esse inter nos quod numquam locuti sumus, sed nosti morem dialogorum*).[16]

Varro did know the conventions of dialogues, and he knew how to parody them: both the character of Scrofa and the pretentious debate he has with Stolo may be read as witty parodies of Ciceronian dialogue,[17] and I would suggest their presence in Varro's agricultural dialogue is motivated more

---

[15] Jones (1939) 312 also notes that "[Cicero's] willingness to change the date to his time and to assume the principal role himself" suggests that "the views expressed in the *De Republica*, especially in the two books he had thus far written, were his own."

[16] Cf. Jones (1939) 325: "It is not to be expected, however, that in a dialogue [i.e. the *Academica*] that had been changed so much there would be a very realistic representation of Varro or of any of the other characters."

[17] Rösch-Binde (1998) 324–46 has recently discounted the possibility that the *De Re Rustica* parodies Ciceronian dialogue, but she does so on an extremely limited basis – namely, by comparing the formal features of the *De Re Rustica* with the *De Finibus*. As noted in my introduction, she does allow the possibility that Varro's dialogue has parodic aspects to it, similar to Menippean satire (345). Diederich (2007) 180–81 sees elements of parody in the *De Re Rustica*'s engagement with the *De Oratore*.

by their punning names ("sow" and "plant shoot") and famous relatives than their actual knowledge.[18] Even the idea of writing a philosophical dialogue on the topic of farming might be read as a retort to Cicero, who has Antonius present farming as a empirical art and not a rational one in *de Orat.* 1.249, and who writes in *Fin.* 3.4 that farming is not a suitable subject for polished elegance.[19] However, rather than seriously challenging Cicero's presentation of farming, as Martin (1995) argues, I would suggest the *De Re Rustica* uses it as a starting point for a more general send-up of the intellectual tendencies of the age. While both Cicero and Varro were leading representatives of these tendencies, I will argue that Varro had a more self-conscious and ironic attitude towards encyclopedic and analytic knowledge, and that he displays this attitude even in his more serious works of scholarship, a suggestion I will return to later in this chapter.

RATIO VS. CONSUETUDO

The dialogue proper begins with a typical dialogue setting during a festival, which provides the necessary *otium* for intellectual conversation (*R.* 1.2.1).[20] Two experts on agriculture just happen to drop by, Scrofa and Stolo, the latter known for his diligence in farming ("who, on account of his diligence in cultivation, confirmed that he deserves the family name of Stolo," *et qui propter diligentiam culturae Stolonum confirmavit cognomen,* 1.2.9) and the former for his skill ("who is considered to be the Roman most skilled in agriculture," *qui de agri cultura Romanus peritissimus existimatur,* 1.2.10). The contrast between Stolo's *diligentia* and Scrofa's skill hints at a juxtaposition between two types of knowledge, namely empirical (*consuetudo*) and rational knowledge (*ratio*); this juxtaposition is reminiscent both of Antonius' debate with Crassus on the type of knowledge required by oratory and the discussion between Ischomachus and Socrates on the nature of

---

[18] As Speranza (1974) 58 notes regarding Stolo, "Varro relates more information about Stolo's ancestors than about our Stolo" (*plura de C. Licinii Stolonis maioribus tradidit Varro quam de nostro Stolone*). Indeed, there is even less external evidence for the agricultural expertise of Stolo than there is for Scrofa. Pliny never cites Stolo as an authority, and Columella does not include him in his list of Roman agricultural writers (1.1.12), a bibliography which Martin (1971) calls "très complete" (255 n. 1). There are two vague mentions of Stolo in Columella (1.pr. 32, 4.11.1), but there is no strong evidence that Columella has a source other than Varro for the character. On Varro's punning names throughout the dialogue, see Linderski (1989) esp. 114–20. "Significant names" are a distinct feature of satire and comedy, on which, see Rudd (1966) 132–59, Braund (1989b) 29, and Freudenburg (1993) 48–49.

[19] Cf. Rawson (1985) 137: "Possibly Varro was taking up the challenge of a passage in Cicero's *De Finibus*, which claims that the subject of agriculture is quite unsusceptible of literary refinement."

[20] Cf. the settings of Cic. *Rep.* 1.14 and *N.D.* 1.15.

the farming *technē*.[21] A dichotomy between their approaches to agriculture is further suggested when we learn that Scrofa is now (*nunc*) the master of agriculture and that Stolo once was (*olim*) (1.2.12). This contrast between *nunc* and *olim* seems to associate Scrofa with modern, trendy methods and Stolo with an older, and now less popular, approach.

Scrofa takes the lead in answering Agrius' initial, theoretical question about the ends of agriculture ("tell us what is the purpose of agriculture, utility or pleasure or both?" *docete nos, agri cultura quam summam habeat, utilitatemne an voluptatem an utrumque,* 1.2.12) with a long digression on how to limit and define the meaning of agriculture (1.2.12–28). In doing so, he follows good Ciceronian practice of starting an investigation by defining the topic under debate.[22] Stolo inserts his view into the discussion that *agri cultura* proper should be firmly separated from the related field of *pastio* (1.2.13) and again seems quite similar to Antonius in the *De Oratore*, who argues for a more limited definition of oratory (1.209–18). Scrofa and Stolo are joined in this attempt to define agriculture by the other participants in book 1, namely Varro, Agrius, Agrasius, and Fundanius. It immediately becomes clear that while Scrofa and Stolo may be the "experts," the other participants share an equal penchant for intellectualism, as they eagerly toss in etymological explanations of different agricultural terms (1.2.14), quote Greek authorities (1.2.16), give aetiological explanations of religious ritual (1.2.18–20), and scoff at earlier Latin authorities (1.2.22–28). While Varro had said in his preface that after defining the proper realm of agriculture, he would follow the natural divisions of the subject (1.1.11), the many different categories and definitions of agriculture put forth in this debate seem to indicate that there are no *natural* divisions, but only the schematic contrivances of intellectuals.[23]

After they have defined the limits of agriculture, Agrasius asks Scrofa to discuss whether farming is "an art or something else" (*ars id an quid aliud,* 1.3.1). Scrofa readily responds: "it is not only an art, but a necessary and great one; and it is also a science" (*non modo est ars, sed etiam necessaria*

---

[21] Ischomachus tells Socrates that farming is a pleasant, noble, and useful art (*Oec.* 15.4), which is easy to learn and requires not *epistēmē* (knowledge), but *epimeleia* (diligence) (20.2–15). In the *De Oratore*, Antonius, who is less ready than Crassus to give oratory the status of an *ars* (2.30–33), gives a veritable ode to *diligentia* (2.147–51) and explicitly notes that good oratory owes more to *ingenium* ("natural ability") and *diligentia* than to *ars* (2.150). He also associates *ars* with knowledge (*scientia*) as opposed to opinion (*opinio*) (2.30). Crassus, on the other hand, associates oratory with *ars* and skill (1.109). See further Martin (1995) on the debates in the *De Oratore* and *De Re Rustica* over the types of knowledge required by the arts of oratory and farming.

[22] E.g. *Rep.* 1.38.

[23] Cf. Rawson (1985) 138: "One wonders if Varro, in imposing this elegant symmetry [in his subdivisions in book 2], really thought he was following the *naturales divisiones* of the subject."

ac magna; eaque est scientia, 1.3.1). This response puts him in the tradition of Crassus, who extolled the importance of oratory (*de Orat.* 1.29–34) and allowed it to have the status of an art form (1.107–09); it opposes him to the less theoretical conception of both farming (1.249) and oratory (2.30–33) put forth by Antonius. Yet, even Crassus had hesitated to apply such a fancy theoretical framework to the topic of oratory (1.102–03), and Scrofa's comparative eagerness to apply it to an arguably less appropriate subject underscores his pedantic nature.[24]

Scrofa firmly establishes the intellectual pretensions of his agricultural art by giving it a tripartite structure akin to the Hellenistic division of philosophy into physics, ethics, and logic or dialectic.[25] He explains the physical aspect of farming with a quotation from Ennius ("the basic elements of farming are the same as those of the universe as Ennius writes: water, earth, air, and sun," *eius principia sunt eadem, quae mundi esse Ennius scribit, aqua, terra, anima et sol*, 1.4.1), the ethical aspect with a statement of its *summum bonum* or *summa bona*, as the case is here ("farmers ought to aim at two goals, utility and pleasure," *agricolae ad duas metas dirigere debent, ad utilitatem et voluptatem*, 1.4.1), and the dialectical aspect with an extensive display of the divisions of agriculture (1.5.3–4).[26] He further solidifies the reputation of the farming art by comparing it to that of medicine in its ability to improve the lives of mankind and lessen the risks of nature (1.4.3–5).

Indeed, a distinctive feature of most *technai* or *artes* is their ability to increase man's control over *tuchē* and *casus*, or the uncontrollable elements of nature,[27] and Scrofa fully exploits this aspect of *ars* and *scientia* in his discussion of agriculture. There is a double level at which agriculture represents this ordering power of *ars* and *ratio* in Scrofa's teaching: in a physical sense, farming fights against the power of nature to destroy human production, and in an intellectual sense, by being made into an archetypal *ars*, farming represents the ordering power of the human mind. On both levels, however, Scrofa's confident faith in human skill proves to be misplaced, and the parodic aspects of Scrofa's character are most clearly

---

[24] One is perhaps reminded of the figure of Catius in Hor. *S.* 2.4, who turns dining into an *ars* with philosophical pretensions.

[25] On this division, which may have originated with the post-Platonic Academy of Xenocrates, see Algra *et al.* (1999) xi–xvii and Long and Sedley (1987) I.158–62. One of the metaphors used by philosophers for this tripartite scheme is that of a fertile field or orchard, with the wall corresponding to logic, fruit to ethics, and the land or trees to physics (e.g. D.L. 7.39–41).

[26] As Diogenes Laertius notes, definitions and divisions are part of dialectic (7.43–44). See also Algra *et al.* (1999) 66–67.

[27] See Nussbaum (1986) 89–121 and Roochnik (1996) 17–88.

seen when his supposed expertise on farming is revealed to be anything but expert.

Scrofa loses control of his "art of farming" early in his discourse: after dividing the topic of agriculture into four main divisions with two sub-divisions each (1.5.3–4), he completely bungles his own categories when he actually discusses them.[28] It is not just his organizational skills that are faulty, and Skydsgaard has well documented the further failings in both Scrofa's and Stolo's teachings. In addition to giving generally impractical instructions, which substitute etymologies for the most important farming information,[29] Scrofa and Stolo also frequently misquote Theophrastus, or use his advice in the wrong contexts,[30] and at times give complete mis-information about farming.[31] Thus, both Scrofa and Stolo come across as out-of-touch pedants, who know very little about actual farming.

Another way in which the intellectual pretensions of Scrofa and Stolo are undermined is that the distinction between Stolo's old-fashioned approach and Scrofa's modern one collapses in the course of the dialogue. While Scrofa scoffs at past authorities[32] and Stolo frequently quotes them,[33] in the end, their discourses on farming sound more alike than different. Not only are Scrofa's criticisms of his predecessors superficial,[34] but his own prescriptions at times resemble the simple and lowly advice of a Cato or Saserna.[35] For his part, Stolo quotes Theophrastus (e.g. 1.37.5 and 1.40.3) despite his initial statement that his work was more suited for philosophers (1.5.1–3), and he throws in as many arcane etymologies as Scrofa (e.g.

[28] For details of Scrofa's deviations from his original outline, see Skydsgaard (1968) 12–21. See also Ross (1979), who suggests emending the text to avoid the difficulty posed by Scrofa's errors in organization. No emendation is necessary, however, if Scrofa is read as a satirical character.

[29] As Skydsgaard (1968) notes, Stolo's discourse seems designed to fill in the gaps left by Scrofa's, namely by describing the practical farming operations, but Stolo, too, misses the mark: "Stolo's discourse deals with some, but only some, of the points we missed in Scrofa's discourse. Many points of vital importance to agriculture are mentioned peripherally or not at all, and more technical instructions are rather scarce" (25).

[30] See Skydsgaard (1968) 64–88.

[31] See Skydsgaard (1968) 118: "Varro has put some of the farm operations at the wrong time, e.g. the planting of thyme and lily . . . or of suckers and layers . . . On the same grounds, the information about the rotation of crops in Olynthos must be said to be misleading . . . Further, the description of grafting and shield budding is so confused that it leaves a very distorted [*sic*] picture."

[32] E.g. 1.2.25 (The Sasernas) and 1.18.1–7 (The Sasernas and Cato).

[33] E.g. 1.7.1–2 (Cato), 1.7.9 (Cato), and 1.9.7 (Diophanes).

[34] Skydsgaard (1968) 16 defends his superficial polemics but only on the grounds that "the pervading feature of ancient polemics seems to have been to misunderstand the opponent, twisting his arguments, and carrying them *in absurdum*." He cites as a comparison, "Cicero's censure of the Epicureans in the *De Finibus*" (16 n. 14). Varro may indeed have imitated Ciceronian polemics, but that does not mean he could not have a parodic intent in doing so.

[35] For instance, he quotes Cato in 1.24.4, but it is Varro as narrator who makes clear the source of the quotation, not Scrofa.

1.48.2–3). Finally, Scrofa's explanation of how human beings should learn the principles of farming further conflates *ratio* and *consuetudo*:

bivium enim nobis ad culturam dedit natura, experientiam et imitationem. antiquissimi agricolae temptando pleraque constituerunt, liberi eorum magnam partem imitando. nos utrumque facere debemus, et imitari alios et aliter ut faciamus experientia temptare quaedam, sequentes non aleam, sed rationem aliquam. (1.18.7–8)

For Nature has given us two paths to culture/agriculture, experiment and imitation. The most ancient farmers settled on most things by experimenting, their descendants mostly by imitating. We ought to do both, to imitate others and to try certain things in a different way by experiment, following not chance but some rational method.

Scrofa emphasizes the importance of *both* experience and rational method, and there suddenly seems to be little difference between his approach and Stolo's.

This converging of Scrofa's and Stolo's approaches to farming finds a model once again in the *De Oratore*: while Crassus and Antonius each puts forth his own version of the art of oratory, it becomes clear that their opinions are not that different after all, especially regarding whether or not oratory is an art. As Crassus himself points out, the whole controversy turns on the definition of the word *ars* (1.107). Cicero uses this semantic strategy elsewhere, as well: the last two books of the *De Finibus* underscore the similarities between the ethical beliefs of the Stoics, Peripatetics, and Academics and suggest that the differences are mainly terminological. The difference in the *De Re Rustica* is that Varro's competing farming experts never explicitly acknowledge the convergence of their views; thus, they come off not only as incompetent "experts," but as academics who seem more passionate about arguing competing claims and guarding their turf than about advancing the knowledge of their field – the very type of know-it-all experts who populate Menippean satire.

VARRO: SATIRIST OR PEDANT?

While Skydsgaard and others have noticed the failings of Scrofa's and Stolo's teachings, they have resisted reading the characters as parodies since their flaws seem so Varronian.[36] Perhaps, however, we have been taking

---

[36] E.g. Skydsgaard (1968) 36: "Applying the analytic method at every opportunity is so much part and parcel of Varro's method of approach that he just cannot help schematizing. One would, therefore, expect that he would be able to do it with much greater virtuosity than he actually does . . . We

Varro too seriously not just in the *De Re Rustica*, but in other works, as well, and so the strict division of Varro's work into satires and scholarly treatises may be misguided. While certainly it is difficult to prove too much about lost or fragmentary works, I would like to briefly suggest different ways in which we might understand the tone of two of his "serious" works, namely the *De Philosophia* and *De Lingua Latina*.

Skydsgaard (1968) cites as a comparison to Varro's analytic method in the *De Re Rustica* his listing of 288 philosophical sects in the *De Philosophia*, a work which he notes has "caused even more laughter – or indignation – than Book II of *De Re Rustica*" (36 n. 15). He does not think that Varro intended his work to be funny, but what if Varro did? Our knowledge of the *De Philosophia* is sketchy: Cicero does not mention it in the *Academica* and nor does Jerome in his catalogue of Varro's works. Our knowledge of it is based only on quotations from Augustine. Thus, it seems likely that it was hidden in Jerome's catalogue as part of a larger work, and Tarver (1997) has recently supported the view that it was one of the *Logistorici*. He further suggests that the words that Augustine attributes to Varro were probably spoken by an interlocutor in a dialogue (Tarver [1997] 152–59). This suggestion raises the possibility that a know-it-all type of speaker created these pedantic divisions, and that they were meant to be amusing.[37]

In the *De Lingua Latina*, Varro is the speaker, and he makes use of pedantic divisions, academic debates, and etymologies throughout the work. Even so, Varro's satiric and parodic wit is not necessarily absent from this endeavor. For instance, books 8–9 of the work are devoted to detailing a supposed great quarrel between analogists (those who argue that language should be regularized according to rational principle) and anomalists (those who favor the anomalies of actual usage). Once again, Varro has created a debate between proponents of *ratio* (analogists) and *consuetudo* (anomalists). Yet, most scholars believe Varro either exaggerated or completely invented this bizarre quarrel.[38] Not only is Varro our only source for the quarrel, but the quarrel itself comes across as rather ridiculous. While there did exist an opposition between the Alexandrian

---

cannot help asking how such things can happen at all to an experienced writer like Varro. The answer may simply be that he has been pressed for time." Skydsgaard goes on to question the possibility that Scrofa's character is meant as a parody but rejects it (see my further discussion in the introductory section of chapter 3).

[37] I would offer the further suggestion that the *De Philosophia* could have been a *Menippean Satire*. We know that book 2 of the *Menippean Satire* entitled Περίπλους was called Περὶ φιλοσοφίας, and it thus seems a possible candidate for Augustine's source.

[38] See esp. Fehling (1956–57) and Collart (1963).

approach to editing Homeric texts and teaching Greek (in favor of analogy) and the Stoic approach (in favor of anomaly), and thus a tradition of defenders of analogy (including Julius Caesar), there was no one who seriously argued that analogy had no role in language. The "anomalist" position in Varro's debate is carried to an extreme and is a severe deformation of the Stoic position.[39] In addition, each side of the debate in the *De Lingua Latina* is given specious (but amusing) arguments to support its cause, such as the anomalists' argument that analogy does not exist even if it is present in some aspects of language by the same reasoning that Ethiopians are not considered white because they have white teeth (8.38).

Scholars who recognize the absurdity of this debate have proposed serious reasons for Varro's creation of it and thus avoid reading it as parody or satire,[40] but once again, I would raise the possibility that we have been taking Varro too seriously here. Varro's debate in books 8–9, like the debate between Stolo and Scrofa, could be a witty parody of academic debates such as those found in Ciceronian dialogue. Varro even provides the ultimate Ciceronian conclusion to his debate by reconciling the two opposing camps: not only does he provide a synthesis of the two in book 10, but he explicitly suggests that the whole controversy is a semantic one (10.6; cf. Crassus in *de Orat.* 1.107) and that analogy and anomaly are connected and work in conjunction with one another (9.2–3; cf. Scrofa in *R.* 1.18.7–8). In fact, the influence of Ciceronian dialogue technique, and particularly his academic tendency "to argue both sides of a debate" (*disputare in utramque partem*), has been well documented in Varro's construction of books 8–10, and it has also been noted that this sort of debate is out of place in a handbook, as opposed to a literary dialogue. Instead of agreeing with Ax (1995), that Varro originally intended books 8–10 to be a literary dialogue, I would argue that Varro gears his style in this part of the work to his dedicatee, Cicero.[41] The result is not necessarily a flattering one, however, because he produces a contrived and strange debate that makes sense as parody.

[39] See Fehling (1956) 267, Collart (1963) 128–29, and Bloomer (1997) 63–64.

[40] Collart (1963) 131 suggests that Varro uses the debate to give the field of Roman philology some autonomy so that it is not completely dependent on Greek doctrine. Cf. also Bloomer (1997) 64: "Varro found in an exaggerated contrast of the modes of analogy and anomaly a theoretical weapon with which to decry the influence of the theorists."

[41] Ax (1995) argues that Varro originally intended books 8–10 to be in dialogue form with different speakers. See also Bloomer (1997) 52 n. 30, 55–56, 64 and Cardauns (2001) 36–37. Books 2–4, which no longer exist, may have followed a similar Ciceronian structure, as Varro's recapitulation of their topics seems to indicate (7.109).

CICERO AND VARRO

Why would Varro go out of his way to parody Cicero? Much work has been done on analyzing the often uneasy relationship between Cicero and Varro, and there is extensive evidence of it in Cicero's letters, as well as in their dueling dedications to each other in the *Academica* (2nd edn.) and *De Lingua Latina*.[42] Besides being leading intellectuals of their day, the main thing that Cicero and Varro had in common, it seems, was a friendship with Atticus. Cicero frequently used Atticus as a "middleman" to facilitate his (Cicero's) requests for Varro's support in various political and literary matters, and Cicero's letters make clear that these requests were frequently disappointed.[43] Indeed, the very presence of Varro in the *Academica* is the result of Atticus' advice to Cicero, and Cicero clearly hopes that his compliance with this advice will encourage Varro to follow through on a long-awaited dedication to Cicero.[44]

Once Cicero does put Varro in his dialogue, he is very nervous about Varro's response to his work (*Att.* 13.24, 13.25) and characterizes him with a quotation from the *Iliad* (11.654): "a fearsome man, he would find fault with the faultless" (δεινὸς ἀνήρ· τάχα κεν καὶ ἀναίτιον αἰτιόῳτο, *Att.* 13.25). In an earlier letter, Cicero had characterized Varro's thoughts as "twisted" with the beginning of a quotation from the *Andromache*, which maligns the Spartans as "thinking twisted thoughts and nothing wholesome" (E. *Andr.* 448; cf. ἑλικτὰ καὶ οὐδέν, *Att.* 2.25). In the preface of the *Academica*, Cicero even has "Varro" voice some implicit criticism of Cicero's project of presenting Greek philosophy in Latin by saying that he (Varro) prefers to send his "friends who are interested in philosophical study to Greece, that is, I bid them go to the Greeks so that they can draw right from the source rather than seek out the rivulets" (*sed meos amicos in quibus id est studium in Graeciam mitto, id est, ad Graecos ire iubeo, ut ex fontibus potius hauriant quam rivulos consectentur, Ac.* 1.8). In turn, Cicero offers implicit criticism of Varro's version of philosophy mixed with *hilaritas* by saying in the same dialogue: "In many places you have made a start of philosophy, but only enough to interest the reader and not to teach him thoroughly" (*philosophiamque multis locis incohasti, ad impellendum satis, ad edocendum parum, Ac.* 1.9).[45]

---

[42] See Kumaniecki (1962), Bloomer (1997) 53–55 and 251–53 n. 14, Baier (1997) 15–70, Rösch-Binde (1998), and Leach (1999).
[43] E.g. *Att.* 2.20, 2.21, 2.25, and 3.15.
[44] See *Att.* 13.12–14. Cicero explicitly reminds Varro of his promise in *Ac.* 1.1–3.
[45] Relihan (1993) 51 detects the subtle jab: "Cicero stresses Varro's poetic and literary achievements against his philosophical inadequacy."

Cicero also takes several subtle jabs at Varro in a series of letters addressed to him in 46–45 BC (*Fam.* 9.1–8). In these letters, Cicero professes to admire Varro's contemplative lifestyle, particularly now that political life has become untenable; yet, attached to these praises of the life of *otium* is also criticism.[46] Cicero makes it clear that he is more concerned with public affairs than Varro: while Varro has been exclusively living a retired life away from Rome, Cicero has been more actively involved in politics and is now falling back on scholarship and passivity as a second choice option – not a first choice.[47] Far from expressing a desire to imitate Varro, Cicero urges Varro to imitate *him* and to use his scholarship as a means to help the state until he can do so through action:

> modo nobis stet illud, una vivere in studiis nostris, a quibus antea delectationem modo petebamus, nunc vero etiam salutem; non deesse si quis adhibere volet, non modo ut architectos verum etiam ut fabros, ad aedificandam rem publicam, et potius libenter accurrere; si nemo utetur opera, tamen et scribere et legere πολιτείας, et, si minus in curia atque in foro, at in litteris et libris, ut doctissimi veteres fecerunt, navare rem publicam et de moribus ac legibus quaerere. (*Fam.* 9.2.5)

Only let this be our plan, to live together in our studies, from which previously we sought only joy, but now in truth also salvation; and if someone wishes to call us in not only as architects but also as carpenters for building the republic, let us not be absent but rather willingly rush forward; if no one will use our aid, nevertheless let us write and read *Republics*, and, if not in the Senate Building and Forum, then at least in our letters and books, as the most learned men of old have done, let us assist the Republic and investigate morals and laws.

Varro responded not with a *De Re Publica* but with works like *De Lingua Latina* and *De Re Rustica*.[48] However, as I will argue more fully in chapter 5, the *De Re Rustica* also presents a Varronian version of the *Republic* – though one that is full of *hilaritas*, "twisted thoughts," and a defense of *otium*.

---

[46] I read more of an "edge" in these letters than does Leach (1999), who notes: "What is striking in the eight letters written directly to Varro is the way in which Cicero portrays Varro as a figure who has pursued a better course of action than himself" (166). Her final conclusion, however, is more in line with mine: "The Cicero who looks with ambivalent envy upon Varro's philosophical life remains the Cicero motivated by ambition" (176).

[47] See *Fam.* 9.1.2, 9.2.2–5, 9.3, and 9.6.4–6. Dahlmann (1935) 1176–77 contrasts Varro's relationship with the contemplative life to Cicero's and notes Varro's comparatively apolitical nature, as well as his greater dedication to the life of the mind. For Cicero's relationship to *otium* and intellectual pursuits, see Kretschmar (1938), André (1966) 279–334, and Fox (2007) 29–37. See also Wirszubski (1954), who elucidates Cicero's politically active conception of *otium* in the phrase *cum dignitate otium* ("leisure with dignity").

[48] On the interplay between the works of Varro and Cicero, see further Bloomer (1997) 53–55 and 253 n. 14, though Bloomer does not see Varro's responses to Cicero's works as parodies or satires.

THE TRIUMPH OF NATURE

I have been emphasizing the humorous elements of the academic debates in the *De Lingua Latina* and *De Re Rustica*, but I would now like to focus on the more serious part of the satire in book 1 of the *De Re Rustica*. As I mentioned before, the type of theoretical, expert knowledge that was celebrated in the Late Republic and associated with Scrofa's art of farming implied an optimism towards mankind's ability to impose order on the chaotic external world. Yet, in book 1, it becomes clear not just that there are logical flaws in the *ratio* of Scrofa, but that there are serious limitations on the ability of the agricultural art to control the natural world.

The first indication that Scrofa's rational optimism might be misplaced comes in a statement by Agrius immediately before Scrofa arrives on the scene. Agrius has just finished extolling the amazing natural fertility of Italy, but he ends with the sobering advice that if a farmer is not able to recoup his expenses in farming or if his land is in an unhealthy environment and liable to pestilence, he would be crazy to go through with cultivating it and should be committed to the care of his family if he persists (1.2.8–9). Even in a land like Italy, which is naturally blessed, pestilence lurks around the corner, and no human *ars* can prevent its attack. Agrius' reminder of the vulnerability of human life to the vicissitudes of nature is reminiscent of Socrates' emphasis on the vulnerability of agricultural life just after he has praised farming (*Oec.* 5.18–20);[49] however, just as Ischomachus focused instead on the powers of *technē* to control nature and human nature, so too does Scrofa.

While Scrofa adheres to the optimistic mantra of science in his opening discussion and states that theoretical knowledge can diminish the element of risk in farming (1.4.4–5), his agricultural instructions nonetheless emphasize the great control the natural world has over the farmer. For instance, in discussing the soil of the farm, he admits that the soil determines whether the farm is "good or bad" (*bonus aut non bonus*) and also determines what types of crops can be planted (1.7.5). Soon after, when Fundanius asks how pestilence should be prevented if an unhealthy farm is inherited, Agrius repeats his earlier pessimistic advice to sell or abandon the farm immediately. Scrofa reiterates his view that agricultural science can find solutions to alleviate such problems (1.12.2–4); however, this time, Scrofa multiplies the potential aggravating factors: not just pestilence, but rain storms and bands of robbers are threats to the farm, as well (1.12.4). In 1.16.2, Scrofa

---

[49] Perhaps this reminder is what earns Agrius the designation *Socraticus* (1.2.1)?

recommends being in a neighborhood with lots of artisans whose services the farmer can rely on since "sometimes the death of one artisan destroys the profit of the farm" (*non numquam unius artificis mors tollit fundi fructum*, 1.16.4). Suddenly, the ordered world of *ars* and agriculture is looking a lot less secure, even in the words of Scrofa.

Scrofa's agricultural calendar (1.27.1–37.5) similarly underscores the limited power of *ars* to control and keep up with nature since the required precision in the timing of agricultural operations indicates how critical it is to conform to nature's laws. For instance, Scrofa advises that after the winter solstice, "unless a necessary reason compels you" (*nisi quae necessaria causa coegerit*, 1.34.1), you should not sow because it makes the difference between seeds that sprout in seven days and seeds that sprout in forty. His conditional phrase, "unless a necessary reason compels you," is a reminder that there are some necessities outside of our control that prevent proper planting even though the results for the seeds are disastrous.

The world of chance decisively gains the upper hand at the end of book 1 with the dramatic entry of the sacristan's freedman, who announces to the group that his master has been mistakenly killed (1.69.2–3). After this, the participants depart, "more complaining about human misfortune than showing surprise that it happened at Rome" (*de casu humano magis querentes, quam admirantes id Romae factum*, 1.69.3). It is perhaps now understandable why Varro began the book with an invocation to the agricultural gods and put in prominent last position the god of "Good Outcome" (1.1.6 *Bonum Eventum*). *Ratio* is not enough to ensure control over the haphazard world of nature. However, *religio* does not necessarily fill the void left by *ratio*, and the gods never helpfully intervene in the course of the dialogue; rather, it simply becomes clear why there is a human *need* for the divine.

BOOKS 2 AND 3

While the parody of expert knowledge and intellectual culture is most clearly seen in book 1, books 2 and 3 continue to satirize the excessive pedantry of the dialogue participants, as well as to point to the limitations of human *ratio*. In book 2, on the pastoral art, Stolo disappears, and Scrofa shares the spotlight with several other participants. Scrofa is still honored as the man "to whom this age grants the palm in all rustic endeavors" (*cui haec aetas defert rerum rusticarum omnium palmam*, 2.1.11), but his discourse does not seem more expert than that of the others; it is, as usual, simply more subdivided. Just as in book 1, Scrofa is closely associated with *ars* in book 2: while Varro plays on his own reputation as an antiquarian by taking on the job of discussing the *origo* ("origin") and *dignitas* ("merits") of the pastoral science, he defers to Scrofa when it is time to discuss it *qua* art (2.1.2).[50]

Scrofa's organization of his discourse is better than it was in book 1, but it still leads to some humorous difficulties, which the other participants point out. For instance, Atticus asks how Scrofa will fit all nine of his subdivisions into the category of herd that includes mules and herdsmen since one of the categories is breeding (2.1.25–26). Varro himself steps in with the suggestion that perhaps they can simply drop the categories related to breeding when speaking about mules (Atticus had already reasoned that herdsmen can breed) and that maybe the number of divisions does not need to be precise (2.1.26). Scrofa will have none of that and remains fixated on finding eighty-one divisions (2.1.28). Yet, the two categories he adds to make up for the loss of the two for the mules, i.e. shearing and the making of milk and cheese, do not rationally belong to a scientific discussion of pastoralism – at least, not by the strict standards set forth in book 1 for the definition of *agri cultura*. So, just as in book 1, the theoretical logic of Scrofa's *ars* is shaky.

There are also hints in book 2 that the pastoral art, like the agricultural art, is liable to the whims of nature and promises no great defense against disaster. For instance, Scrofa makes an important division of the pastoral art the care of the herd's health, which is "a multifaceted and important matter, because a sick herd is defective, and men are often afflicted with disaster because it is not healthy" (*res multiplex ac necessaria, quod morbosum pecus est vitiosum, et quoniam non valet, saepe magna adficiuntur calamitate*, 2.1.21). In addition, the causes of disease which he lists are so general and all-compassing (i.e. either heat or cold, too much work or too little exercise, and eating too quickly after working, 2.1.22) that the effect is to make disease seem inevitable despite medical treatments.[51]

In book 3, Scrofa does not appear, but *ars* still has an important role thanks to Appius' description of the bees, which are now the representatives of *ars* and *ratio*.[52] Yet, there is something deflating about this switch since *ratio* is usually considered the unique province of man.[53] In a telling description of how the bees gather material from flowers, Appius mentions

---

[50] As Henderson (2002) 132 notes, of these three divisions, "the 'art' gets all the coverage."
[51] Cf. also the discussion of the health of goats, who are said to be never without fever (2.3.5), and of the fast spreading plagues among large herds (2.3.10).
[52] Appius speaks of both the *ingenium* ("natural ability") and *ars* ("skill") that nature has given to bees (3.16.3), as well as of their *ratio atque ars* ("reason and skill," 3.16.4).
[53] Man's unique possession of *ratio* is a common theme in Cicero (e.g. *Off.* 1.11).

that they follow a certain method of selection but then corrects himself and says that the method follows them (3.16.26). Unlike human beings, bees do not derive scientific principles from nature or experience; they *are* nature, and science follows them. This subsuming of *ratio* into the realm of nature was actually foreshadowed in the preface to book 3 when country life was suddenly placed in the domain of nature, not human skill ("divine nature gave us fields, human skill built cities," *divina natura dedit agros, ars humana aedificavit urbes*, 3.1.4) and agriculture was said to predate the invention of all the *artes* and to be a superior lifestyle ("all the arts are said to have been discovered in Greece within a span of one thousand years, but there were never *not* fields on the earth to be cultivated. Agriculture is not only older but is also better," *artes omnes dicantur in Graecia intra mille annorum repertae, agri numquam non fuerint in terris qui coli possint. neque solum antiquior cultura agri, sed etiam melior* 3.1.4). The *De Re Rustica*, then, traces the progression of *ars* and *ratio* from their height in book 1, as the unique tools of mankind to control nature, to their absorption into the realm of nature in book 3 – though of course the fault lines in the confident world of *ratio* were already visible in book 1.

CHAPTER 4

The morality of farming

In Greek and Roman satire and comedy, the city is the place of vice and the country the place of virtue. These genres pick up on the moralizing tendencies of their cultures and decry the greed and luxury of the city as opposed to the country, as well as the loose morals of the modern age as compared with those of the past.[1] That said, moralizing in satire and comedy often has an ironic edge, and the moralizing characters frequently appear hypocritical or are somehow undermined in the course of the work. Recent studies have located this kind of ironic moralizing in Horace's and Juvenal's *Satires* and the plays of Plautus, as well as in Varro's *Menippean Satires*; however, the moralizing of the *De Re Rustica* has generally been taken at face value.[2] I hope to show that Varro undermines moralizing in this work, too, and that he also undermines the conventional morality of Roman culture. There is again a humorous and a serious aspect to Varro's satire as he reveals that behind the Roman esteem of farming lies a profit-motive that is at the core of the Roman value system.

GENEALOGY OF MORALS

In the preface to the *De Agri Cultura*, Cato equates farming with a moral lifestyle: he says that when the Roman ancestors wanted to praise a "good

---

[1] On these themes in comedy, see Hunter (1985) 109–13 and in satire, see Braund (1989a).

[2] Diederich's (2007) recent examination of moralizing in the *De Re Rustica* (298–368) allows for an element of irony and tension in Varro's presentation of nostalgia for the past and valorization of the agrarian life, but does not go so far as to suggest that Varro undermines this moralizing. On Horace's ironic moralizing in his *Satires*, see Freudenburg (1993); on Plautus', see Moore (1998) 67–90. On moralizing in comedy in general, see Hunter (1985) 139–47. On Varro's ironic moralizing in the *Menippeans*, see Relihan (1993) 65–74. On the irony in Umbricius' diatribe against the city in Juvenal's *Satire* 3, see Braund (1989b) 26–39. See also Braund (1988) for further discussion of Juvenal's irony and parodies of moralizing. Clayman (1980) 70 makes a similar argument for Callimachus' *Iambi*: "Callimachus' *Iambi* seem at home in the general context of Hellenistic moralizing literature . . . Callimachus' intent, however, is not to create legitimate diatribes and moralizing choliambs, but to parody them."

man" (*virum bonum*), they would call him a "good farmer and husbandman" (*bonum agricolam bonumque colonum*, pr. 2) and that farming is an
"especially moral source of income" (*maximeque pius quaestus*, pr. 4). Yet,
it is also clear from this preface that what has made farming moral in the
eyes of the Romans are the material benefits it provides them: compared to
trading, farming provides a less dangerous and more stable form of income,
and it also readies men to be good soldiers (pr. 3–4). Indeed, after the preface, farming is presented not as an inherently virtuous lifestyle but as a way
of making money, pure and simple.[3] If Cato does provide an ethical precept
in the course of his work, it always has an underlying self-interested and
materialistic goal, such as when he advises his readers to be good neighbors
because doing so makes it easier to sell your produce and to find helpers on
the farm (4). Religious references in the *De Agri Cultura* are also intimately
bound up with the material benefits that prayer and proper observance of
ritual can give the farmer (e.g. 83, 131, 132, 134, and 139–41). While Cicero
in the *De Senectute* transformed Cato from a cold-hearted businessman
into a philosophical farmer who found virtue and "splendour in the grass,"
Varro replicates the true spirit of Cato's manual in the *De Re Rustica*: Varro
makes profit the overwhelming focus of agricultural instruction and also
the originating force behind Roman values, religion, and politics.

The profit motive of agriculture and its related fields is clearly identified
in each book of the *De Re Rustica*. Scrofa states in book 1 that the two
ends of agriculture are *utilitas* ("utility") and *voluptas* ("pleasure"), and
that *utilitas*, which seeks profit, is the more important goal (1.4.1).[4] As
the work progresses, the profit motive only increases: Scrofa's definition
of the pastoral science in book 2 makes money-making inherent in its
very nature ("There is a science of raising and feeding farm animals such
that the greatest profit possible is obtained from them, from whom money
itself got its name. For herds are the foundation of all wealth," *est scientia
pecoris parandi ac pascendi, ut fructus quam possint maximi capiantur ex eo,
a quibus ipsa pecunia nominata est. nam omnis pecuniae pecus fundamentum*,
2.1.11), and in book 3, a villa is defined by the fact that it makes a profit,
regardless of what kind of animal the profit is from ("This also for a similar
reason ought to be called a villa, in which great profit is obtained because

---

[3] As Martin (1971) 85 puts it, the fundamental teaching of the treatise was "how a landowner could
quickly obtain wealth" ("comment un propriétaire foncier pouvait rapidement atteindre la richesse").

[4] Maggiulli (1994) has noted the traditional association of these twin motives with agriculture, but the
only sources he cites prior to Varro are Xenophon, Cicero, and Scrofa. I would argue, then, that they
all lead back to Xenophon and to Socrates' subtle critique of the materialistic nature of agriculture
(and political life). While Cicero did not interpret these twin motives in a negative way, I hope to
show that Varro replicates Socrates' critique.

of pasturing [small animals around the farm]. For what does it matter if you obtain the profit from sheep or from birds?" *haec quoque simili de causa debet vocari villa, in qua propter pastiones fructus capiuntur magni. quid enim refert, utrum propter oves, an propter aves fructus capias?* 3.2.10). Indeed, *pastio villatica* ("the pasturing of small animals around the farm") is the most profitable of all the rustic enterprises, and one of book 3's main characters, aptly named Axius ("worth"), obsessively focuses on the money to be made from *pastio villatica*. While Varro's prefaces to books 2 and 3 give voice to the traditional associations of farming with a virtuous lifestyle, they also explain the underlying materialistic reasons for these associations, much as Socrates did in his Praise of Farming (*Oec.* 5).

In the preface to book 2, Varro explains that agricultural labor produces productive lands and physically healthy Romans (2.pr. 1–2). In the book 3 preface, he notes that country folk are responsible for feeding Romans in time of peace and for protecting them in time of war (3.1.4). He also connects the worship of Ceres and her mysteries with the benefits that "mother earth" brings to civilization. He further suggests that these connections lie behind the belief that rustics live a pious and useful life and are the remnants of the race of Saturn (3.1.5). Thus, Varro's approach here is more anthropological than moralizing. He is not providing proof that farmers really are more virtuous than everyone else but instead is showing how this belief arose among the Romans based on their recognition that the agricultural life is beneficial to them. His further demonstration of the close connection between religious institutions, like the mysteries, and agriculture seems to be influenced by the anthropological theories of Prodicus, who connected the origins of religious practice to agriculture.[5]

Indeed, throughout the *De Re Rustica*, religion seems to be introduced more for the sake of intellectual curiosity than serious reverence,[6] and even

---

[5] Cf. Henrichs (1984) 143: "Demeter and Dionysus, the providers of bread and wine, occupy a prominent place in Prodicus' theory because he advocated a close connection between religion and agriculture. This emphasis is borne out by Themistius, a late but well-read source, who observes that Prodicus 'derived all religious practices, mysteries and initiations from the benefits of agriculture, believing that the very notion of the gods came to men from this source and making it the guarantee of piety.' The last part of this quotation is corrupt, but what precedes is unambiguous and confirms that Prodicus placed the beginnings of religion in an ambience that was not merely cultural but agricultural." Varro could have been exposed to Prodicus directly or indirectly through Euhemerus, whom Ennius translated and whom Varro has Stolo quote in *R.* 1.48.2. Cf. Henrichs (1984) 151: "It is hardly an exaggeration to say that the essential features of Euhemerism are in fact the property of Prodicus." There could be a further reference to Euhemerizing theories in Varro's mention of Saturn as a "king" (i.e. a human being who was later deified) in 3.1.5 (*Saturni regis*) . Cf. Ennius' narration in his *Euhemerus* of the fight over kingship between Saturn and Titan (8–19).

[6] For example, cf. Fundanius' aetiology of two different Greek goat rituals, which he explains have their origin in the recognition that goats destroy vines and olives: in one version, a goat is offered to

the opening hymn to the agricultural gods reads more like an anthropological commentary on the creation of religion than an actual religious invocation.[7] Like Prodicus, Varro focuses in the invocation on the importance of the "sun and the moon" (*Solem et Lunam*, 1.1.5), "Demeter and Dionysus" (*Cererem et Liberum*, 1.1.5), and other personified natural forces that promote survival (1.1.5–6).[8] Each invocation makes explicit the beneficial function of the god being invoked, and the explanation attached to the invocation of Ceres and Liber, "because their fruits are especially necessary for life" (*quod horum fructus maxime necessarii ad victum*, 1.1.5), is particularly reminiscent of Prodicean phraseology.[9]

The *De Re Rustica* debunks the myth of the virtuous farmer by revealing that the farming life became associated in Roman culture with morality and religion because of the material benefits it provides the Romans. In addition, Varro explicitly contradicts key elements of that myth, such as the belief that a farmer's life is not characterized by greed.[10] According to the instruction in the *De Re Rustica*, farming is about nothing if not profit, and what is profitable is simply assimilated to what is moral. Indeed, in Scrofa's discourse on the moral aspect of farming, this assimilation of the profitable and the moral becomes clear. As already mentioned, he states that the two ethical ends of farming are *utilitas* and *voluptas*, and that *utilitas* is the more important of the two (1.4.2). However, he goes on to reconcile the two in a manner reminiscent of Cicero's reconciliation of morality (*honestas*) and utility (*utilitas*) in the *De Officiis* (e.g. 2.9, 3.11): Scrofa states that land which is made "more attractive" (*honestiorem*) by being planted with rows of trees is also more productive and profitable, whereas "ugly" (*turpis*) land, even if

---

Bacchus as punishment for hurting vines; in the other, goats cannot be sacrificed to Minerva because of the damage they cause olives and are allowed in Athens only once a year for a sacrifice (1.2.18–20). These explanations reinforce the idea that religion is a local, cultural institution that reflects human needs and values.

[7] Cf. Baier (1997) 149, who notes the lack of religious sentiment in Varro's opening hymn.

[8] Cf. Henrichs (1984) 141: "The belief that gods were deified men is the main component of Prodicus' doctrine, but there is another part that turned out to be almost equally influential. In an earlier stage of cultural evolution, primitive man deified those aspects of nature that were conspicuously useful to his survival, including the sun and moon, rivers, springs, and lakes as well as meadows and the fruits of the earth." Cf. also *P. Herc.* 1428 fr. 19: "[Prodicus] maintains that the gods of popular belief do not exist and that he does not recognize them, but that primitive man [out of admiration] deified the fruits of the earth and virtually everything that contributed to his subsistence" (trans. Henrichs [1975] 107–08).

[9] On variations of this phrase and its likely use by Prodicus, see Henrichs (1975) 107 n. 56.

[10] Cf. Cicero's description of the rustic life in *Pro S. Roscio Amerino* as a "life which is entirely removed from greed and connected with duty" (*quae vita maxime disiuncta a cupiditate et cum officio coniuncta est*, 14.39). However, he has a very different assessment of rustics in a letter to Atticus, in which he complains that "they care for nothing at all but their fields, their little farms, and their money" (*nihil prorsus aliud curant nisi agros, nisi villulas, nisi nummulos suos, Att.* 8.13).

productive, is not as profitable (1.4.2). In this ethical framework,[11] it is hard to forget that *honestus* and *turpis* are words that can have an inherently moral meaning, though their meaning here is purely aesthetic. Scrofa's reconciliation of *utilitas* and *honestas* is entirely different from Cicero's then: whereas Cicero invests *honestas* with purely moral significance and argues that being virtuous is always expedient, Scrofa's discourse leads in the other direction by emptying the moral words of any properly moral content and dealing only in the realm of pleasure and utility.

The specific example Scrofa uses to show how *honestas* can be reconciled with *utilitas*, namely the planting of trees in quincunx rows,[12] connects nicely back to the passage in the *Oeconomicus* in which Socrates recounts how Lysander praised Cyrus for his trees planted in quincunx formation and proclaimed Cyrus to be not only a "fortunate" (εὐδαίμων) man but also a "good" (ἀγαθός) man (*Oec.* 4.21–25). Cicero presumably translated this vignette in his *Oeconomicus*, and it shows up again in the *De Senectute*: he has Cato quote Lysander by saying, "Rightly do men say that you are blessed, Cyrus, since fortune has been joined to your virtue!" (*recte vero te, Cyre, beatum ferunt, quoniam virtuti tuae fortuna coniuncta est, Sen.* 17.59). Prior to Scrofa's version in Varro, the "moral" of this story was that true virtue is found not in the aesthetic beauty of the trees, which merely made Cyrus fortunate, but in the industry that went into planting them. When contrasted to these versions, Scrofa's sole emphasis on the aesthetic aspect of the trees and how that aspect adds to the land's profitability shows that Scrofa sidesteps the underlying moral altogether.

Of course, I suggested in Part I that there is another way of reading the underlying moral of the tale: Socrates presents the vignette with Cyrus and Lysander not to endorse Lysander's judgment but to prod his pupil Critobulus into realizing that, in fact, being ἀγαθός involves more than simply being industrious in farming. Whether or not Varro read an ironic *Oeconomicus*, he could still be making a similar point in his adaptation of the quincunxes. Perhaps he leaves out the moral aspect of the vignette not just because Scrofa is focused only on profit but because there *is* no inherently moral aspect. Just as Varro has shown that the myth of the virtuous farmer derives from the utility of the farming, so

---

[11] Martin (1995) 88 calls Scrofa's discussion of the ethical ends of farming "a sort of *De Finibus* in miniature" ("une sorte de *De Finibus* en miniature").

[12] In a later discussion, when Scrofa again mentions the planting of trees in rows and the added value that this arrangement gives the land, he specifically mentions the name for this formation of trees, the quincunx, which refers to trees planted in staggered rows (1.7.2).

he makes the essentially Epicurean point in Scrofa's discourse that conventional moral language derives its meaning from the realm of pleasure and utility: what is *honestus* is both pleasant and useful, but nothing more.[13]

While I have argued that Varro uses the myth of the virtuous farmer, as well as the non-moral uses of moral terms, to reveal that morality is derived from materially based self-interest, he does not critique this derivation by suggesting there is a higher moral plane that everyone is missing. Unlike in the *Oeconomicus*, there is no strong moral figure in the *De Re Rustica* to advocate replacing conventional morality with a quest for true moral goodness, and, in that sense, Varro's work remains more Menippean (or Mandevillian) than Socratic, and also a more open text, whose irony is ultimately "unstable." Yet, I would suggest that Varro's work is different from a work like the *De Agri Cultura* in that Cato showed no obvious awareness that there was anything contradictory about presenting farming as both a uniquely moral occupation and one whose sole purpose is making money.[14] The *De Re Rustica*, in contrast, seems to revel in exploiting these contradictions and in satirizing moralistic and know-it-all characters, who never acknowledge their own mistakes or hypocrisies.

HYPOCRITES AND MORALIZERS

In the opening invocation of the *De Re Rustica*, Varro tells his readers that he is not going to invoke the Muses, as Homer and Ennius did, but instead the twelve gods of Rome – and not the usual urban ones, whose gilded statues stand in the forum, but rustic gods (1.1.4). With this rejection of the

[13] There are many other examples of potentially moral terms used in a non-moral sense in the *De Re Rustica*, such as at 1.7.5, in which *bonus* ("good") is applied to a farm, or 2.6.2, in which *honestus* ("handsome"), *bonus* ("good"), and *optimus* ("excellent, best") are applied to desirable features of donkeys. Cf. also Murrius' odd command that it is best to choose a male and female ass for breeding who are marked by *dignitas* ("dignity, merit,") (*cum dignitate*, 2.6.3), since their progeny will resemble them. On the Epicurean derivation of moral virtues from *voluptas*, see Cicero's quotation of Epicurus in *Tusc.* 3.41–42.

[14] Habinek (1998) 49 makes a related point about the hypocrisy of elite Romans in regards to their different moral valuations of commerce and agriculture: "Cato the man was evidently not disturbed by the prospect of accumulating wealth through means other than agriculture. But the insistence on the traditional privileging of landowning allows Cato and his class to have their cake and eat it too – enjoying the material benefits of a new economy, increasingly oriented toward commerce and manufacturing, as well as the social and political privileges associated with traditional aristocratic hegemony." Cf. also Pagán (2006) 118: "[T]he moral condemnation of turning a profit, so strenuously voiced by Cato in the preface to his *On Agriculture*, contrasts with what we are told by Plutarch of Cato's own practice of earning wealth (Plutarch, *Life of Cato* 21.5). One thing is certain: The contradictions between the theory and practice of wealth left the Romans in a deep moral predicament."

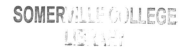

Muses and gilded statues, Varro gives voice to the moralizing dichotomies
that characterized the distinction between city and country life: the city is
associated with luxury and things Greek, whereas the country is associated
with frugality and "Romanness."[15] While it might seem, then, that the *De
Re Rustica* is going to present a typical moralizing sermon on the superiority
of the country over the city, I would suggest that there is an underlying
ironic treatment of such moralizing, and that this irony is present from
the beginning: not only does Varro's bibliography on farming contain only
Greek sources despite his claim to include Roman ones, as well (1.1.7),
but the dialogue is a self-consciously Greek genre.[16] It is also revealed that
the setting of this work on farming is in fact a fancy part of Rome (the
temple of Tellus in the Carinae district),[17] and the participants in it are
city folk, including both a follower of Socrates (G. Agrius) and a tax-
collector (P. Agrasius). As Tatum notes, "one thinks of Horace's famous
second epode."[18] Indeed, the setting of the dialogue and description of
its participants prepare the reader to interpret the moralizing of the *De
Re Rustica* like the moralizing of Horace's Alfius in *Epode* 2 – namely, as
hypocritical, superficial, and contradictory.

Varro's preface to book 2, in which he takes on the persona of a stodgy
old Roman who decries the modern world, provides an excellent example
of what I would call the ironic moralizing of the *De Re Rustica*. He starts
by explaining why Rome's great ancestors preferred country life to the city
and, as already discussed, cites the benefits that the country provides in
terms of keeping the land productive and the Romans healthy (2.pr. 1).
He then goes on to disparage the current prevalence of Greek gymnasia
in the city and the use of Greek names for every room in the villa, such
as the *palaestra* (wrestling-room), *ornithon* (aviary), or *oporotheca* (fruit-
room) (2.pr. 2). Next, he laments that Romans would rather applaud
in the theater or circus than work in fields or vineyards with the result
that grain and wine must be imported (2.pr. 3).[19] Finally, he criticizes the

---

[15] On the ideological associations of country and city life in Greece and Rome, see the initial section
of my introduction.

[16] For a discussion of the "Greekness" of philosophical dialogue, see Cic. *de Orat.* 2.13–22.

[17] On the "not quite appropriate" setting of books 1 and 3 in the city rather than a country villa, see
Green (1997) 430.

[18] Tatum's (1992) full quote is: "In Book One we also meet C. Agrius and P. Agrasius, men who,
despite their names, know nothing of agriculture whatsoever (cf. e.g. 1.12.2). Indeed, Agrasius is a
publican (1.2.1)! One thinks of Horace's famous second epode" (196). On *Epode* 2, see my Part II
introduction.

[19] Whether or not there is direct influence (or parody), commentators frequently note the appearance
of a similar moralizing statement in a letter of Cicero to Atticus: "the Roman people use their hands
not in defense of the Republic but in applause" (*populum Romanum manus suas non in defendenda
re publica, sed in plaudendo consumere, Att.* 16.2).

prevalence of pastoralism and says it is the result of the greed and ignorance of Romans who turned grain fields into pastures (2.pr. 4). This preface is controversial because nearly every claim is contradicted in the course of the work. Instead of proposing complex chronologies of composition to explain away the contradictions or attributing them to Varro's haste or old age, as others have done, I would argue that they are signs of the ironic nature of Varro's moralizing.[20]

For instance, in book 1, Varro praises Scrofa's magnificent estates for having more fruit-rooms (*oporothecas*) than picture-galleries (*pinacothecas*), in contrast to the fancy houses of people like Lucullus (1.2.10). Yet, according to the anti-Greek rhetoric of the book 2 preface, an *oporotheca* has as negative a connotation as a *pinacotheca*.[21] In addition, Scrofa's fruit-rooms are compared to the top of the Via Sacra, where "fruit is exchanged for gold" (1.2.10). Thus, the proposed dichotomy between luxury and simplicity is subverted with this reminder that the purpose of a farm is the profit to be made. The *oporotheca* is not the only Greek-inspired room to be praised in the *De Re Rustica*: a large portion of book 3 is dedicated to the management of the *ornithon* despite its dismissal in book 2. Similarly, book 2 focuses on the profit to be made from pastoralism, despite its negative characterization at the opening of the same book. Finally, it might also be pointed out that the *gymnasium* and *palaestra* are the settings for Greek philosophical dialogue (cf. *de Orat.* 2.20), of which the *De Re Rustica* is obviously a descendant. Thus, the moralizing denigration of all things Greek in the preface to book 2 is dramatically undercut throughout the dialogue, as is the denigration of pastoralism.

Also undercut is the lament in the book 2 preface that so many Romans have abandoned the fields that wine and grain have to be imported from abroad. In book 1, precisely the opposite situation is outlined, both in the jingoistic praise of Italy for being the most fully cultivated and fertile land in the world (1.2.3–7), and in Scrofa's statement that their ancestors made less wine and grain than the current generation because they did not have sophisticated methods of cultivation (1.7.2). Of course, one could instead argue that the pessimistic claim in the preface of book 2 undercuts the optimism of book 1; in fact, as discussed in chapter 1, the optimistic rationalism of book 1 *is* undercut throughout the book, which ends not in triumph but with the report of the sacristan's death and the participants'

---

[20] Cf. my discussion of internal contradiction as a commonly cited sign of irony in the introduction, "Irony in Xenophon, Varro, and Virgil."

[21] *Oporotheca* also seems to be a completely contrived word and is attested in neither Greek nor Latin literature beyond the *De Re Rustica*. See Heurgon (1978) 111 and Flach (1996) 332–33 (*ad* 1.59.2).

complaining about the misfortunes of human life (1.69.3).[22] Thus, both the overly optimistic viewpoint of book 1 and the overly pessimistic moralizing of the book 2 preface are shown to represent only partial and superficial understandings of the world.

Book 3 has the most moralizing about the luxury of the modern age; yet, it is also the book that focuses the most intensely on profit and on agricultural topics that are associated with luxurious villas, not the idealized Roman farm.[23] Thus, book 3 underscores most powerfully the hypocrisy of Roman moralists. The dialogue proper opens with a discussion of how to define a villa, which is prompted by Appius Claudius' moralizing commentary on the Villa Publica, where they are gathering: "But is not this villa, he said, which our ancestors built, more frugal and better than that fancy villa of yours in Reate?" (*sed non haec, inquit, villa, quam aedificarunt maiores nostri, frugalior ac melior est quam tua illa perpolita in Reatino?* 3.2.3). Axius responds by bursting the frugal illusion created by Appius and revealing his hypocrisy: "'Are you sure your villa here,' said Axius, 'on the edge of the Campus Martius is simply useful and not in fact more sumptuous in its luxuries than all of the villas of everyone in all of Reate?'" (*scilicet tua, inquit Axius, haec in campo Martio extremo utilis et non deliciis sumptuosior quam omnis omnium universae Reatinae?*, 3.2.5).[24]

---

[22] Hunter (1985) in his chapter on moralizing in comedy notes, "No subject for general reflection is more common in New Comedy than the role of Luck or Chance (Τύχη, Fortuna) in human affairs" (141).

[23] Cf. Martin (1971) 215, who registers surprise that Varro devotes so much space to warrens and fishponds, "which had nothing to do with the traditional rural economy, but served to enrich a minority of very rich owners" ("qui n'avaient rien à voir avec l'économie rurale traditionnelle, mais servaient à l'enrichissement d'une minorité de très riches propriétaires").

[24] Tatum (1992) 198 n. 43 notes the confusion among critics about whether Axius is referring to the *Villa Publica* itself or a private villa of Appius (or, as Green [1997] 432 has more recently suggested, to the symbolic Villa Publica, i.e. Rome itself). I think it could symbolically refer to all three, and, as Tatum notes, whichever interpretation is accepted, "Axius' retort still has the effect of deflating Appius' pretensions" (198 n. 43). Cicero also makes disparaging remarks about fancy villas (e.g. *Leg.* 2.2 [Atticus is the speaker]; *Leg.* 3.30–31), and these remarks are similarly hypocritical since, as Miles (1980) 25 notes, "For all of his criticisms [of luxurious villas], Cicero *did* own six country villas plus assorted *deversoria*; he *did* employ Greek gardeners; and he *did* send to Greece for well covers and other such adornments for his villas." On Cicero's hypocrisy on this score, see also Linderski (1989) 108, Tatum (1992) 198 n. 44, and O'Sullivan (2006) 145. There are, in fact, many striking similarities between Appius' character in the *De Re Rustica* and Cicero. For example, when Appius first appears in book 3, he mentions his recent stay with Axius when he (Appius) was on his way to settle a dispute between the people of Interamna and Reate (3.2.3); we know from a letter Cicero wrote to Atticus (*Att.* 4.15.5) that *he* did precisely that, i.e. stayed with Axius when settling a dispute between Reate and Interamna. In addition, in 3.2.7, Appius mentions that he wants to buy a villa from M. Seius near Ostia, and we know Cicero had a villa near Ostia and was a friend of Seius (see Guiraud [1997] 60). Cicero even mentions dining with Seius in a letter to Varro (*Fam.* 9.7). There was a strained personal relationship between Appius and Cicero, which we can reconstruct from Cicero's letters (e.g. *Fam.* 2.13, 3.7), but their political careers were quite parallel: they both served as consul, augur, and governor of Cilicia. In the next chapter, I will argue that book 3 polemically

Appius Claudius is a perfect character to symbolize hypocritical moralizing: as augur and censor, he is *the* representative of Roman morals,[25] and as a wealthy politician plagued with scandals both personal and political,[26] he is also a representative of the hypocrisy of such moralistic stances. Indeed, Caelius suggests in a letter to Cicero that Appius' obsession with regulating luxurious artwork was, among other things, an (ineffective) means of washing away his own stains (*Fam.* 8.14.4). In another letter, Caelius calls him greedy (*Fam.* 8.12.1) and says he (Caelius) will bring proceedings against him to get back a public shrine that Appius appropriated for his own house (*Fam.* 8.12.3). Thus, in the context of his personal life, Appius' praise of frugal villas in the *De Re Rustica* rings false. Varro provides Appius with more false moralizing later in the book: just as Appius is about to discourse on fishponds, Axius reminds him to speak first about bees by asking if Appius' frugality (*parsimonia*) in his youth, which prevented him from drinking honey-wine, is now causing him to neglect honey (3.16.1). This comment prompts Appius to launch into a tale of his supposedly impoverished past: he claims he was so poor after his father died that he gave his sister to Lucullus without a dowry, and that he did not drink honey-wine at home himself until Lucullus relinquished an inheritance in his favor, even though honey-wine was served to his guests at almost daily banquets (3.16.1–3).

While most scholars have taken this story as evidence for the poverty of the Claudii Pulchri during the 70s BC,[27] Tatum has pointed out the

---

engages with Cicero's *De Re Publica*, especially during Appius' discourse on the bees. Thus, the noted similarities between them may not be coincidental.

[25] Cf. Tatum (1992) 197 on Appius' moralizing comment in 3.2.3: "Such old-fashioned rectitude recalls Fundanius in Book One, who likewise was critical of new-fangled overly fancy villas. It also recalls the actual public posture assumed by Appius during his censorship, a pose which drew the disgust of the thoroughly modern Caelius Rufus, but not necessarily all other Romans (since one might properly expect a degree of moralism in a Roman censor)." Cf. also Gruen (1974) 354: "By the early fall of 50, [Appius] became censor, basking in authority and indulging in rancor. He imitated the shades of greater ancestors, and expelled numerous individuals from the senate."

[26] Cf. Gruen (1974) 352: "Ap. Claudius Pulcher, elder brother of Publius and Gaius, was next to come under fire. The devious politician had constructed and shed alliances with dizzying frequency throughout his career . . . He utilized marital links with other noble houses when they were profitable, discarded them when they were inconvenient. Double-dealing was his stock in trade, most visibly instanced by his scandalous electoral pact in 54. A rapacious tenure in Cilicia followed. The list of transgressions is long. Ap. Claudius was twice indicted in 50: of *maiestas* and of *ambitus*"; (354–55): "The censor promoted a charge of unnatural vice against Caelius . . . Caelius, enraged and bitter, retaliated by bringing the same charge against his tormentor. It was a shrewd move. The allegation fitted the character of Appius at least as well as Caelius, as all men knew."

[27] See Tatum (1992) 191: "This passage is the sole evidence for the poverty of the Claudii Pulchri in the seventies – and, as I hope will be obvious, it is at the most summary inspection far from straightforward. The evidence of Varro's text, however, has been taken as gospel in biographical discussions of Appius Claudius or his siblings – or of Lucullus for that matter – by scholars of the calibre of K. W. Drumann, F. Münzer, and J. van Ooteghem."

many absurdities in the passage. For instance, the fact that Appius had almost daily banquets at which all of his guests drank honey-wine hardly speaks of poverty, and when he does finally come into money, he admits to drinking honey-wine himself at home – a custom which even wealthy Romans limited to dinner parties, as the commentaries note (e.g. Tilly [1973] 294–95 [*ad* 3.16.2]). There is also something odd about the story of his undowered sister and the inheritance from Lucullus. First of all, the very mention of this marriage between Claudia and Lucullus is an embarrassing reminder of the great scandal and divorce that came of it.[28] In addition, Tatum and others have noted how embarrassing it is for senatorial families to be unable to provide a dowry, and that since dowries did not have to be big, this would be an indication of extreme poverty – not just humble beginnings.[29] Finally, as Tatum notes, "[Appius'] assertion that he was rescued from poverty by the generosity of Lucullus ought also to arouse our scepticism. Lucullus' wealth – and his avarice – were proverbial" (198).

This combined evidence has led Tatum to suppose that the facts of the story must be quite different,[30] and that Appius is casting himself in the New Comedy role of the "poor-but-honest brother struggling to secure the position of his sister, while yet maintaining the family's pride" (199). I would also add that Appius' pose of childhood poverty and frugality places him in a tradition of cynic moralizing, just as Horace's tale of humble beginnings likens him to Bion.[31] Thus, Appius' story adds to his moralizing persona in book 3 and also undercuts it, since the autobiography not only seems unlikely in a historical context, but is contradicted within the text by the mention of daily banquets. I disagree with Tatum's conclusion that instead of containing any implicit critique of Appius Claudius, "Appius' brief tale was meant to provoke a laugh from the reader . . . Appius' resort to irony does him no disgrace: as Aristotle put it, irony is something rather gentlemanly" (199). Yet, the irony is Varro's, not Appius'. There is no suggestion that Appius himself understands the absurdities of his tale or the hypocrisy of his moralizing.

[28] Cf. Tatum (1992) 193: "[B]y 50, which is the dramatic date of Book Three, Lucullus had divorced his Claudian wife amidst accusations of adultery and incest, slanders that most certainly echoed through the proceedings of P. Clodius' sensational trial for sacrilege."

[29] See Tatum (1992) 192–93 and his references for further discussion of dowries in Roman society.

[30] He proposes that instead of being overwhelmed with degrading poverty, "the Claudii Pulchri were, upon the more or less simultaneous execution of Appius pater's will and the arrangements for Lucullus' marriage to Clodia, caught merely in a cash crunch, which was eased by Lucullus' willingness to make special arrangements" (194).

[31] On the adoption of a humble persona by Horace and by cynic moralists and satirists, in general, see Freudenburg (1993) 5, 213 and Braund (1996) 29.

Appius does utilize a form of irony in his response to Axius' deflationary reminder (3.2.5–6) that Appius' villa is hardly a true villa since it is so luxurious and has no agricultural purpose: "Appius, smiling, replied, 'Since I am ignorant of what a villa is, I would like you to teach me, lest I slip up from lack of knowledge, because I wish to buy a villa from Marcus Seius near Ostia'" (*Appius subridens, quoniam ego ignoro, inquit, quid sit villa, velim me doceas, ne labar in imprudentiam, quod volo emere a M. Seio in Ostiensi villam*, 3.2.7). Yet, I would argue that even this type of irony is not the self-aware sort that Tatum implies.[32] If there is self-aware irony in this statement, then it is on the part of Varro, who seems to have Appius allude to the opening discussion of Xenophon's *Oeconomicus*, in which Socrates asks Critobulus what an οἶκος is (*Oec.* 1.5). Appius, then, steps into the role of Critobulus in the *Oeconomicus*, who wants Socrates' advice on increasing his estate (*Oec.* 2.1). Of course, Socrates has in mind an entirely different definition of a true *oikos* than Critobulus does, one that involves investigating what is truly beneficial in human life and not simply how much material profit an estate can make. Not surprisingly, Appius and the participants in the dialogue of book 3 never get beyond the monetary focus of their estates and so end up defining a villa solely by the material profit it produces. In this way, they reconcile the traditional farmhouse villa with the modern luxurious residences since the latter can also make a great profit through raising small game like birds, bees, and fish (3.2.10).[33] While Axius is more openly focused on profit than the others, Appius, beneath his moralizing exterior, is not essentially different from Axius.

After hearing of the great profit that can be made from *pastio villatica*, Axius immediately wants to become a student of this discipline and asks Merula to "show [him] the way" (*induce me in viam*, 3.2.18) and teach him the art "of small animal farming" (*villaticae pastionis*, 3.2.18). In discussing the three main topics of *pastio villatica*, namely "aviaries, game preserves, and fishponds" (*ornithones, leporaria, piscinae*, 3.3.1), Merula states that each topic has two stages to it: "the earlier, which ancient frugality contributed, and the later, which modern luxury added" (*superiores, quos frugalitas antiqua, inferiores, quos luxuria posterior adiecit*, 3.3.6). Axius has

---

[32] Tatum (1992) 198: "Varro's Appius, plainly, is aware of the potential for humour lurking in his censorious posture, and he is alert to the tactic of irony."

[33] As Martin (1971) 221–22 notes, this redefinition of the villa in book 3 so as to not only include but to emphasize the luxurious modern villa over the traditional farmhouse contradicts Fundanius' moralizing emphasis in book 1 on the traditional farmhouse villa over the modern luxurious one (1.13.6–7).

no compunction about the modern descent into *luxuria* because he believes it has resulted in greater profit, and so he asks Merula to begin with the later stages of each topic (3.4.1). Merula begins with aviaries and further subdivides this topic into those which are kept "for the sake of pleasure" (*delectationis causa*, 3.4.2) and those which are kept "for the sake of profit" (*fructus causa*, 3.4.2). Of course, it is the latter that Axius wants to hear about (3.5.1). Even Axius, however, takes his turn as a moralizer. When it comes time to discourse on fishponds, he inveighs against the fishponds of the nobility that "are more agreeable to the eyes than the wallet" (*magis ad oculos pertinent quam ad vesicam*, 3.17.2). In other words, because they are designed for pleasure instead of for profit, he condemns them and ridicules Hortensius' concern for his fancy fish (3.17.5–9). While the *piscinarii*, like Hortensius, are a common target of moralizing, particularly from Cicero,[34] Axius is a strange moralizer. Not only does he elsewhere celebrate the innovations that modern *luxuria* has brought, but his reason for condemning the fishponds that are designed for pleasure is motivated by his single-minded concern with profit – and not some higher moral purpose.

Indeed, the reader is reminded of Fundanius' moralizing contrast between the farmhouses of the ancients and those of the moderns: Fundanius says the former were "more profitable" (*fructiosior*, 1.13.6) because they were built with the needs of the crops/profit in mind (*ad fructum rationem*, 1.13.6), whereas the latter are built to accommodate unrestrained passions (*ad libidines indomitas*, 1.13.6). He goes on to condemn the fancy villas of Metellus and Lucullus which he claims have been built to the detriment of the public good (1.13.7). In one sense, Fundanius is advocating the exact opposite of Axius in that Axius had rejected the ancient version of *pastio villatica* as being *less* profitable than the modern. However, where Fundanius and Axius agree is on their use of profit as a gauge of ethical value. They both reject luxury when it is aimed at pleasure and accept frugality when it brings profit. In the *De Re Rustica*, then, moralizing all comes down to money, and it is not the *absence* of old-fashioned farming values that has corrupted the modern age, but the pervasive presence of them.

At the end of his study on Plautus' moralizing, Moore notes "it is moralizing rather than morality that Plautus mocks" (90). Varro, however, makes both a target in the *De Re Rustica* because he implicates all of Roman morality in the hypocritical act of cloaking self-interested motivations in moral dress. Of course, moralizers and those who have pretensions

---

[34] For Cicero's scorn of the *piscinarii*, see *Att.* 1.18.6, 1.19.6, 1.20.3, 2.1.7, and 2.9.1.

to knowledge, but no self-knowledge, are the worst offenders, and, like Socrates, Varro makes a point of revealing their ignorance; unlike Socrates, however, Varro does not imply that there is a source of value beyond *utilitas* and *voluptas*. The *De Re Rustica* also continues to polemically engage with Cicero, who made a point of defining a moral realm apart from *utilitas* and *voluptas* (e.g. *Off.* 3.118) while at the same time engaging in hypocritical moralizing of the sort that we see in the *De Re Rustica*. I will continue to discuss Varro's satire on Roman morality and his polemical dialogue with Cicero in the next chapter as I show how Varro tackles the ultimate hypocrite: the politician.

CHAPTER 5

The politics of farming

In a letter from 46 BC (*Fam.* 9.2.5), Cicero encourages Varro to join him in writing and reading πολιτείας and to devote himself to the republic in his scholarship. While we do not know Varro's exact response to that letter, we do know that he did not write a *De Re Publica*. The *De Re Rustica*, however, might be conceived as a polemical answer to Cicero's suggestion, just as Xenophon's *Oeconomicus* has been conceived as a response to Plato's *Republic*. In this chapter, I hope to show that the *De Re Rustica* uses agricultural and pastoral metaphors not to support the Republic but instead to model the deficiencies of political life. According to these political analogies, politics is about maximizing the profit of those in charge and treats people like animals – lessons familiar now from my discussions of Xenophon's *Oeconomicus* and Plato's *Republic*. Indeed, throughout the *De Re Rustica*, but particularly in book 3, Varro engages with Plato's *Republic*, Xenophon's *Oeconomicus*, and Cicero's *De Re Publica*, and his work may be read not just as a satire of political life, but as a parody of political philosophy.[1] However, in Varro's discourse on the *res publica*, there is no "ideal" state; instead, he undercuts the central thesis of Cicero's *De Re Publica*, that *virtus* is fully realized in political life (e.g. *Rep.* 1.2, 3.6), and instead defends his own choice of a life of *otium*.[2]

---

[1] Varro is not the first to create a comic utopia or dystopia, and Green (1997) 435 has noted the influence of Aristophanes' *Birds* on book 3 of the *De Re Rustica*. In addition, as already suggested, Socrates himself may have been speaking in a comic vein in Plato's *Republic* when he constructs his "beautiful city" and fills it with animal-like humans, and scholars have noted the influence of Aristophanes on Plato's *Republic* (e.g. Saxonhouse [1978] and Howland [1993] 94–118). As with Varro's reading of the *Oeconomicus*, it is difficult to sort out whether Varro read an ironic *Republic* and is importing some of its satirical take on political life or whether he is simply parodying it and creating his own satire.

[2] It is worth recalling in this context that *otium* is the first word of the *De Re Rustica*, though Varro is humorously claiming not to have enough of it to write a well-polished work (1.1.1). Diederich (2007) 180 n. 1033 detects here "an ironic sideswipe at the long-winded preface of the *De Oratore*" ("einen ironischen Seitenhieb auf die weitschweifige Vorrede von *De Oratore*"), in which Cicero complains of not having enough *otium* for intellectual activity – but in Cicero's case, his lack of *otium* is due to political and personal troubles, and not because he is old and near death!

BOOK I: THE FOUNDATION OF THE STATE

In both a literal and a metaphorical sense, Cicero's *Republic* integrates farming into the foundation of Rome. In *Rep.* 2.5, he uses the metaphor of planting ("to sow a republic," *rem publicam serere*) to discuss Romulus' foundation of Rome, and he also notes that Romulus and Remus were raised by shepherds "who nourished them with rustic life and labor" (*in agresti cultu laboreque aluissent*, 2.4). Agriculture is an even more important part of the peaceful reign of Numa, who distributed land to all the men and taught them to farm so that they could have everything they needed without war and so that *iustitia* ("justice") and *fides* ("faith") would flourish (2.26). Thus, farming enables the growth of both justice and the state, the origin of which, according to Cicero, is not some need or weakness in human beings, but is instead their natural social impulse ("the first cause of their assembling together is not so much weakness as a certain natural herding instinct in human beings," *eius autem prima causa coeundi est non tam imbecillitas quam naturalis quaedam hominum quasi congregatio*, 1.39). I will argue that in book 1 of the *De Re Rustica*, Varro reverses Cicero's metaphor, and instead of sowing a perfect republic, he shows the foundation of an ideal farm or *villa*, which in turn may be interpreted, like the Greek *oikos*, as a microcosm of the state.[3] While the connections between the private villa and the *res publica* become more explicit in book 3, which takes place in the symbolic Villa Publica, a reader alert to the political symbolism in the later parts of the work will find that it is foreshadowed by the discussions in book 1.

The actual discussion of the farm proper takes up chapters 11–22 of book 1, and Scrofa's initial precepts resemble Scipio's description of the foundation of Rome in Cicero's *De Re Publica*. Scrofa begins by discussing ideal location: he says that the farm should have a water source nearby (1.11.02) and should not be exposed to noxious influences, such as unhealthy winds or airborne swamp creatures (1.12.1–4). Similarly, Scipio begins by extolling Romulus' decision to locate the city of Rome near a water source

---

[3] In this foundational context, the name of Varro's dedicatee, his wife Fundania, takes on more significance, as do those of Fundanius, his father-in-law and a participant in the dialogue, and Fundilius, the absent host who is the reason everyone has gathered at the Temple of Tellus. Cf. Green (1997) 447: "The first book of *De Re Rustica* opens with the pun on Varro's new wife's name. She is Fundania, and she has just bought a *fundus*, an estate. We must not forget, however, that *fundus* also means the ground, the foundation of a thing. The verb *fundo*, 'to establish, fix, confirm' (LSJ [*sic*] s.v. 2.11) is used particularly of the foundation of the city and the power of Rome." The location at the Temple of Tellus takes on more significance, as well, for it is where the senate convened after the assassination of Julius Caesar to re-establish the government and where Cicero says he tried to lay the "foundations of peace" (*fundamenta pacis*, *Phil.* 1.1).

but away from disease (2.11) and the noxious (cultural) influences associated with the coastline (2.5–10). Scipio also mentions the strong fortifications of Rome, situated as it was on a mountain and protected by a wall (*murus*), rampart (*agger*), and trench (*fossa*) (2.11). Likewise, Scrofa mentions the safety of an elevated location (1.12.4) and the importance of surrounding the farm with an enclosure, whether it is a hedge, a wooden fence, a trench and rampart, or a stone wall (1.14.1–4).

Scrofa's next topic concerns the situation surrounding the farm (*quae est extra fundum*, 1.16.1–6), namely the relation between the farm and wider society; Scrofa's precepts here have similarities to Socrates' discussion of the origin of the polis in book 2 of the *Republic*. Socrates presents the thesis that Scipio rejects in Cicero's *Republic* (1.39), namely that our needs and lack of self-sufficiency lie at the origin of society (*R.* 369b–c). He notes that the chief needs are food, housing, clothing, and health and theorizes that the original society must have consisted of farmers, doctors, shepherds, artisans, traders, and shopkeepers (369d–371e). Scrofa's discussion of the farm's connection to the wider society emphasizes these same basic needs, namely, access to the marketplace for trading (1.16.1–3) and access to doctors and other artisans (1.16.4). He particularly underscores the farm's lack of self-sufficiency by noting that those who try to have all of the artisans they need within their own farm may be taking an unnecessary risk since the death of one artisan can destroy the profit of the farm (1.16.4).

Another similarity between Plato's dialogue and Varro's is that each presents two different kinds of farms/cities, a simple and a luxurious one. Socrates' initial "healthy" and "true" city (372e) does not last long since Glaucon dismisses it as a "city of pigs" because it is not luxurious enough (372c). So, Socrates enlarges his city, brings in luxury and, with it, a need for more land, war, and military guardians (372e–374d); this is the luxurious and "fevered" city (372e) that he constructs in the rest of his work with the help of his interlocutors. In Varro's work, Fundanius contrasts two kinds of farms, one built according to the diligence of the ancients and one built according to the luxury of the moderns (1.13.6), and he advises in favor of the former. Yet, the reason Fundanius urges this course is not because the frugal and diligent farm is more "healthy" or "true," but merely because it is more profitable (*fructuosior*, 1.13.6). Scrofa's farm is certainly built with diligence and profit in mind, but the society in which it is placed is not without conflict and does not seem particularly healthy. For instance, Scrofa mentions the need to protect the farm from bands of robbers (1.12.4), thieves (1.13.2, 1.16.2), and quarreling neighbors (1.15.1) and notes that no villa is safe without watch dogs (1.19.3).

Finally, there are also possible traces of the *Oeconomicus* in Scrofa's discussion of the farm, and particularly in his discussion of training the slaves, freedmen, and animals that work the farm (1.17.1–7). As analyzed in Part I, a large portion of the *Oeconomicus* is devoted to Socrates' recollection of how Ischomachus trained his wife in her duties, as well as the housekeeper and foreman, and there is both an implicit and explicit comparison between training members of the household and the art of ruling politically (e.g. *Oec.* 9.14, 13.5). He uses the language of taming an animal when he mentions domesticating his wife (7.10), and he explicitly compares the reward and punishment method for training animals to that for training slaves (13.6–9). All of the rewards that Ischomachus gives to those under his command, whether praise, food, or superior clothing (13.9–10), are designed to secure loyalty and more profit for himself. Thus, he is like Thrasymachus' shepherd (*R.* 343a–b), who cares for the flock only to the extent that it benefits himself.

While Scrofa does not mention training a wife,[4] he does focus on training the farm's slaves, hired help, and foremen. In doing so, he produces a remarkable conflation between man and beast by dividing the instruments of the farm into three classes (1.17.1): those that can speak (i.e. slaves), those that can make noise (i.e. cattle), and those that are mute (i.e. wagons).[5] He goes on to discuss the proper age and temperament of the slaves (1.17.3–4) as if they are the herd animals that will be discussed in book 2. He notes that the foremen who control the slaves should be educated and have some humanity (1.17.4) but only so that the slaves respect him. Like Ischomachus, Scrofa suggests earning loyalty via a system of rewards and punishments (1.17.5) and by making the foreman think that he is valued (1.17.6–7). Whether Scrofa's farm is read as a model of early Rome, the origin of the state, or the art of ruling, the political implications are the same: the world of politics is not an arena for realizing *virtus* but for fulfilling material needs.

BOOK 2: GUARDIANS AND RULERS

There is a long tradition in Greek literature, going back to Homer, of using pastoral metaphors to discuss political rule, and Socratic literature

---

[4] It is perhaps significant in this context, however, that Varro dedicates the *De Re Rustica* to his wife Fundania (1.1.4).

[5] Scrofa even outdoes Cato in this blatant lumping together of the human and non-human tools of the farm. Cf. Cato *Agr.* 2.7, in which Cato includes slaves in the group of tools and animals that should be sold when defective or worn-out, a passage which Plutarch found offensive for its inhumanity (*Cat. Ma.* 5.1).

seems to have been particularly fond of these analogies.[6] Plato focuses a considerable portion of the *Republic* on Socrates' discussion of how to train the guardians of his "city in speech," a group that is eventually split into the military class and the ruling class (412c–d), and their education is discussed as if they were animals being trained and bred. I would suggest that book 2 of the *De Re Rustica* presents shepherd and animal analogies similar to those in the *Republic*, but this time shepherding is the text and politics the subtext.[7] Because of this inversion of text and subtext, the metaphorical aspect of the analogies is less explicit and pervasive than in Plato, but is sufficient to connect this book to the increasingly political framework of the *De Re Rustica*.[8]

Before examining Varro's version of these pastoral metaphors, I will give a brief summary of Plato's animal-human analogies.[9] Socrates initiates the animal analogy by asking whether there is a difference between the nature "of a noble dog" (γενναίου σκύλακος) and a "well-born youth" (νεανίσκου εὐγενοῦς) with regard to their guarding ability (375a). He immediately suggests that the horse, and especially the dog, is a great model for the guardian, because both have the capacity to be brave and fearless (375b–c), while the dog has the more important ability to be both fierce to its enemies and gentle to its flock (375c–376b). The guardians, then, are to be trained to be protectors of the flock. They must be taught not to fear death and so cannot be exposed to stories that present death as an evil (386a–388d). Other animal analogies are used to model their need to avoid harmful images, an act which is compared to grazing on bad grass (401b–c), as well as their need to be tested with fears and tempting pleasures, a test which is compared to confronting a colt with loud noise to see if it is afraid

---

[6] See my introduction, "Allegory in Xenophon, Varro, and Virgil," for examples and bibliography.

[7] Unfortunately, the crucial intermediary between Plato's *Republic* and Varro's *De Re Rustica*, namely Cicero's *De Re Publica*, is missing the book on the education and training of Roman citizens (book 4). Thus, it is not possible to know if Varro is also engaging pastoral analogies in Cicero's work; however, an intriguing fragment preserved in Nonius suggests that pastoral analogies were used: "when they employ shepherds for the farm animals" (*cum adhibent in pecuda pastores*, Non. p. 159.16). On this fragment, Zetzel (1999) 82 n. 12 suggests: "Guardianship of women is being compared to shepherds' supervision of sheep." In book 5, there is also an elaborate analogy between the farm-overseer and the statesman (5.4–5).

[8] An APA talk by C. M. C. Green at the 2007 conference in San Diego ("The shepherd of the people: Varro on herding for the Villa Publica in *RR* 2"), which I heard after this chapter was written, also references the political subtext of book 2 and argues that "throughout the *RR* Varro uses the cultivation of the farm as a model for the care of the city of Rome" (quoted from the abstract). Her overall interpretation of Varro's use of farming and pastoral analogies continues to be different from mine, however, since she sees Varro's agricultural framework for the most part as a positive model for statecraft instead of a symbol of its flaws.

[9] For a detailed treatment of the animalization of Socrates' guardians, see Saxonhouse (1978).

(413d). Most importantly, the dog guardians must learn not to attack the flock, thereby becoming wolves instead of dogs, or savage despots instead of kind allies (416a–b). Indeed, their own interests and happiness are to be subordinated entirely to those of the city as a whole (419a–421c), and, in particular, they are to be subject to the rulers, who are the "shepherds of the city" (ποιμένων πόλεως, 440d).

Socrates' analogies between the guardians and animals become more bizarre as the topics of female guardians and breeding are broached; like dogs, women are to guard and hunt together with the males (451d), and they are to breed like dogs, birds, and horses (459a–b). In order for the city not to degenerate, the best specimens of the guardian class must mate with each other at the prime of their lives, and only those offspring are to be reared (459d–e). So, a secret breeding process must be set up whereby lots are drawn, and those chosen are shut up in breeding pens.[10] It is up to the shepherd/philosopher-king to decide on the size of their flock since it must not be either "too large or too small" (460a). Even these philosopher-kings are to be treated like animals, for when they get too old to be of use to the city, they should be set out to pasture like bulls destined for sacrifice (498c).

As discussed in Part I, Socrates' philosopher-kings are problematic, since true philosophers have no desire to rule a city and must be forced to become "leaders of the hive" (520b); thus, those who become shepherds *willingly* must do so from a materialistic motive, and this is the model of shepherd that is found in Varro's "republic." As mentioned in chapter 4, Varro associates pastoralism with greed (*avaritia*) in the preface to book 2 (2.pr. 4), and Scrofa defines the pastoral art as the science of making the maximum profit out of the flock (2.1.11). He even suggests that the word *pecunia* ("money") is derived from *pecus* ("herd") since the herd is the foundation of all wealth (2.1.11). Indeed, throughout the book, the goal of profit and the self-interest of the shepherd are kept at the forefront of the discussion,[11] and any incidental benefits for the flock, such as soft bedding (2.2.8) or warm shelter (2.5.15), are motivated only by a concern for profit.

The political subtext of the book is also emphasized by its setting: it takes place in Epirus,[12] and Varro tells us that he was at the time in command

---

[10] Cf. Saxonhouse (1978) 897: "Once the partners have been matched, they do not retire to a private bedchamber. Rather, they are shut up together as if the rulers were breeding cattle or dogs. The word *sunerxis* used twice in this short passage (460a and 461b) to indicate the enclosing of the mating couple is one 'properly used of penning animals' (Jowett and Campbell 1894, p. 230)."

[11] E.g. 2.pr. 5, 2.1.11, 2.1.14, 2.3.1, 2.4.22, 2.5.17, and 2.6.2.

[12] Dahlmann (1935) 1190 interprets *R.* 2.11.12 ("a freedman of Vitulus coming into the city," *Vituli libertus in urbem veniens*) as meaning that the book takes place in Rome, though I do not think this

of the Greek fleets between Delos and Sicily and was fighting pirates (2.pr. 6), which would make the year around 67 BC.[13] Thus, Varro has not yet abandoned political life for the life of *otium* and has experienced first hand what it is like to be a shepherd – in both the literal and metaphorical sense. Indeed, later in the book, Varro is explicitly addressed by the senator Lucienus as a "shepherd of the people" (ποιμένα λαῶν, 2.5.1).

In addition to the presence of this political and military framework, there are several ways in which the equation between ruling people and herding animals is effected in book 2. An obvious one is through the punning asso-ciation of the participants in the dialogue with the animals they discuss, and Varro notes that many Roman names are derived from herd animals (2.1.10). Assembled at Epirus are Scrofa ("sow") and Vaccius (cf. *vacca*, "cow"), and, in the course of the book, a Q. Modius Equiculus (cf. *equus*, "horse") and Vitulus ("calf") are mentioned (in 2.7.1 and 2.11.12, respec-tively). While these puns might seem to represent a superficial conflation of man and beast, the connections between the real and metaphorical herds of book 2 gain more significance in the discussion of the animals themselves.

For instance, the repeated emphasis on the importance of selecting animals of good lineage[14] finds a counterpart in the importance Roman families placed on their own lineage. Scrofa illustrates this importance when he feels a need to assure his audience that he is not from a family of swineherds, despite his name, and that the name instead derives from the military exploits of his grandfather, who scattered the enemy "just as a sow scatters pigs" (*ut scrofa porcos*, 2.4.2).[15] Similarly, the repeated focus on the physical health of the flock[16] recalls the point made in the preface to this book that the Roman ancestors valued farming because it made the

---

vague reference to a "city" should override the more specific references to Epirus (2.pr. 6, 2.1.3, 2.2.1, 2.5.1). See also Flach (1997) 41–42, who suggests Buthrotum as the locale.

[13] I would also speculate that there could be a political allusion in the dedication of the book to the mysterious Turranius Niger (2.pr. 6), whose identity is unknown. While it is certainly likely, as Tilly (1973) 230 (*ad* 2.pr. 6.) suggests, that "his name is probably connected with *taurus*, 'a bull', which in Umbrian is *turu*: his name is also spelt Turannus," I would add that it might also bring to mind *tyrannus* ("tyrant"). Turranius Niger is said to enjoy shopping at the cattle market (Campi Macri) in Mutina (2.pr. 6), and in the same sentence, Varro makes a reference to having once possessed great herds (*ipse pecuarias habui grandes*). Boissier (1861) 2 n. 1 and Guiraud (1985) 82 cite the confiscations during the civil wars as one possible explanation for why Varro no longer has his herds. Might Turranius Niger be an ironic allusion to the ultimate greedy shepherd and tyrant, Mark Antony, fresh from his invasion of Mutina and confiscation of Varro's property?

[14] E.g. 2.2.3, 2.1.14, 2.3.4, 2.4.4, 2.5.9, and 2.7.6.

[15] Macrobius (1.6) tells a more embarrassing story about Scrofa's name: he says that Scrofa's slaves killed a neighbor's sow, and, when the neighbor came looking for it, Scrofa hid it under his wife's bed and swore an oath that there was no sow in the house except the one lying on the bed. If this story was well known, then Scrofa's suppression of it adds to the humor of his character.

[16] E.g. 2.1.21–23, 2.2.20, and 2.3.8.

Romans healthy (2.pr. 2).[17] Indeed, nearly all of the instructions on raising and breeding animals have a human counterpart, and while these implicit connections can be made throughout the book, they become suddenly explicit at the end of it when the last type of "herd" is considered, namely the shepherds themselves and their families (2.10.1–11). As with Socrates' guardians, they are to be bred like animals,[18] and the women take on equal duties as the men (e.g. 2.10.1 and 2.10.7).

Echoes of Socrates' guardians perhaps also appear in the discussion of horses and dogs. For instance, just as Socrates details the necessary physical qualities of the guardians by discussing the brave and spirited natures of well-bred horses and dogs (375a–b), so the speaker Lucienus notes that signs of an *equus bonus* include the horse's competitive spirit in the pasture or race and his boldness in crossing a river without looking back (2.7.6). An even closer parallel to the *Republic* is found in the instruction to expose the colt to the sight and sound of the harness so that it does not get frightened when he must put it on (2.7.12; cf. *R.* 413d). Finally the emphasis on the importance of having both "fierce" (*acres*) and "gentle" (*placidos*) horses for different jobs (2.7.15) is reminiscent of Socrates' emphasis on finding guardians that are both fierce to the enemy and gentle to their own flock (e.g. *R.* 375c). While Varro's horses are not explicitly compared to military men, there is an implicit comparison at the start of the section when Quintus Modius Equiculus is mentioned and called "a most brave man, whose father was also in the military" (*vir fortissimus, etiam patre militari*, 2.7.1). Like the horses to be discussed, Equiculus is praised for possessing a brave spirit and good lineage.

The dog is Socrates' preferred model for his guardian class, and Varro has Atticus introduce the dog explicitly as a "guardian" (*custos*) of flocks which needs this ally for their defense (2.9.1). In addition, just as Socrates had divided his city into a producing class, a guardian class, and a ruling class, so essentially does Varro when he has Scrofa note that dogs belong to the type of herd which is kept not for profit but for its service to the profitable group (2.1.12); he also later comments on the dog's complete obedience to the shepherd (its "ruling class") (2.9.5–6). Finally, just as Socrates had cautioned against the dogs attacking the flock (416a–b), so Atticus notes that dogs are not allowed to feed on dead sheep lest it lead them to attack

[17] Scrofa also explicitly compares the medical science that treats animals to that which treats people (2.1.21).

[18] Atticus emphasizes this point early in the dialogue when he decides that Scrofa's category of "breeding" can apply to the human herd as well (2.1.26). The discussion of breeding herdsmen is in 2.10.6–8 and begins with a topic sentence that uses a breeding term (*fetura*, "breeding") more suitable to the breeding of animals than humans.

the flock (2.9.10). While none of the human participants in the discussion in book 2 has a dog-like name, the military setting evokes the human kind of guardian-soldier for whom these dogs might serve as models. Of course, by the time of the book's composition in the midst of the Roman civil wars, many such "guardians" had attacked their own flocks instead of a foreign enemy.

Book 2, then, builds upon the political and moral foundation of book 1, which placed need and greed at the origin of the state and made the utility and pleasure of the farmer the ultimate goal of the farm. The political subtext becomes more pronounced in book 2 as a more familiar metaphor for ruling people is introduced via the shepherd analogy, and as possible echoes of Plato's own political use of that analogy surface, along with his barnyard of other animal analogies. Book 2 underscores the similarities between what a state values in its people and what a shepherd values in its flock, and these similarities imply that human *mores* and institutions, instead of having inherent moral worth, simply enshrine values that promote group profitability. Of course, Socrates' explicit goal in the *Republic* was not to build a city but to prove that justice is an inherent good. Whether or not Socrates actually thought that justice could be found in his "beautiful city," and however Varro interpreted the *Republic*, it seems clear from book 2 that the only justice that exists among Varro's shepherds is of the Thrasymachean kind – i.e., the advantage of the stronger (*R.* 343c). Just as all states (or households) held together by these bonds of material self-interest eventually decline in the works of Xenophon (or after the work takes place, in the case of the *Oeconomicus*), so the Roman Republic of the *De Re Rustica* is hurtling towards civil war and is in complete disarray at the time of its composition.

BOOK 3: THE ACTIVE AND CONTEMPLATIVE LIFE

While I have suggested that readers alert to a political subtext may detect one in the agricultural and pastoral discussions in books 1 and 2, it is in book 3 that the political metaphor is most explicit. Like book 2, book 3 has a distinctly political setting. This time, however, the setting is not a war abroad, but an election at home. The participants in the dialogue have all gathered in the Villa Publica, during the aedile election of 50 BC – the last before Julius Caesar seized control of the state[19] – and the Villa Publica is presented as an idealized symbol of the Republic. Appius says

---

[19] The dating of this book is somewhat controversial, though most scholars agree it is set in 50 BC. See Badian (1970), Nicolet (1970), Linderski (1985) (*contra* Richardson (1983), who places it in 54 BC), and Flach (2002) 29–30.

it was built by the Roman ancestors and is more frugal and better than Axius' fancy villa at Reate. It is the "common property of all the people" (*communis universi populi*, 3.2.4) and is "useful" (*utilis*) "for administering the state" (*ad rem publicam administrandam*, 3.2.4).[20] In addition, as in book 2, most of the participants in book 3 have animal names,[21] so the reader is again encouraged to draw connections between the human and non-human "flocks" being discussed. Not only does the election take place in the "sheep pen" (ovile), but the dialogue proper begins when Axius asks Appius, who is sitting in the Villa Publica with Merula, Pavo, Pica, and Passer, if he will welcome them (i.e. Axius and Varro) into his aviary, where he is sitting among birds (3.2.2). Thus, the Villa Publica is identified both with the Republic and with an aviary, and this symbolic identification sets the stage for a discussion about aviaries that in turn represent the *Res Publica*.

Green (1997) agrees that "the setting of the dialogue is a signal to the reader that Rome, in the guise of the Villa Publica and its flocks, is also under discussion" (436); however, as already noted, she has a different interpretation of Varro's political analogies. According to Green, farming is a "metaphor for wise government" (431) and "Rome, in Varro's view, never could be separated from the farmers who were its true founders, or from the land, its true foundation" (447). She also argues for a symbolic difference between the herding of animals in book 2 and the keeping of flocks in book 3 based on the Roman law of *usucapio* ("ownership by possession"). According to that law, human beings and wild animals have a "natural liberty," and while they may be hunted and captured, they regain their liberty if they escape (Green [1997] 436–38). Thus, according to Green, book 2 focuses on domestic animals and the hunting of legitimate prey (i.e. pirates) during a better period in the Republic. Book 3, on the other hand, focuses on the keeping of wild animals with natural liberty and, symbolically, the hunting and ruling of Roman citizens during the proscriptions and civil wars (Green [1997] 439–45).[22]

---

[20] Cf. also Green (1997) 432: "The Villa Publica is a symbolic representation of the concept of the *res publica*: specifically, it symbolizes the origin of Rome's republic (idealized, of course) as a collective of farmers, countrymen, who elected magistrates to manage their estate (*res publica, villa publica*)." On the definition of the Republic as the "property of the people," see Cic. *Rep.* 1.39.

[21] There is Cornelius Merula (blackbird), Fircellius Pavo (peacock), Minucius Pica (magpie), and Marcus Petronius Passer (sparrow). Appius Claudius, in his guise as augur, is connected with both bees (Appius) and birds. Only Quintus Axius and Varro do not have animal names. On the significance of Axius' name, see chapter 4, "Genealogy of morals."

[22] Cf. Green (1997) 439: "Book 3, on both levels, is about animals that have natural liberty, animals which were free, if sometimes hunted, but which have come in times recent to Varro's own to be kept in villa enclosures."

While I certainly agree with Green that the *Res Publica* is the underlying subject of book 3 and that the discussion of *pastio villatica* presents the current Roman state as corrupt and flawed, I disagree that books 2 and book 3 present fundamentally different visions of political life. Human beings were among the "herds" in book 2, as well, and not just in the slave herds: the Roman nobles were also conflated with beasts and shown to be enslaved by political and military life as much as the domesticated animals. The pessimistic vision of book 3 represents the natural result of the political analogies of books 1 and 2 instead of a falling away from some ideal. As mentioned previously, *pastio villatica* is presented as the most profitable agricultural practice, and, accordingly, book 3 focuses most intensely on the profit to be made from the herd; however, according to the *De Re Rustica*, the point of *all* agricultural practice is the profit of the farmer/shepherd.[23]

I would suggest that what is different about book 3 is not its negative vision of political life, but the fact that for the first time, an alternative to political life is considered. Indeed, there are two different kinds of aviaries in book 3: one is presented by Merula, and it is an aviary whose purpose is profit; the other is presented by Varro, and its purpose is not profit but enjoyment (3.4.2). Green does not distinguish between Varro's and Merula's aviaries, but I would argue that there is an important symbolic difference that develops from these different motives. Varro's description of his aviary becomes a symbol not of the Villa Publica or of the *Res Publica*,[24] but of his literary dialogue; his goal of enjoyment instead of profit stands for his choice of a contemplative life over a political one. Thus, book 3 is the ultimate answer to the dialogue Cicero began with Varro on the contemplative and political life; in it, Varro defends the life of the mind and his decision to "step into the shade."[25]

Indeed, there are many similarities between book 3 of the *De Re Rustica* and book 1 of the *De Re Publica*. Just as book 1 of the *De Re Publica* contains a lengthy exposition on the definition of a *res publica* and the different kinds of governments (1.38–69), so book 3 of *De Re Rustica* begins with a discussion of the different kinds of villas and the proper definition

---

[23] Indeed, Varro reiterates this underlying similarity between the three agricultural enterprises he describes in his work at the beginning of book 3: "Therefore since I reckoned that there are three types of agricultural enterprises, which are established for the sake of profit . . ." (*itaque cum putarem esse rerum rusticarum, quae constituta sunt fructus causa, tria genera . . .* 3.1.9).

[24] *Contra* Green (1997) 441: "There is, we should notice, a certain similarity between Varro's aviary and the Villa Publica."

[25] Book 3 begins with Axius asking Varro if he would like to use the shade of the Villa Publica with him (3.2.1).

of one (3.2.3–18). In addition, just as Cicero's Scipio speaks of three forms of government (1.44), so Merula mentions three kinds of *pastio villatica*, namely aviaries, hare-warrens, and fish ponds (3.3.1). Also, like Scipio, Merula divides each type into an earlier pure form and a later depraved form ("the earlier, which ancient frugality contributed, and the later, which modern luxury added," *superiores, quos frugalitas antiqua, inferiores, quos luxuria posterior adiecit*, 3.3.6. Cf. *Rep.* 1.44). Finally, the *De Re Publica* begins with a lengthy preface in Cicero's own person (1.1–13), in which he defends the superiority of the active, political life over the contemplative life of *otium* and *voluptas*. This is a topic that Cicero continued to debate with Varro in his letters and that Varro engages throughout book 3 of the *De Re Rustica*.[26]

As already mentioned, the main way in which Varro approaches this debate is through the discussion of aviaries, the first type of *pastio villatica* and the topic to which the majority of book 3 is dedicated (3.4.2–3.11.4). While Merula had initially divided *pastio villatica* into an earlier frugal phase and a later luxurious one (3.3.6), he further subdivides the topic of aviaries into those which are kept "for the sake of pleasure" (*delectationis causa*, 3.4.2), such as Varro had at his villa near Casinum, and those kept "for the sake of profit" (*fructus causa*, 3.4.2). This *opposition* between profit and pleasure is unusual for the *De Re Rustica* since most of the agricultural advice aims at both *utilitas* and *voluptas* ("utility and pleasure") or *fructus* and *delectatio* ("profit and pleasure") (e.g. 1.4.1, 1.23.4, and 3.3.1). Yet, with regard to aviaries, it is immediately suggested that it is difficult to combine these two goals: Lucullus tried to do so by placing a dining room in his aviary so that he could eat birds and watch them at the same time, but it

---

[26] I would even suggest that perhaps the dedication of book 3 to a certain "Pinnius" could refer to the recently deceased Cicero. While it is of course possible that the name is simply a pun on "wing" and nothing more, there are a few odd details about the dedication that make it seem as if Varro had someone specific in mind. Varro notes that this dedication is "owed" to Pinnius ("I seemed to owe," *visus sum debere*, 3.1.9), which could be an allusion to the dedication Cicero felt Varro owed him (cf. Cic. *Fam.* 9.8 and *Ac.* 1.2–3). Pinnius is described as having a fancy villa that is not complete until "adorned" (*exornati*) with his own writings (3.1.10). Cf. *Leg.* 1.5, in which Atticus expresses the belief that Rome should be "adorned" (*ornata*) with Cicero's historical writings. Finally, Varro references conversations he had with Pinnius on the *villa perfecta* ("complete/perfect villa," 3.1.10). If the metaphorical equation between the *villa* and the *res publica* holds, then it is perhaps significant that Cicero speaks of the *res publica perfecta* in the *De Re Publica* (e.g. *Rep.* 2.22). Diederich (2007) 180 also suggests that the phrase *villa perfecta* might be understood "as an ironic allusion to Cicero's *perfectus orator*" ("als eine ironische Anspielung auf Ciceros *perfectus orator*") in *de Orat.* 1.34. Other suggestions for the identity of Pinnius have included a certain T. Pinnius, who appears in one of Cicero's Letters and who made Cicero the guardian of his son (*Fam.* 13.61), though there is nothing in Varro's text to suggest they are the same man. See Guiraud (1997) 53. Green (1997) 446 proposes that the dedicatee is Asinius Pollio, since he founded a library next to the Villa Publica and was "a close friend and admirer of Varro's."

turned out that the stench of the aviary overwhelmed the pleasant sight of the birds (3.4.3). There seems to be a more subtle distinction being made here between types of aviaries, and one that has nothing to do with the opposition between luxury and frugality or the past and the present. After all, both of these types of aviaries belong in the luxurious present since Axius had requested that Merula start with the more profitable modern age (3.4.1). Instead, the focus of the distinction is on the ethical purpose of each aviary.

Also notable in this regard is the use of the term *delectatio* instead of *voluptas*. While there is certainly semantic overlap between them, and at times Varro uses *voluptas* and *delectatio* without distinction, Cicero tended to reserve *delectatio* for higher, intellectual pleasures, while *voluptas* was used for baser, carnal ones.[27] Indeed, Cicero often associates *delectatio* with the life of the mind and *otium*, as opposed to utility and public life.[28] In his letters to Varro, he specifically associates *delectatio* with the contemplative life Varro has chosen,[29] and in the *Academica*, he has Varro praise the study of philosophy, which he uses "for the delight of the mind" (*ad delectationem animi*, *Ac.* 1.7). It is also interesting to note that when it is Varro's turn to discuss his aviary, Appius replaces *delectatio* with *animi* in describing its purpose: "Varro tell us about that other kind of aviary, which you are said to have built near Casinum for the sake of the mind/pleasure" ("*dic illut alterum genus ornithonis, qui animi causa constitutus a te sub Casino fertur*," 3.5.8).[30] While other translators and commentators have limited the meaning of *animi causa* to "for the sake of pleasure," it is the only time in the work that Varro substitutes *animus* for *voluptas* or *delectatio*. Therefore, I would argue its full semantic range comes into play here and helps to set up the description of an aviary that symbolizes not just pleasure, but the pleasures of the mind.[31]

If Varro's aviary is associated with the delight of the mind and the contemplative life, then I would suggest that Merula's profit-based aviary brings to mind the political life, which has thus far been symbolized

[27] Cf. Maggiulli (1994) 498.   [28] E.g. *Tusc.* 5.66, *Tusc.* 5.72, and *Leg.* 2.14.

[29] E.g. *Fam.* 9.2.5. In *Fam.* 9.6.4, Cicero mentions the *delectatio* that comes from Varro's intellectual pursuits and says it is to be preferred to the pleasures (*voluptatibus*) of others. While he goes on to profess admiration for Varro's lifestyle and an inclination to join him in it, he also subtly restates his belief that *otium* should only be a way of life when an active life is not possible (9.6.5–6).

[30] I would also note that Cicero describes Varro's villa at Casinum specifically as a retreat for his intellectual pursuits and thus is all the more outraged at Antony's ransacking of the place (*Phil.* 2.104–05).

[31] One might also be reminded of Socrates' metaphorical use of an aviary full of birds to symbolize the mind in Pl. *Tht.* 197c–d.

in the *De Re Rustica* by the profit-making enterprises of agriculture and pastoralism.[32] Merula begins the description of the aviary-for-profit by emphasizing its physical features, which immediately make it seem like a miniature bird-*res publica*. In addition to using architectural terms to describe the shape of the cage (3.5.1), he introduces a water system reminiscent of aqueducts (3.5.2), which in turn require a sewer system (3.5.2). The cage is further equipped with doors and windows (3.5.3), which are fortified against beasts (3.5.3), and a seating arrangement, which is compared to that of a theater (3.5.4). Food and drink are provided down below (3.5.4).

These birds, like the Romans in the Late Republic, are provided with plenty of food and drink and protection from external attack – but the real predator is not a *bestia* ("beast") but the owner of the aviary. Indeed, Merula makes clear that the whole purpose of keeping the birds physically comfortable and well fed is so that they will bring greater profit, and he notes they are fed particularly well right before they are killed (3.5.4). Merula also reveals the importance of skillfully manipulating the birds' psychology so as to bring the greatest profit: there should not be too many windows, and the birds should not be able to see the trees or birds outside because the sight makes them thin with longing (3.5.3). They only need enough light to be able to see their food and water (3.5.3). When it comes time to kill the birds, they should be taken to a room and killed *en masse*. It is important that this room be hidden from the other birds since their knowledge of their eventual fate might make them so depressed that they die at an inconvenient time for the seller (3.5.6).

The aviary owner's effort to deceive and manipulate the birds recalls the lies that are utilized in Socrates' animal-city to keep the citizens in check (e.g. 389b and 414c–d), and it is a short leap to make between the owner's manipulation of the birds and a politician's manipulation of people. Similarly, the command that the birds live in near darkness, with only enough light to see their food and water, recalls the lives of the prisoners stuck in the cave in Plato's *Republic* (514a–517a), who never see the light of

---

[32] I would also suggest that perhaps Lucullus' attempt at combining the two types of aviaries (3.4.3), in the context of book 3's symbolism, might bring to mind Cicero's ideal of a combined political and intellectual life. Cicero presents Lucullus' lifestyle precisely as such an ideal in the first version of the *Academica* (*Ac.* 2.1–7). Of course, Varro presents Lucullus' attempt to combine the two types of aviaries as a humorous failure, and in "real life," Lucullus did end up choosing an exclusively private life in his gardens, one that became an infamous symbol of dissolute *luxuria* in the mind of Cicero and other moralizing Romans. On Lucullus' retirement from public life, see Keaveney (1992) 143–65, who gives a modest defense of Lucullus' character and luxurious lifestyle character against the biased reports in Cicero and Plutarch, and Hillman (1993). Varro describes the three types of lives, the contemplative, the political, and the combined contemplative/political, in a part of the *De Philosophia* quoted by Augustine (*C.D.* 19.2).

the sun, and do not even know it is there. In Green's (1997) words, "the Varronian aviary is a study of – shall we say? – physically comfortable but spiritually tormenting confinement. There is a theater, as in Rome; basic food and water are supplied in abundance, as in Rome; but there is no way out. The birds are in a *huis clos*. Readers could draw their own conclusions" (443). This comment is appended to her description of Merula's aviary in particular, and she does not distinguish the ethical purpose of Varro's aviary or its (a)political implications from Merula's, but I hope to show that Varro's non-profit aviary is different in several important respects.

First, the description of the aviary emphasizes its metapoetic features and transforms it into a symbol of Varro's literary production.[33] Varro carefully lays out the setting for his aviary (3.5.9–10): a "stream" (*flumen*), which is "clear and deep" (*liquidum et altum*), runs from the aviary to his *museum* and is bordered by an *ambulatio*. Each of these items is significant: water is a common symbol of poetic inspiration for Roman writers, presumably taking their cue from Callimachus.[34] His *museum* obviously evokes the muses and the intellectual atmosphere of Alexandria,[35] and the *ambulatio* evokes philosophical dialogue.[36] Lastly, "the location of the aviary is turned towards the country" (*in agrum versus ornithonis locus*, 3.5.10) and, implicitly, away from the city and Rome. Thus, before the aviary proper is even described, the stage is set for it to be a symbol of *otium* and intellectual pursuits.

When Varro describes the aviary itself, the literary symbolism intensifies. He first explicitly compares the shape of his aviary to a "writing tablet" (*tabulae litterariae*, 3.5.10) and then continues the writing metaphor by describing an *ambulatio* which is inscribed at the bottom of the "tablet" (3.5.11). The birds which populate the aviary evoke poetry and particularly the multigeneric nature of Varro's literary production: he twice says that birds "of every kind" (*omnigenus*, 3.5.11 and 3.5.14) are within, though he

---

[33] While many scholars have given detailed reconstructions of the literal contours of Varro's aviary, the literary symbolism has gone unnoticed. For a visual compendium of these reconstructions, see Flach (2002) 341 ff. ("Abbildungen").

[34] For water imagery in Callimachus, see Kambylis (1965) 110–23, Crowther (1979), and Knox (1985). For examples of Callimachean water imagery in Latin poetry, see Lucr. 1.927–28, Hor. *S.* 4.11, Prop. 3.1 and 3.3. It is also relevant to note that Varro's terms to describe his stream (*liquidus* and *altus*) can both be used to describe literary style (e.g. Cic. *Brut.* 274, 276 and Hor. *Ep.* 2.2.120).

[35] Perhaps Timon of Phlius' famous designation of the *Museum* at Alexandria as the "bird-cage of the Muses" (Ath. 1.22d, fr. 12 Diels) is also relevant. Timon, a writer of satires with many similarities to Cynic satire, would presumably have appealed to Varro. On the Cynic aspects of Timon's satire, see Long (1978) esp. 74–76.

[36] Cicero frequently sets his philosophical dialogues in an *ambulatio* (e.g. *de Orat.* 1.28, *Tusc.* 4.7, and *Fin.* 5.1). On the philosophical connotations of the *ambulatio* in Roman culture, see further O'Sullivan (2006) and (2007).

specifies that most of them are songbirds (*cantrices*), such as nightingales (*lusciniolae*) and blackbirds (*merulae*) (3.5.14). The nightingale is a frequent symbol of poetry,[37] while the inclusion of *merulae* encourages the mirroring effect of this aviary since Varro's dialogue, too, contains a Merula. Thus, his aviary might be interpreted as a *mise en abyme*, or an image of his dialogue in miniature. Varro's birds also take part in the theater and symposium, perhaps signaling the dramatic, philosophical, and Menippean aspects of Varro's work.[38] There is a little bird theater within the aviary (*theatridion avium*, 3.5.13), and the birds are described as "guests" (*convivae*) at a dinner party (3.5.14–15).[39] Varro provides entertainment for his birds not in order to fatten them up or distract them from their impending deaths, but because pleasure and not profit is the goal of the aviary, and the pleasure is of a distinctly artistic and intellectual kind.

There is another important difference between Merula's aviary and Varro's. While Merula had hidden the trees, the birds outside, and the light from his confined birds, because it would make them grow thin with longing (3.5.3), Varro shows his birds the outside world: he replaces the wall with a net "so that there is a view into the woods and the outside world can be seen" (*ut perspici in silvam possit et quae ibi sunt*, 3.5.13). Though Varro's birds are no more able to escape from the aviary than Merula's (3.5.13), at least they are not killed for profit and, in the meantime, are provided with enjoyment and knowledge of the world beyond the aviary. Indeed, they have more than just a view of the woods; the description of the aviary ends with a mention of a dome through which they can see the morning and evening stars, and there is even a *horologium*, which allows them to know which way the wind is blowing from within (3.5.17). The very last words of

---

[37] See Chandler (1934–35). Cf. also Pl. *R.* 620a, in which the singer Thamyras chooses to be reincarnated as a nightingale.

[38] Relihan (1993) 65 discusses the close connection between the symposium and Menippean satire: "The symposium, exploited by Menippus, is frequently encountered in the *Menippeans* [of Varro] as a scene of absurd debate." See also Relihan (1993) 25–26, 54–57, and Bakhtin (1984) 120.

[39] There has been much discussion about whether the *convivae* described in this passage are meant to be human or bird guests, and certainly those who interpret the aviary literally are less inclined to see the birds personified in such a manner. I think Green (1997) 441–42, however, gets it right: "The majority of scholarly opinion holds that the guests at this dinner table must be real, human guests. This cannot be so... An aviary is a beautiful thing to look at from the outside; but, as Lucullus discovered (3.4.3), a confined place where the droppings of hundreds of birds fall is *not* a pleasant place to dine... Besides, the rather clever device of the single boy serving all the guests food and water indiscriminately is entirely antithetical to the *luxus* of such an implicitly extraordinary dining room – and we would expect wine, not warm and cold water, to flow to human guests... Thus I share Keil's view that in fact the ducks do own the place, or the dinner wheel at least, and that when they visit the island – their equivalent of the insula Tiberina – they are the *convivae*. They come from under where the couch covers would be, if there were covers, which there aren't. Varro mentions humans not at all."

Varro's aviary description emphasize their access to this knowledge of the outer world ("... so that you are able to know from within," ... *ut intus scire possis*, 3.5.17). To return to the cave analogy, these birds may not be able to leave the cave, but at least they can see the light.

After the description of Varro's aviary, chapter 5 ends with a brief "real world" intrusion: there is a commotion, and Pantuleius Parra ("the owl," a bird of bad omen) arrives with the news that there has been electoral fraud; someone was caught "stuffing ballots in the ballot-box" (*tesserulas coicientem in loculum*, 3.5.18). Virlouvet (1996) has provided a convincing argument that the strange language used to describe these ballots being stuffed evokes the *tessera frumentaria* (i.e. corn ticket) and the money-box (*loculus*) more than the ballot and the ballot-box. This language, then, reinforces Varro's assimilation of political life to concerns about material goods and profit.[40] Both the human-birds and the literal birds in book 3 exchange their freedom (and, perhaps, their lives), for food and other material benefits. Only Varro presents an alternative to this exchange with his aviary designed for pleasure. While the contemplative life that it symbolizes is not immune to the constraints of the outside world and does not literally set the birds free, it does offer pleasure and, more importantly, knowledge.

The rest of Merula's discourse on birds (chs. 6–11) continues to emphasize the deception and manipulation of the birds for profit (e.g. 3.7.7) and the importance of confining them so they do not get away (3.9.19), even if it means breaking the legs of nurslings in the nest (3.7.10). Some birds are turned loose for a time – but only because they are sure to return to nurse their young (3.7.6), are trained to return (3.7.7) or prevented from escaping by a net (3.9.15). Thus, the birds have the illusion of freedom, but not the real thing. While the birds generally appear as innocent victims of the bird keeper's greed, some are not without complicity in the arrangement. For instance, the geese are described as being so eager for food that they need to be restrained from breaking their necks "on account of greed" (*propter cupiditatem*, 3.10.5) by pulling on a root too hard.

In chapter 12, Appius takes over from Merula and begins discussing the second topic of *pastio villatica*, namely *leporaria* ("hare-warrens"), which includes the keeping of hares, deer, goats, boars, snails, bees, and mice. Though more picturesque in style, Appius' instructions on raising these animals are similar to Merula's in that he emphasizes how to keep them

---

[40] Green (1997) 431 also notes, "Books 1 and 3 are therefore linked by this offstage but significant character, the aedile" – i.e. the provider of bread and circuses.

captive and fatten them, and this topic is dispatched quickly. However, as Appius is about to move on to the third topic of fishponds, Axius stops him and asks if he is neglecting honey because of his youthful frugality (3.16.1). This comment leads Appius into a lengthy disquisition on bees, through which Varro continues his critique of the active life and his engagement with Cicero, Xenophon, and Plato.

According to Appius, bees are gifted by nature with incredible "skill" (*ars*) and "natural talent" (*ingenium*) (3.16.3). They are social creatures, like people (3.16.4); they are partners in work and building (3.16.4), and they learn how to do their various tasks through *ratio* and *ars* ("here there is reason and skill; from these they learn to do work," *hic ratio atque ars, ab his opus facere discunt*, 3.16.4). They produce a sweet substance that is pleasing to both gods and men (3.16.5) and "seek everything pure" (*secuntur omnia pura*, 3.16.6). They have governments like men with a "king" (*rex*), "power" (*imperium*), and "society" (*societas*) (3.16.6), and they are completely devoted to their king (3.16.8). They are industrious, hate the "lazy" (*inertes*) and keep out the drones (3.16.8). They live and sleep as if in an army, send out colonies, and obey the trumpet-like signal of their leader (3.16.9). In short, Appius presents the bees as an ideal political society and, in doing so, engages a long history of political thought that compared human and apian societies.

In particular, it is likely that Cicero used the bees as an example of an ideal society in book 2 of the *De Re Publica*. Unfortunately, the description itself is lost, but we have the introduction (2.64–66): Tubero is dissatisfied with Scipio's discussion of the Roman state because Laelius had asked Scipio to talk not about Rome in particular but about the *res publica* in general. Scipio replies that if Tubero wants to understand "the nature of an ideal state" (*genus ipsum . . . optimi status*, 2.66) without using the example of any people, he will have to use an "image of nature" instead (*naturae imagine*, 2.66). While there have been several suggestions for what this *imago naturae* is,[41] I find Richter's (1969) arguments persuasive that Scipio's example of an ideal state is that of the bees.[42] Even if Cicero did not use the bee state as a model in the *De Re Publica*, he made comparisons between bees and human society elsewhere (e.g. *Off.* 1.157); more importantly, he translated

---

[41] Pöschl [1936]/(1990) 120–27 has argued that the *imago naturae* is Plato's city-soul analogy, while Ferrary (1984) 97–98 has suggested the image of the universe and divine demiurge from Plato's *Timaeus* (see also Ferrary [1995] 59–60). Zetzel (1995) 26 and 222–23 tentatively supports Ferrary's conclusion.

[42] In arguing against Pöschl, Richter (1969) 285 notes that Plato's hierarchy of the parts of the soul is only a theory and not an *imago* that can be empirically perceived.

Xenophon's *Oeconomicus* and presumably included Ischomachus' version of the bee-human comparison, in which Ischomachus tells his wife that her control of the household should resemble that of a queen bee's control of her hive (*Oec.* 7.32–34). Plato, too, makes use of bee analogies in the *Republic*: Socrates calls the philosopher-kings the leaders of the hive (520b) and later compares drones to the type of spendthrift man who is ruled by unnecessary desires (552c–d, 559d, 564b–565a). Thus, whether Varro is responding directly to Cicero's *De Re Publica* or not, Appius' encomium of the bee-state fits into a tradition of political theorizing about ideal states.

Appius does not, however, have the last word on the bees. Instead, he passes the torch on to Merula to talk about the profit that can be made from them since he knows that this is what Axius is dying to hear (3.16.9). Merula's advice breaks the illusion of Appius' ideal society: he includes instructions on how to stop "civil discord" (*seditiones*) among the bees by making sure that more than one king does not arise (3.16.18). He notes in particular that the black bee is a problem and should be killed because when he is with another king, he is seditious and destroys the hive (3.16.18). Later, he gives advice for preventing the stronger bees from imposing on the weaker ones and for stopping fights between bees (3.16.35). In addition, the illnesses that plague bees are suddenly mentioned (3.16.19–20), as are the dangers of exposure to heat, cold, or rain (3.16.37). Finally, the bees are shown to be just as easily manipulated as the birds by attractive substances that are used to lure them to new homes (3.16.31), and they also greedily get drunk on mead (3.16.35).

While Appius presents the miraculous society of the bees as if it were some divine manifestation of virtue, Merula presents the underlying truth: beneath the pious and moral exterior of bee society is self-interest and survival of the fittest.[43] While the greedy bees' self-serving instincts lead them to form a complex, ordered society, this society is not without its fault-lines, and it seems to be constantly riven by conflicts of interest within the group. Thus, just as Axius had revealed the hypocrisy of Appius' moralizing about villas, so Varro (through Merula) more subtly reveals the hypocrisy of his idolization of bee society. More importantly, Varro has a chance to show that it is not just the corrupt state of the Late Republic that is imperfect; political society, even in its ideal form as an *imago naturae*, is based on self-interest and greed. Varro may have finally given himself an animal role in his dialogue as the wasp in the hive, who can injure bees

---

[43] In this point, Varro anticipates the thesis of Mandeville's *Fable of the Bees*.

with its sting but takes no part in bee society (3.16.19). After all, the wasp
is the animal of the satirist, and it is the satirist's job to attack society with
his words.[44]

After the discourse on bees, Appius and Merula go off to hear the
results of the election (3.17.1), and the third topic of *pastio villatica* is
briefly treated by Axius, namely fishponds. While the treatment is brief,
I would suggest that Varro uses the contrast between bees and fishponds
to model once again the differences between the active and contemplative
life. If according to the conventional moralizing of Romans like Appius or
Cicero, the society of bees connotes an ideal state and the virtues of the
active life, then fishponds represent precisely the opposite, namely private
luxuria and *otium*.[45] Indeed, fishponds are the symbol of *luxuria* that
Cicero most consistently criticizes, and he condemns the *piscinarii* (owners
of fancy fishponds) for caring more about their fish than the Republic.[46]
Similar moralizing critique makes it into the *De Re Rustica* in the words
of both Merula (3.3.9-10) and Axius (2.17.2-9).[47] In fact, Axius' entire
discourse on fishponds consists of a critique of the nobility's *piscinae* that
were kept for the sake of pleasure instead of profit (3.17.2). Yet, Axius is not
exactly a moral exemplar himself, and his dislike of fishponds-for-pleasure
is explicitly connected to their lack of profitability (3.17.2) and not to any
inherent moral badness. More importantly, through Axius' discourse on
fishponds, Varro once again creates a symbol of the contemplative life, both
because of their associations with *otium*, and because of certain metapoetic
qualities emphasized in their descriptions.

There are several ways in which Varro has Axius associate luxurious
fishponds with art. First, his description of their purpose, that "they are

[44] As Clayman (1980) 57-58 notes, "Hipponax was well-known in antiquity for his waspish character.
An epigram of Leonidas (*A.P.* 7.408) warns its readers to pass quietly by Hipponax's tomb lest they
wake the sleeping wasp whose burning verses have the power to harm even in Hades." He also
notes that "[Archilochus] too is a wasp in Callimachus' own estimation [fr. 380.1-2], who stings his
opponents such as Lykambes." (61). See also Freudenburg (1993) 77. On the anti-social nature of
satirists in general, see Braund (1996) 37-41.

[45] Wallace-Hadrill (1998) 2-6 makes the related point that the luxurious *horti* of the late Republic
frequently made (a)political statements: "Because the garden is a denial of the forum, it flags an
abstinence from politics of a particular sort" (6). Cf. also Edwards (1993) 23: "A life devoted to
literature and contemplation was often elided with a life devoted to pleasure." She cites Tac. *Hist.*
4.5 as an example.

[46] For Cicero's scorn for the *piscinarii*, see references in chapter 4, "Hypocrites and moralizers."

[47] Merula ends his critique with a rhetorical question that seems a sly reference to the *piscinarii*'s
notoriety at the hands of Cicero: "For who is unaware of the fishponds of Philippus, Hortensius,
and the Luculli on account of their celebrity?" (*quis enim propter nobilitates ignorat piscinas Philippi,
Hortensi, Lucullorum?*, 3.3.10). Indeed, it is precisely these three whom Macrobius (3.15.6) cites as
being called *piscinarios* by Cicero. For more on the *piscinarii* and fishponds in the Late Republic,
see Higginbotham (1997) 55-64 and Weeber (2003) 37-42.

more agreeable to the eyes than the purse" (*magis ad oculos pertinent, quam ad vesicam*, 3.17.2), brings to mind a work of visual art. This association is reinforced by the comparison of the compartments for separate kinds of fish to the compartments that painters use to keep their colors separate (3.17.4). Axius also ridicules the fishpond owners for treating their fish as if they were more sacred than those in Lydia, which once gathered around Varro at the sound of a flute while he (Varro) was sacrificing (3.17.4–5). The intrusion of Varro's character at this point directly connects him to the luxurious fishponds[48] and presents him as a quasi-Orpheus figure, summoning animals to music. Axius also adds that in Lydia, Varro watched the "dancing islands of the Lydians" (3.17.4), which, according to Pliny, moved to the singing and dancing of choruses (*Nat.* 2.209). Though commentators will note that Varro was in Lydia to fight pirates, there is no mention now of his being the "shepherd of the people." Instead, Varro is exclusively associated with music and dancing, and in the process, fish become a symbol of sacred art – not profit.

The rest of Axius' critique of luxurious fishponds ridicules the extreme care that Hortensius lavished on his fish. Indeed, Axius notes that Hortensius was more generous with his fish than he (Axius) is with his asses at Rosea. He also notes that Hortensius cares for them when sick (3.17.8) and that he leads his "beloved fish" (*amicos pisces*) to cooler locations when it is hot, just as Apulian shepherds do in the Sabine hills (3.17.9). While there is of course humor in Hortensius' excessive concern for his fish, in the symbolic context of the dialogue, there is perhaps something more: in Hortensius, we finally have an image of a shepherd who is concerned for the welfare of his flock not because of the profit the flock will bring him but because he loves them. Thus, fishponds-for-pleasure, like aviaries-for-pleasure, might evoke the superiority of the life of contemplation, which values art, as well as fish and birds, for their own sake. While Cicero found fault with the *luxuria* of the Late Republic, Varro presents the *frugalitas*- and *fructus*-loving nature of farmers and politicians as more destructive.

Varro began his work on farming by comparing his writing to the singing of the Sibyl and particularly to the benefits of her songs for mankind (1.1.3). By the end of the *De Re Rustica,* the nature of Varro's benefit to mankind has become more complex: it seems he has not tried to teach anyone to farm but instead to have a better view into the forest and some *delectatio* along the way. He does not replace the moral and political views that he

---

[48] Varro is also connected to fishponds-for-pleasure via his aviary, which has them within its structure (3.5.12).

satirizes with any dogmatic system of his own, nor does he indicate a path to true virtue; he simply advocates a life guided by intellectual pursuits – though even the intellectual life is not immune to Varro's parodic (and self-parodic) wit. That at least one ancient reader read Varro's work as more than a farming manual or moralizing discourse will hopefully become clear in the next section, in which I present Virgil's incorporation of Varro's satire on farming into the *Georgics,* which ultimately molds the Menippean spirit of Varro's dialogue into something more tragic and Virgilian.

PART III

Virgil's Georgics

Much excellent work has been done on the poetic influences on Virgil's *Georgics*.[1] My goal in this section is not to discount the importance of these poetic models but simply to reintegrate equally important sources of inspiration for the *Georgics*, namely Xenophon's and Varro's philosophical dialogues on farming. The *Georgics* has frequently been read as a generically self-conscious work, but when that genre is limited to didactic poetry, the reader loses sight of aspects of the work that might be read profitably against the background of philosophical satire and dialogue.[2] In particular, I would suggest that connecting the *Georgics* to works like the *Oeconomicus* and *De Re Rustica* usefully recontextualizes the parodic, ironic, and satiric aspects of the *Georgics*, as well as its use of polyphony, allegory, and the contrast between the active and contemplative life. More importantly, it highlights what Virgil does differently with these common devices of Socratic dialogue (and Menippean satire). While all three works require the careful attention of the reader to sort out the attitude of the author towards the different voices in the work, Virgil perhaps trumps them all in his destabilization of the authorial voice and in the challenges of his polyphony. In the following two chapters, I propose one specific way of making sense of the dialogue between the voices in the text and beyond the text, while at the same time acknowledging that "the diversity of compelling interpretations is part of the *Georgics'* larger value and meaning" (Batstone [1997] 125).

---

[1] E.g. Farrell (1991), Thomas (1999), and Gale (2000).
[2] On the *Georgics* as a generically self-conscious didactic poem, see Schiesaro (1997) and Volk (2002).

CHAPTER 6

Virgil's satire on farming

While my analysis of the *De Re Rustica* presents an unfamiliar way of reading that work, many of the conclusions I have drawn about it (and the *Oeconomicus*) are commonly made about the *Georgics*. For example, many readers find in the *Georgics* lessons about the failure of *ars* or *ratio* to control the chaos of nature (and human nature);[1] an association of the farmer with materialistic ethics;[2] contradictory moralizing about the life of the farmer and the land of Italy;[3] analysis of the deficiencies of political life via animal-human analogies,[4] and the presentation of a contrasting contemplative ideal.[5] Thus, it will not be as difficult to demonstrate that these themes appear in the *Georgics*, and my goal is not to give an exhaustive analysis of them so much as show how deep an imprint Varro's work, in particular, left on the *Georgics*. Ultimately, my analysis of Virgil's incorporation of Varro's satire on farming will bring into relief the ways in which the *Georgics* differs from the works of both Xenophon and Varro, as I will explore more in the next chapter.

THE FAILURE OF KNOWLEDGE

In book 1 of the *De Re Rustica*, Varro parodies Late Republican intellectual culture via the dialogue between Scrofa, the modern expert, and Stolo the old-fashioned teacher. Not only do Scrofa and Stolo end up sounding

---

[1] E.g. Thomas (1988), see index under "failure (of man's endeavour)." See also Gale (2000) 97–100 on Virgil's critique of "Lucretius' faith in the power of *ratio*" (97).
[2] E.g. Perkell (1989).
[3] E.g. Ross (1987) 109–45, Thomas (1988) 1.179–90 (*ad* 2.136–76), 1.244–63 (*ad* 2.458–540), and Gale (2000) 170–73.
[4] E.g. Griffin (1979) 63–69, Connor (1979) 43–45, and Perkell (1989) 123–30.
[5] E.g. Perkell (1981). See also Thomas (1988) II.169–75 (*ad* 4.125–48). Gale (2003) suggests there is an unresolved tension in the *Georgics* between two different ways of conceptualizing the relationship between the active and contemplative life, namely, the relationship may be viewed as either interdependent or antagonistic.

more alike than different, but they both come off as incompetent pedants. The book ends with an eruption of violence, which serves as a reminder that the realm of intellectual pursuits provides no safe-haven from or control over external chaos. In this section, I will argue that the first half of Virgil's *Georgics* treats similar themes; however, instead of using fully developed characters like Scrofa and Stolo to represent different approaches to knowledge, Virgil utilizes allusions to the poetic tradition as his "characters" and transforms the debate from one between *ratio* and *consuetudo* to one between *ratio* and *religio*.[6]

Farrell has convincingly demonstrated the existence of a program of allusion in the *Georgics*: he suggests that book 1 is primarily composed of allusions to Hesiod and Aratus and book 2 of allusions to Lucretius.[7] I would argue that Virgil conjoins Hesiod and Aratus not just for a literary purpose,[8] but for an ideological one: the worlds reflected in the *Works and Days* of Hesiod and the *Phaenomena* of Aratus are different and even conflicting in many respects, but they find common ground in their presentation of a universe that is controlled by divinity. Both works begin, quite literally, with Zeus, even if their conceptions of Zeus are different.[9] In contrast, the allusions to Lucretius in book 2 evoke a universe guided not by gods but by scientific principles. This contrast between a divinely controlled world and a scientifically structured one, or between *religio* and *ratio*, is ultimately undermined in the course of the two books, but before I show how Virgil conflates *religio* and *ratio*, I will present some of the ways in which he sets up the dichotomy.[10]

---

[6] While books 3 and 4 of the *Georgics* match up nicely with Varro's books 3 and 4 on pastoralism and *pastio villatica*, it seems that Virgil has expanded book 1 of the *De Re Rustica* into two books – another indication that books 1 and 2 of the *Georgics* might profitably be read as a unit. In addition, Virgil's "coda" at the end of book 2 (541–42) strengthens the structural unity of books 1 and 2.

[7] Farrell (1991) 131–68 (on Hesiod and Aratus in book 1) and 169–206 (on Lucretius in book 2, as well as book 3).

[8] Cf. Farrell (1991) 166: "According to my analysis, the allusive program of the book, which incorporates the structure and central thematic elements of both Hesiod's *Works and Days* and Aratus' *Phaenomena*, is based on Callimachus' polemical epigram identifying Aratus as a consummately Hesiodic poet."

[9] Cf. *Op.* 1–10 and Arat. 1–4. On their different conceptions of Zeus, cf. Hunter (1995): "The *Works and Days* presents us with an all-powerful and all-seeing Zeus (cf., e.g., 267–9) who is concerned with justice, but whose mind (*nóos*) is changeable and hard-to-know (483–4)...The Zeus of the *Phainomena*, however, while also being all-seeing and concerned with justice, openly assists mankind through the omnipresence of 'signs' (*Phain.* 10–13)." Hunter goes on to suggest, however, that "Aratus 'reads' Hesiod not merely as a forerunner of the Stoics, but as the seed from which they grew."

[10] I am using the terms *religio* and *ratio* as shorthand for a constellation of various words and images that tend toward either a religious or a scientific and rational view of the world. The *ratio/religio* dichotomy particularly structures the opposing ideologies evoked in the *De Rerum Natura*, with

Book 1 does not begin with Zeus or Jupiter, as the *Works and Days* and *Phaenomena* do, but it does begin with a hymn to the agricultural gods, similar to Varro's,[11] and throughout book 1, the divinities are presented as having a tangible effect on the farmer's life. The first didactic passage in book 1 includes a reference to the "vows" (*votis*, 1.47) of the greedy farmer, as well as to the mythological creation of human beings from the stones of Deucalion (62–63). Ceres is said to look down on the work of the farmer (96) and to have taught man to plough (147) after Jupiter introduced the age of *labor* (121–46). The instruments of the farmer are connected to religious mysteries (162–66). The field is said to be "divine" (*divini*, 168). The zones of the world have been organized by the gods (238), and the underworld exists at its bottom (243). "Divine and human law" and "religion" (*fas et iura... religio*, 269–70) govern the activities of life and the days on which things may be done (276–78). Jupiter himself wields his thunderbolt during rain storms (328–29), after which the importance of venerating the gods in order to prevent disaster is reiterated and the yearly rites for Ceres described (335–50). Jupiter is said to provide clear signs in the sky about the weather forecast (351–55), as does the personified Sun, who hid his face after Caesar's death (461–68). A vast array of portents accompanies Caesar's murder (469–97), and the book finishes with a desperate plea to the gods and to Octavian to restore order to the universe (498–514). Thus, book 1 is suffused with the powers of divinities, which alternately resemble the mysterious gods of Hesiod and the providential Zeus of Aratus.

For most of book 2, skill and human ingenuity are given prominence over the power of divinities. The gods, when they appear, are allegorized or metaphorical, and religious rites are explained in a rational or anthropological manner. For instance, Bacchus is invoked at the outset of book 2 to signal the topic of the work, but, as Thomas notes, he seems to appear as a metapoetical symbol.[12] The next eight times he is mentioned, it is

---

ratio indicating the rationalism of Epicureanism and *religio* the superstitions and religious beliefs of non-Epicureans. This dichotomy is set up early in book 1 and continues throughout the poem (e.g. Lucr. 1.51, 63, 77, 78, 81, 83, 101, 105, 108, 109, 110, etc.). I will show that there are many ways in which Virgil invokes this dichotomy in books 1 and 2, though he usually does not use the particular words *religio* or *ratio* but creates more nuanced and complex references to the opposing world views that were more bluntly set forth in the *De Rerum Natura*.

[11] Unlike Varro's hymn, which begins with Jove, Virgil's begins with the sun and the moon and culminates in an address to Octavian (1.24–42). Thomas (1988) 1.73 (*ad* 1.24–42) notes that "Octavian has virtually replaced the absent Jupiter."

[12] Thomas (1988) 1.156 (*ad* 2.7–8): "Bacchus is invoked, and invited to participate in the pressing of the new wine. The image is clearly metaphorical, with wine-pressing, and V.'s involvement in it (*mecum*), standing for the poetry of Book 2. There is perhaps a further, more profound, metaphorical reference in the lines, to generic preference. Bacchus' (or Dionysus') traditional involvement with

simply as a metonymy or periphrasis for wine or the vine (37, 113, 143, 191, 228, 229, 240, and 275). While there is a description of an elaborate ritual feast for Bacchus in book 2 (380–96) to match the ritual feast to Ceres in book 1, it is not introduced with a pious injunction to worship the gods as in book 1 (cf. 1.335–38) but instead by way of an intellectual aetiology of the festival rites, as in Varro (380–81; cf. Var. *R.* 1.2.18–20).[13] Virgil further emphasizes the aetiological focus of his description by connecting the ritual to the origins of drama in Greece and poetry in Italy, and only at the end of the description is there a reference to the Roman worshipping of the god (393–96).[14] Even in this description of religious worship, however, the tone of the narrator's voice is distinctive from the tone in the corresponding scene in book 1: instead of commanding the reader to worship the gods and Ceres with a series of imperatives and hortatory subjunctives (1.335–50), the narrator simply uses future tenses to explain why and how Romans will worship Bacchus.[15] The focus is still on rational explanation and not pious pronouncement.

Jupiter appears rarely in book 2, and when he does, it is not as the powerful, anthropomorphic deity of book 1 but as an allegorized, natural force. In 2.15–16, there is a reference to the "oak trees, which are deemed oracular by the Greeks" (*habitae Grais oracula quercus*, 16), but the phraseology is distancing and does not imply the speaker's own belief in its powers.[16] In 2.325–27, Jupiter is presented in the allegorical guise of "father Heaven" (*pater . . . Aether*, 325) who fertilizes the earth in the spring and recalls Lucretius' own rationalizing *hieros gamos* ("holy marriage") description (1.250–53), as well as his allegorization of Venus.[17] It seems that the

---

poetry is specific – he is the god of drama, particularly tragedy; hence V. refers to his buskins (*coturnis*), the footwear of the tragic actor. But for the Augustan poets he came to occupy a new position, as favourable to the new poetry . . . Programmatically, V.'s lines may be taken to mean 'Remove the buskins [of tragedy], Bacchus, and join me in soaking your naked legs in the new must [of Virgilian poetry].'"

[13] Cf. Gale (2000) 106: "[T]he digression is introduced as an *aetion* for the sacrifice itself."

[14] Cf. Thomas (1988) 1.226 (*ad* 2.380–96): "His main interest is to present the figure of Bacchus, the tutelary deity of the book (1–8, 2nn.), and to make connections between him and the origins of Greek drama and poetry." Thomas also notes (1.229 [*ad* 2.393]), "[T]here is no attempt to link religious observance with the actual *practice* of the farmer, or to show how it affects the realities of scientific agricultural endeavor."

[15] In addition, Mynors (1990) 148 (*ad* 2.380 ff.) makes the interesting point that "in Rome the sacrifice seems to be a literary fiction: the goat as a sacrificial animal in the State-cult is extremely rare (W. Krause in *RE* 5A, 250 ff.), and it is not offered to Bacchus or Liber except in what may well be derivatives of our passage."

[16] Cf. Thomas (1988) 1.159 (*ad* 2.16): "V.'s words seem almost to express *diffidentia*" and Gale (2000) 210: "[O]aks are held to be oracular by the Greeks (though there may be a note of scepticism here)."

[17] On Virgil's complex allusions to these Lucretian passages, see Farrell (1991) 100–01, who notes: "It is through Venus especially that one finds the Lucretian link between the *hieros gamos* and the other ideas with which Vergil associates it in the 'Praise of Spring'" (101). On Lucretius' use of allegory

"god" who is in control of the universe in book 2 is no god at all, but *natura*, which is the subject of the first line of the didactic portion of the book (2.9). As Gale notes, *natura* is frequently a personified subject in Lucretius,[18] and "Virgil's discussion opens with a very Lucretian-sounding line."[19] The narrator immediately launches into a Theophrastean-influenced discussion of the different types of vine propagation, namely those created by nature and those created by man (9–34).[20] The opposition that this passage sets up between *natura* and *usus* ("nature" and "practical experience") further recalls Lucretius and foregrounds man's abilities to compete with nature in exerting control over the world.[21] Thus, *natura* is not the only powerful force in book 2 but is matched by *ratio*, *ars*, and *usus* – the intellectual powers of mankind.

Indeed, it is appropriate that the book dedicated to vine growing should emphasize human cleverness and skill, as Cicero presents vine tending, and particularly grafting, as the most clever invention of agriculture in the *De Senectute* (15.54), and in the *De Finibus*, Cicero twice uses the metaphor of tending a vine as an analogy for the work of *ratio* in shaping a human being (*Fin.* 4.38 and 5.39). In book 2, Virgil extends the metaphor of the *cultura vitium* to cover all forms of human *cultus* based on *ratio*.[22] Thus, it is not just the grafting of the vines that symbolizes man's conquering and transformation of nature, but the achievements of Italy, detailed in the famous Praise of Italy (136–76), also symbolize the work of *cultus*. This praise obviously picks up on Agrius' Praise of Italy in *De Re Rustica* 1.2.3–7, but whereas Agrius had focused primarily on the *natural* fertility of Italy, Virgil's praise moves quickly out of the realm of natural achievements and into the realm of technical, human ones (e.g. 155–57).

---

in the *hieros gamos*, see Gale (1994) 40–41, who calls it "a rejection, not a justification of the myth" (41).

[18] Gale (1994) 212–13: "Therefore, *natura* is frequently personified as the force which brings all things to birth and controls the natural world" (see 213 n. 21 for the list of Lucretian passages).

[19] Gale (2000) 209. She further explains, "*principio* ('in the first place') is a favourite Lucretian *incipit*, and the second half of the line combines two phrases from Lucretius' culture-history, *in variis mundis* varia *ratione* creatis ('in the various worlds, variously created', 5.1345) and *specimen . . . / ipsa fuit rerum primum* natura creatrix (' the first model was nature the creator herself', 5.1362" (209). Farrell (1991) 194 notes, "Of the first six paragraphs in the book (9–135), five begin by mentioning the variety motif. Four of them also open with obvious Lucretian echoes."

[20] On Virgil's use of Theophrastus, see Thomas (1987) 253–60.

[21] See Farrell (1991) 195 and Gale (2000) 86–87 and 208–10. Gale (2000) 209–10 notes, "The progression from *natura* to *usus* strongly recalls the rationalistic basis of Lucretius' culture-history as a whole, and the agricultural section in particular: first of all, natural processes provide the *specimen* or model for human creativity, and then the arts and sciences are gradually refined by a process of trial and error (*usus*, 1452)."

[22] Cf. Wilhelm (1976) 66: "Although on a literal level Vergil is concerned with the *cultus* of plants and trees, poetically his choice of language suggests a symbolic expansion to man's civilization."

While I have argued that book 1 presents a *predominantly* religious view of the world (though one that is by no means uniform in its religious outlook) and book 2 a *predominantly* Lucretian or rationalistic view, I would also suggest that each book subverts this dichotomy between *religio* and *ratio* and undermines both approaches to understanding the world. As Farrell acknowledges, Lucretius actually has a large presence in book 1,[23] and Gale has extensively documented how Lucretian, Hesiodic, and Aratean voices are intertwined throughout the *Georgics* with the effect of subverting the attempt to make one of their world views dominant.[24] I would still argue, however, that all of these voices are not evenly balanced in books 1 and 2, and that recognizing this fact opens up further possibilities for how the reader might interpret their interactions. For instance, the intrusion of a scientific-sounding passage within a predominantly religious one could serve to undermine the dominant voice instead of simply presenting an equally valid way of viewing the world – and vice versa. It seems to me that while the voices of *ratio* and *religio* are intertwined, there is a larger story arc in books 1 and 2 that presents a progression from predominantly religious views of the world to predominantly rationalistic ones, and back again, as each fails to provide "the answer." *Ratio* and *religio* are merged and intertwined at key points in books 1 and 2 to underscore that they each serve the same basic need in human life – the need to understand and control the external world.

This progression from religion to science is seen in book 1 in the transition from primarily Hesiodic to primarily Aratean voices in the last section on weather-signs (351–463).[25] While Aratus shares with Hesiod a view of a universe guided by divinity, he merges a scientific approach to the natural world with a providential outlook.[26] The opening lines of Virgil's adaptation of Aratus' weather-signs section indicate both the scientific ("so that we might learn from certain signs," *certis possemus discere signis*, 351)

[23] Farrell (1991) 172: "Despite the general importance of Hesiod and Aratus in *Georgics* 1, in several important passages their influence is far from obvious; and not surprisingly, these passages contain what look like allusions to other authors. By far the most prominent of these is Lucretius."

[24] While this theme is present throughout Gale (2000), see esp. ch. 3 (58–112), ch. 4 (113–42), and ch. 6 (196–231). Examples of passages she particularly highlights as combining Lucretian voices with Hesiodic or Aratean ones are 1.60–63 (see Gale [2000] 60) and the "aetiology of *labor*"(1.118–59; see Gale [2000] 61–67). I will discuss the aetiology/theodicy of *labor* further in the next section.

[25] Cf. Thomas (1988) 1.127 (*ad* 1.351–463): "The influence of Hesiod gives way to that of Aratus, specifically the Aratus of *Phaenomena* 733–1154." See also Farrell (1991) 79–83 on Virgil's transition to and incorporation of Aratus.

[26] As many have suggested, Aratus' poem seems influenced by early Stoicism, which itself was a philosophy that merged *ratio* with divinity. He also perhaps drew on a lost treatise of Theophrastus for his section on weather-signs. On Stoicism in Aratus and the use of Theophrastus, see Hunter (1995).

and theological ("the father himself determined," *ipse pater statuit* 353) nature of the discourse. There is even an explicitly anti-religious, scientific intrusion in 1.415–23, in which the behavior of birds after a storm is said to be motivated by a change in the atmosphere instead of by some divinely inspired wisdom.[27] Reliance on the gods seems ultimately to fail in providing the constant emotional and material support the farmer needs in book 1: after two great storms threaten to destroy the farmer's world, namely the rain storm in 311–34 and the storm of civil war in 461–514, the narrator prays not just to the gods of Rome (498–99), but to a human being, Caesar, to bring salvation and an end to the chaos that has erupted (500–14).

By the end of book 1, then, the stage has been set for human beings to rely on *human* powers, and not divine, in their quest to create order and meaning in the world. Yet, while I have indicated the ways in which *ratio* and human *cultus* are valorized in book 2 and divine guidance minimized, *ratio* ultimately comes up short and fails to solve all the problems in the farmer's life, just as *religio* did in book 1. Accordingly, the confident and optimistic tone of the first part of book 2 becomes increasingly more wavering and broken up by emotional intrusions that admit the fearsome power of nature to control man's destiny.[28] Indeed, beginning with 2.397, in which the intense amount of *labor* that goes into caring for vines is emphasized, the style of the didactic content reverts back to the archaic-sounding, epigrammatic instructions of book 1.[29] The narrator no longer expresses absolute faith in *cultus*, and the olive is praised precisely for *not* needing cultivation (420), along with a host of other natural objects that need little care or culture (426–53). This list culminates in the *vituperatio vitis* ("blaming of the vine") (454–57), in which the vine, the symbol of man's great agricultural skill, is now spurned as a cause for blame.[30] Another way in which Virgil subtly undercuts *ratio* in book 2 is by conveying expert

---

[27] Cf. Gale (2000) 84–85 on lines 415–23: "The whole passage could virtually come straight out of Lucretius, were it not for one discordant note – the reference to Jupiter as agent of the changes in atmospheric pressure which motivate the animals' behaviour (418)."

[28] E.g. 2.251–53. Cf. also the epic description of the fire storm in 1.303–14, which ends with victory of nature.

[29] Cf. Thomas (1988) 1.231–32 (*ad* 2.408–13): "The strongly didactic series of imperatives in –*to* looks back to the beginning of the technical tradition, as can best be seen from Cato, *Agr.* 151.1–2 ... By V's time the style is definitely archaic." Also note Hesiod's blatant intrusion into book 2: "Praise large fields but cultivate a small one" (*laudato ingentia rura, / exiguum colito,* 412–13). Cf. Thomas (1988) 1.233 (*ad* 2.412–13): "The sentiment is a clever reversal and correction of Hes. *W.D.* 643 νηῒ ὀλίγην αἰνεῖν, μεγάληι δ' ἐνὶ φορτία θέσθαι, 'praise a small ship, but put your cargo in a big one'."

[30] On the critical discomfort engendered by these lines, see Thomas (1988) 1.242–43 (*ad* 2.454–57).

"misinformation" about vine tending, just as Varro undercut his experts in book 1 with their misinformation and Scrofa's botched organizational schemes.[31]

After the *vituperatio vitis*, book 2 concludes with Virgil's famous Praise of the Farmer (2.458–540), whose outer frame completes the book's move away from the world of *ratio* and back to *religio*, and whose inner frame (475–94) continues to merge the two ideologies. While the praise is frequently excerpted from the work and cited as proof of the *Georgics'* fundamental optimism, it is important to contextualize it within the narrative of books 1 and 2. The Praise of the Farmer, while vacillating between images of *otium* and *labor*, consistently attributes to the farmers a life that is full of the gods and *religio* and not reliant on *ratio* in any sophisticated sense (e.g. "[here are] sacred rites of the gods and the elders are holy," *sacra deum sanctique patres*, 473).[32] Coming as it does at the end of a book that trumpeted the powers of *ratio*, as well as revealed its ultimate failure to provide a complete answer to the farmer's troubles, the praise reads like an emotional reaction to this failure and an expression of a desire for a world more connected to nature and religion. In its rejection of book 2's fundamental premises, it parallels the Praise of the Olive, which incidentally idealizes the olive as much as this praise idealizes the country life.[33]

Within the Praise of the Farmer, there is a crucial passage (475–94) that both reinforces the dichotomy between *ratio* and *religio* and also conflates it; it thus provides a perfect coda to books 1 and 2. In line 475, Virgil breaks into the narrative and expresses a desire to be initiated into the

---

[31] See esp. Ross (1987) ch. 3 (95–148) on the false grafts and other "lies" populating book 2 of the *Georgics*. See also Kronenberg (2000) 351–55.

[32] The religious imagery is somewhat broken up by the Lucretian sounding "relaxation free from care" (*secura quies*, 467); however, Lucretius' version of rational philosophy is not without its own kind of religious symbolism and emotional connection to nature (see my discussion below of lines *G.* 2.475–77), and so the Lucretian voice here does not necessarily disrupt the vision of a life that opposes the *ratio*-controlled world of the earlier parts of the book – it simply underscores the similar mission of both *ratio* and *religio*, that is, to provide comfort and control over nature. I will focus more on this outer frame of the Praise of the Farmer in chapter 7.

[33] Cf. Thomas (1988) 1.235 (*ad* 2.420–25): "To quote White (1970) 226: '"By contrast, olives need no cultivation." Virgil's brief dismissal is not supported by the agronomists.' The olive may not require as much work as the vine (but see 420n.), yet that hardly justifies, from the technical point of view, the fact that the vine occupies 150 lines, while the olive receives a mere six... V.'s preoccupation with the vine at the expense of the olive... must have a literary, rather than a technical motivation. The success of *labor* in book 2 is virtually synonymous with successful viticulture, while the olive is (falsely) removed from the area of *labor*... V., against the facts, presents the growing of olives as an effortless enterprise, placing them in a category with uncultivated trees (426n.), whereas in reality it is, like the vine, a highly cultivated tree." Cf. also Mynors (1990) 156 (*ad* 2.420): "*non ulla est oleis cultura*: this was rightly felt in Antiquity to be an overstatement: Serv. says 'alii *non nulla* legunt, hoc est aliqua, non ut in vitibus nimia'."

ways of the Muses (475–76) and to learn the physical principles of the universe (477–78 and 479–82). As many have noted, he seems to be a Lucretian figure here, or at least a scientific didactic poet guided by *ratio*.[34] Virgil's next lines, however, express doubt that he can actually achieve that kind of understanding (483–84), and he settles instead for appreciating the beauty of the pastoral world (485–86). The pastoral images soon morph into descriptions of places in Greece associated with the Muses, Orpheus, and Bacchus (Spercheus, Taygetus, and Haemus, 486–89).[35] Virgil ends the section by praising both types of poets/intellectuals in a double beatitude:

> felix qui potuit rerum cognoscere causas
> atque metus omnis et inexorabile fatum
> subiecit pedibus strepitumque Acherontis avari:
> fortunatus et ille deos qui novit agrestis
> Panaque Silvanumque senem Nymphasque sorores.
>
> (490–94)

> Blessed is he who is able to understand the causes of things
> and has placed under his feet all fears and unrelenting fate
> and the roar of greedy Acheron.
> Fortunate also is that man who knows the rustic gods:
> Pan, old Silvanus, and the Nymph sisters.

Scholars have come up with many different formulations of Virgil's contrast between these two figures, though they generally distinguish between the rational and scientific approach of the *felix* and the emotional, religious approach of the *fortunatus*.[36] Further questions arise, however, when the two approaches are matched up to Virgil's own poetic career. While in many ways, the *Georgics* could be said to correspond to the scientific, didactic impulses of the *felix*, and the *Eclogues* with the pastoral love of the *fortunatus*,[37] the *Georgics*, too, displays an emotional love of nature (such as in this Praise of the Farmer) and the *Eclogues* contains scientific

---

[34] For a bibliography on the Lucretian allusions, as well as suggestions for other figures alluded to in these lines, see Kronenberg (2000) 344 n. 6. See also Gale (2000) 9–11 and 43 n. 74.

[35] On the poetic associations of these places, see Putnam (1979) 149, Miles (1980) 153–54, Thomas (1988) 1.253 (*ad* 2.486–89), and Mynors (1990) 168–69 (*ad* 2.486–87, 487–88, and 488).

[36] E.g. Clay (1976) 239, Putnam (1979) 150, and Hardie (1986) 44.

[37] Cf. Thomas (1988) 1.249–50 (*ad* 2.475–94): "The passage as a whole is best understood as applying to Virgil and his career. The topics of 477–82 are peripherally agricultural, and many of them were covered in the second half of Book 1; and in that the *Georgics* may be seen as a poem which attempts to understand the workings of nature, these lines, along with 490–2, appear to express a wish for the success of the poem. The alternative (483–9, 493–4) is contentment with a pastoral world, the world represented by the *Eclogues*." See also Dyson (1994) 12–14. La Penna (1995) connects the cosmogonic themes of the *felix* with Amphion's cosmogony in the *Antiope* and suggests that the *Antiope* "stands at the origin of the poetic catalogues of philosophic themes" (324).

didactic poetry (such as in *Eclogue* 6). Indeed, as I have argued elsewhere (Kronenberg [2000]) just as Virgil's poems conflate genres and intellectual attitudes, so too do these lines: they do not just contrast *ratio* and *religio*, but merge them, and they associate both with Dionysian imagery and the irrational inspiration of poetry.[38]

For instance, the beginning of the scientific segment (lines 475–77) alludes to Lucretius' discussion of his poetic inspiration, which is conceived of in Dionysian terms:

> . . . sed acri
> percussit thyrso laudis spes magna meum cor
> et simul incussit suavem mi in pectus amorem
> Musarum . . .   (Lucr. 1.922–25)

> But the great hope of praise has struck my heart with the sharp thyrsus
> And at the same time has shaken into my chest the sweet love of the Muses . . .

In addition, Hardie has shown how Virgil imitates Lucretius' own appropriation of the language of the mysteries and initiation in discussion of his poetic desires.[39] Similarly, while the "pastoral" segment begins with images that recall the *Eclogues*,[40] it ends with an evocation of Dionysian imagery (486–88). More importantly, what the *felix* and the *fortunatus* share with each other and with the farmer of this passage is an ability to conquer

---

[38] I would even suggest that Virgil's discussion of his "split" poetic personality, torn between *ratio* and *religio*, could be an allusion to a Menippean satire of Varro called the *Bimarcus*, which, according to Relihan (1993) 62, involves "a fantastic discussion between two halves of Varro's personality, that of the moralist and that of the litterateur." Bakhtin (1984) 116–17 makes the "split personality" a particular feature of Menippean satire and cites the *Bimarcus* as an example. Cf. also Leach (1981) 40, who notes a Varronian (and Menippean) influence on the antitheses at the end of *Georgics* 2. In addition, I would compare Virgil's mock humility about not being smart enough for science ("but if the cold blood around my heart prevents me from approaching these parts of nature . . . ," *sin has ne possim naturae accedere partis | frigidus obstiterit circum praecordia sanguis*, 2.483–84) to Varro's own mock confession about not reaching the highest level of etymological knowledge in the *De Lingua Latina* ("The fourth [level] is where there is the sanctuary and mysteries of the king: if I am not able to arrive there at knowledge, then I will strive after opinion . . . ," *quartus, ubi est adytum et initia regis: quo si non perveniam ad scientiam, opinionem aucupabor, L.* 5.8). Like Virgil, Varro uses the language of the mysteries to describe the mystical level beyond his reach. On Virgil's use of the language of the mysteries, see my next note.

[39] Hardie (1986) 33–47. In particular, he points out the connotations of religious enlightenment present in *G.* 2.477 ("let them receive me and show me the paths of the sky and the stars," *accipiant caelique vias et sidera monstrent*) and compares the language Lucretius utilized for Epicurus' journey to enlightenment in the proem of book 1 (lines 62–79). Hardie also notes that *G.* 2.483 (*sin has ne possim naturae accedere partis*) evokes Lucretius' poetic initiation in 1.927 ("it is a pleasure to approach the pure springs," *iuvat integros accedere fontis*), a line which in turn exploits "the Aristotelian (and common Hellenistic) idea of the contemplation of the universe as analogous to the shows of the mysteries . . . The language of religious initiation and revelation is picked up in the *makarismos* of lines 490 ff." (38–39).

[40] Cf. *G.* 2.485 with *E.* 2.62 and 10.62–63. Cf. also *G.* 2.489 with *E.* 1.1.

death and destruction and find happiness and meaning in life. The *felix* accomplishes this by rationally controlling the fear of death and understanding the causes of things (490–91) and the *fortunatus* by an emotional or spiritual connection to nature. However, the narrator's voice in the "praises" clearly idealizes these figures and presents them from an outsider's perspective. For instance, he presents the farmers as a group who do not even recognize their great fortune ("O fortunate farmers, too fortunate, if they should recognize their own goods," *O fortunatos nimium, sua si bona norint,* | *agricolas . . .*, 458–59). When Virgil seems to speak in his own voice about the types of poetry he would like to write, the implication is that he has yet to successfully write either type: he preemptively backs down from his quest to write scientific poetry, and his pastoral desires are presented with hortatory subjunctives, as if not yet accomplished.[41] Thus, the voice at the end of book 2 does not present a realistic plan for finding happiness but instead simply projects the desire for a happy life onto figures he thinks have achieved it. The reader of books 1 and 2, however, knows that the farmer's life is not so ideal and that *ratio* and *religio* are not entirely successful at conquering the chaos of nature.[42]

Both Xenophon and Varro showed the ultimate failure of *technē* and *ratio* to provide security in the world of nature, and so too does Virgil, but Virgil expands the scope of his meditation on the shortcomings of human knowledge to include *religio*, as well. While initially presented as contrasting ideologies, ultimately *ratio* and *religio* are brought together in the *Georgics* because of their similar goals of creating order and meaning in the world. Yet, Virgil does not simply satirize or undermine these types of knowledge, because he also explores the real need that they fill in human life and implicates his own persona in desiring some sort of "answer" to the problems of life, whether in the realm of *ratio* or *religio*. I will explore this theme more in the next chapter when I present the ways in which Virgil goes beyond the satire of Varro.

THE AMORALITY OF FARMING

In the *Oeconomicus* and *De Re Rustica*, Xenophon and Varro dug beneath the surface of the conventional belief that the farming life is virtuous to

[41] Cf. Perkell (1989) 64–65 (on 2.475–82): "The poet desires unattainable knowledge . . . The possibility of failing in this aspiration (483 ff.) is very real to the poet. Thus he confronts openly the reality of a poetic quest forever unfulfilled."

[42] Even the voice at the end of book 2 seems to doubt whether the farmers in the present age are truly blessed because he finally pushes back to early Rome the happy lifestyle he has been describing (532–33).

expose the foundations or origins of this belief: the virtues of farming derive from material profit with the corollary that the conventional morality of the polis or city does, as well. While there is perhaps nothing shocking or "wrong" with this exposé of morality from an Epicurean or sophistic point of view, it seems fair to say that neither philosophical trend represented the mainstream of Greek or Roman moral thought, whether of the popular or philosophical kind. Virgil similarly deflates the farmer's pretensions to an objective and inherent kind of virtue in the *Georgics*, but he does so in a more subtle and complex way. As Perkell and others have noted, "Virgil's farmer is never specifically directed towards *fructus* ('profit'), which the poet never mentions."[43] *Voluptas* is used only once, to describe the sexual instinct in mares (3.130), and *utilitas* not at all. Despite her observation about *fructus*, however, Perkell's main thesis is still that the farmer's values, as opposed to the poet's, consist of "material survival and utility" (139). Virgil's farmer certainly is concerned with profit and survival, and the farmer's epithet in the first didactic portion of the work, "greedy" (*avari*, 1.47), could function as a footnote to Varro's presentation of the farmer.[44] Still, the focus of the *Georgics* is less on condemning the farmer's unrelenting focus on material survival than on explaining it as an inevitable part of human life, and indeed of life for all living creatures.

Instead of focusing on the forces of *voluptas* and *utilitas*, Virgil presents the force of *amor* as the prime motivation of all creatures – and not just farmers. While the most explicit statement of this belief comes in a description of sexual desire,[45] which merges into a description of human love through progressive anthropomorphism,[46] *amor* is used to mean more

---

[43] Perkell (1989) 29. *Fructus* appears only twice in the *Georgics* and in the sense of "fruits" (2.36 and 2.500). Nelson (1998) 141 suggests that the profit motive is emphasized more in the second half of the *Georgics*: "The first difficulty arises with a topic which, up until now, has been notably absent from the *Georgics*. The topic is profit. The first two Georgics examined how the farmer raises crops, vines, and trees. They did not mention why he does so. In contrast, Vergil introduces each of the subjects of the third and fourth Georgics with reference to their use, and so to their profit."

[44] Mynors (1990) 11 (*ad* 1.47–48) expresses discomfort with this programmatic description of the farmer and writes, "This is the only place where V. suggests that his husbandman may suffer from the *amor habendi* (Hor. *Ep.* 1.7.85); but it is an extreme and hypothetical case, and is Hesiodic (*Op.* 381)." As I hope to have shown, the emphasis on the greed of the farmer is not just Hesiodic but is also part of a satiric and philosophical tradition that critiques the idealization of the farmer and shows the materialistic underpinnings of conventional notions of virtue.

[45] 3.242–44: "Indeed every race of man and beast on land, the race of the sea and herds and birds of various color rush into passion and fire: love is the same to all," *omne adeo genus in terris hominumque ferarumque | et genus aequoreum, pecudes pictaeque volucres, | in furias ignemque ruunt: amor omnibus idem.*

[46] While the passage that follows is primarily about *amor* in animals, the extreme anthropomorphism implicates human beings in the descriptions. Cf. Thomas (1988) 11.89 (*ad* 3.258–63): "A human *exemplum* for the destructive power of *amor* is inserted in the middle of the examples concerning

than just love and desire for another creature. In the *Georgics, amor* is the emotion that a plant feels for the earth (2.301), that vines feel for the hills (2.113), horses for praise (3.112, 3.186), bees for material profit (4.177) and flowers (4.205), and Virgil for poetry (3.285, 3.292), nature (2.486), and poetic knowledge (2.476). Thus, *amor* appears to be an instinctual force of nature and not a unique preserve of human *ratio* or a moral force. Quite the contrary, it is described as an irrational force not subject to human control, especially in the depiction of love in book 3 when *amor* turns to *furor*, and Virgil never uses *amor* to describe purely altruistic or disinterested motivations. While it is a force that can bring two creatures together, it leads to conflict as much as to love.[47] What Virgil emphasizes, then, is not so much the materialism of farmers as the instinctual and self-interested motivations of all living creatures, whether plant, animal, or human.

As Virgil's farmers look more and more like "creatures" motivated by survival instincts, their moral world looks more and more empty. As in Varro, one of the ways in which Virgil shows the emptiness of man's moral words and their roots in non-moral forces of self-interest is by applying them to the natural and animal world. For instance, *improbus* ("indomitable" but also "morally bad" or "wicked") is used to describe a goose (1.119), *labor* (1.146), a crow's voice (1.388), and a water snake (3.431). *Malus* ("injurious" but also "evil, wicked,") describes snake venom (1.129), rust (1.150), land (2.243), and a snake (3.425). *Sceleratus* ("impious, accursed") describes the cold (2.256). *Turpis* ("ugly" but also "shameful, base") describes vine clusters (2.60), the head of an ox (3.52), old age (3.96), foot disease (3.299), sheep scabies (3.441), rotting flesh (3.557), ugly bees (4.96), and ugly seals (4.395). *Iustus* ("just," "proper") is used to indicate the "right" measure for plant growth (2.251) or space for a constellation (1.35), as well as to describe the earth (2.460) and the right time for "marriage" among cattle (3.60). *Honestus* ("honorable," "proper," "handsome") is only used to describe physical attractiveness (2.392, 3.81, 4.232), not moral goodness. *Bonus* and *optimus* are used usually in conjunction with a noun to indicate what something is "good" or "best" for in terms of its technical use (2.205, 2.262, 2.319, and 2.447). *Virtus* ("excellence," "virtue") is never used,[48] and a positive state of human life is generally described with words whose

---

animals"; (*ad* 3.258): "The reader who has seen human terms applied to animals throughout the first half of the book, who has seen *iuvenis* applied at one moment to animals, the next to men . . . will initially be unsure not of the identity of the youth, but of the nature of the animal." On the conflation between man and beast, particularly in book 3, see Liebeschuetz (1965), Miles (1975) and (1980) 166–225, Rocca (1983) 71–127, and Gale (1991) and (2000) 88–100.

[47] For example, *amor* is the force that leads to the duel between bulls in 3.209–41.

[48] Indeed, *labor* seems to literally replace *virtus* in 1.145 ("labor conquered all," *labor omnia vicit*) if read in conjunction with Sal. *Cat.* 7.5: "virtue overcame all," *virtus omnia domuerat*.

semantic range can denote a thriving state in plants, animals, or people such as *laetus* ("joyful," "fertile") (of people in 1.301, 1.304, 2.382, 3.375, and 3.379) or *felix* ("fertile," "fortunate") (of a person in 2.490).[49]

I would argue that the cumulative effect of Virgil's use of moral language applied to the plant and animal world is to skew the semantic meaning of these words in the non-moral direction, so that even when applied to human beings, the non-moral usage lingers. For example, Virgil does at one point transfer *malus* to the human world to describe "evil stepmothers" (*malae... novercae*, 3.282) collecting "poison" (*virus* 3.281), but because these stepmothers are mentioned in a long line of creatures who hurt mankind or their livestock, they form a continuum with the other savage and poisonous forces of destruction, such as snakes.[50] Indeed, all the major forces of destruction in the *Georgics* are intricately tied together by their similar imagery: the rain storm in book 1 is described as a war;[51] civil war is described like a storm;[52] love is described like a plague,[53] and the plague like a storm[54] and a snake.[55] The end result is to make the concept of "evil" seem equivalent to "harmful to man" and to rid it of any inherent moral

---

[49] Cf. Betensky (1972) 156 on the opening words of the poem: "*Quid faciat laetas segetes* comes first in the poem, opening up unknown terrain. Therefore it may be thought to mean only the obvious 'fertile crops.' However, as the resonance of *laetus* grows through the poem, hindsight and rereading show that the phrase promises instruction not simply in farming but in the potential for a mutually happy life shared by people and the other elements of nature." Cf. also Lyne [1974]/(1999) 163: "The poem's commitment to *life* is symbolized in the continual personification involved in description of nature; we should note particularly the use of suggestive words like *fetus* (55, etc.), *fecunda* (67, etc.), *gravidus* (111, 319, etc.) whose basic sense of 'pregnant' is never dead in good poets, and the recurrent *laetus* (1, 69, etc.) which contributes its full significance of human joy" and Batstone (1997) 130 (on the phrase *laetas segetes*): "The adjective-noun unit, which we know was a farmer's idiom, gives only nominal stability to a process that drifts from cow manure to human joy." Contrast Mynors' (1990) 230 more regimented reading (*ad* 3.318–21): "*laetus*: occurs in *G.* thirty-three times. In some eighteen places (and four times in *A.*) it is applied to the land and its products, vegetable and animal, and means 'fruitful', 'flourishing' (so *G.* 1.1), extending into 'plentiful' in 3.310, as in *E.* 7.60. Eleven times it clearly means 'rejoicing' (as constantly in *A.*), and thrice (*G.* 2.363, 520, 3.63, but not *A.* 2.395) it seems to convey both meanings." Cicero twice uses the example of the phrase *laetas segetes* to illustrate the metaphorical use of language (*de Orat.* 3.155 and *Orat.* 81), and so the metaphor was clearly a "live" one in Virgil's time.

[50] Indeed, very similar language is used to describe the viper in book 3, who is bad to touch (*mala tactu*, 416), or the adder, who sprays his venom (*virus*, 419) on cattle.

[51] E.g. 1.318: "I have seen all the winds rush together in battle," *omnia ventorum concurrere proelia vidi*. See further Thomas (1988) 1.121–22 (*ad* 1.316–34).

[52] Gale (2000) 69–70: "[T]he literal storm anticipates the storm of civil war at the end of the book, where Roman lines 'run together' (*concurrere*, 489) like the winds of 318. Virgil hints that natural violence and human violence are connected by a kind of cosmic sympathy, calling into question the Lucretian view that, while violent conflict is inherent in nature, conflict on the human level arises directly from ambition and fear, and can thus be 'cured' by Epicurus' *dicta*."

[53] See Thomas (1988) II.87 (*ad* 3.244), II.126 (*ad* 3.452, 454), II.127 (*ad* 3.457–58) and II.137 (*ad* 3.511–12).

[54] See Thomas (1988) II.129 (*ad* 3.470–71 and *ad* 3.473).

[55] See Thomas (1988) II.119 (*ad* 3.414–39), II.120 (*ad* 3.419), II.127 (*ad* 3.458) and II.129 (*ad* 3.469, 470–71). Cf. also Putnam (1979) 215: "The snake in *Georgic* 3 is vividly present before our eyes, but it is also the purveyor and hence the emblem of poison and disease."

force. Thus, when the *saecula* ("generations") of the civil wars are deemed
impia ("impious") (1.468) or the *gens* ("race") that first dined on oxen
(2.537), the moral condemnation inherent in *impius* seems superfluous:
death and destruction are embedded in the natural fabric of the Georgic
world and sin and *culpa* ("fault, blame") have nothing to do with it – a
fact also underscored by the attribution of *culpa* and *vitium* ("fault, defect,
crime") to non-human creatures and forces.[56]

   The emptiness of moral words in the *Georgics* is also expressed in Virgil's
version of the now *locus communis* description of rows of vines which, like
Cyrus' trees, are compared to battle lines (2.277–83; cf. *Oec.* 4.21). To briefly
recall the tradition: in the *Oeconomicus*, Lysander had interpreted Cyrus'
well-laid out trees as a symbol of virtue not because they were beautiful
but because Cyrus had arranged them through hard work. While I argued
that Socrates ultimately undermines the Spartan's equation of hard work
with virtue in the *Oeconomicus*, Cicero accepts Lysander's praise at face
value and has his Cato the Elder agree with Lysander's attribution of moral
virtue to Cyrus (*Sen.* 17.60). Varro, however, has Scrofa bypass the moral
point altogether: Scrofa does not attempt to find a symbol of virtue in
his description of quincunxes, but only focuses on how their aesthetically
pleasing rows bring more profit. Virgil goes even further than Varro in
emptying the vignette of moral content. The Virgilian narrator instructs:

> omnia sint paribus numeris dimensa viarum,
> non animum modo uti pascat prospectus inanem,
> sed quia non aliter viris dabit omnibus aequas
> terra, neque in vacuum poterunt se extendere rami.
>   (2.284–87)

> Let all of the vineyard's paths be laid out in equal measure,
> not only so that the image of it may vainly feed the mind,
> but because not otherwise will the earth give equal strength to
> all, nor will the branches be able to extend themselves into the void.

Not only is the focus on the virtue of labor left out, but even the aesthetic
pleasure of the rows is associated now with an image of futility (285).

---

[56] Cf. the *culpa* of a goat (2.380), of wine (2.455), and of a plague-infested sheep (3.468). See also Ross
(1987) 180, who notes the "clear, and indeed striking, designation of this disease as a 'moral wrong.'"
Vitium is applied to a fault in the soil (1.88) and a plague infested body (3.454). Cf. also Miles (1980)
224: "The experience of plague suggests a quite different interpretation of the civil wars. Insofar as
they are analogous to the plague, we must regard them neither as a consequence of human failing,
nor as retribution for wickedness, nor as an expression of divine disfavor. They must be seen, rather,
as a natural phenomenon, neither more nor less than an aspect of the workings of nature. Civil
disorder, like the plague, is inevitable and inescapable; its destructiveness is beyond human power
to check or ameliorate."

Another way in which Virgil empties moral words of their inherent meaning is by emphasizing their relativity. If moral words are derived from notions of material harm and benefit, then it is only from the perspective of the thing harmed or benefited that these words have appropriate meaning. The *Georgics* underscores this relativity of value by frequently forcing the reader to view the world from the perspective of plants and animals.[57] It does this not just by humanizing plants and animals, but by focalizing the narrative from their perspective. Thus, Virgil describes the perspective of the vine as the vinedresser tears away "plant shoots from the tender body of their mother" (*plantas tenero abscindens de corpore matrum*," 2.23); the ploughman who destroys a grieving nightingale's brood is seen from her perspective and described as "harsh" (*durus*, 4.512). I would argue that Virgil's point is less to condemn the aggression of agriculture than it is to point to the conflicting forces at work in the creation of value. After all, he presents the perspective of nature in the face of non-human enemies as well, such as when he describes the enemies of bees:

> absint et picti squalentia terga lacerti
> pinguibus a stabulis, meropesque aliaeque volucres
> et manibus Procne pectus signata cruentis;
> omnia nam late vastant ipsasque volantis
> ore ferunt dulcem nidis immitibus escam.
>
> (4.13–17)

> Let the lizards with painted scaly backs
> be far from the rich stables, and the bee-eaters and other birds
> such as the swallow, her breast marked by her blood-red hands;
> for they destroy everything far and wide and they carry off in their mouth
> the bees as they are flying to be a sweet meal for their cruel nestlings.

The lizards and birds are clearly viewed at first from the bees' perspective, since they are described with dramatic language that portrays them as fearsome enemies. However, this perspective becomes splintered when the purpose of the birds' killing of the bees is revealed and their own perspective is brought into play: they are simply trying to provide a pleasing meal for their young. There are no "good guys" and "bad guys" here – just competing *amores*.

Indeed, even from the same creature's perspective, a particular object or concept might take on drastically different meanings depending on the

---

[57] Cf. Nelson (1998) 142: "Profit is simply a given of Hesiod's farm. On Vergil's it has driven a wedge between the farmer and his farm. This is not because profit is wicked, but because Vergil has given the creatures of nature a voice. They use that voice to make us see their own, individual, point of view. In so doing they disrupt the unity of the farm."

circumstance. Some of the most controversial passages in the *Georgics* can
be explained if interpreted as highlighting this essentially unstable nature
of moral value, such as the "theodicy" in book 1 (121–46).[58] In this passage,
labor is initially praised as a tool of divinely ordained human progress but
in the end is condemned as *improbus* (1.146). Critics have fiercely argued
over which vision predominates in the *Georgics*, good *labor* or bad *labor*.
I would counter that the reader is not being prodded to pick a winner so
much as to reflect on the *source* of this ambiguity, namely the subjective and
relative nature of moral value. Human beings value *labor* because they need
it to survive; but they also hate it because it makes life difficult. Similarly,
as already discussed, the vine in book 2 is praised for most of the book only
to be condemned at the end of it because of the mixture of benefits and ills
it brings mankind. Thus, *fas* and *nefas* are confused in the *Georgics* not just
during the civil war at the end of book 1 ("right and wrong are inverted,"
fas versum atque nefas, 1.505), but in a fundamental way throughout the
text, as Virgil forces the reader to confront the implications of an amoral
world driven by conflicting self-interests and relative value.

Opponents of this interpretation might argue that I am ignoring all
the voices in the poem that posit a providential and divine world in
which absolute right and wrong exist. While I certainly agree such voices
are present, they are carefully contextualized, and the world views they
represent are shown to be motivated by the fear of living in an amoral
world, as I will explore further in the next chapter. Thus, just as Lucretius
examines the emotional fears and confusion that lead to the creation of
religion (Lucr. 5.1161–1240), as well as the misunderstandings that create
sentimental visions of a pious past (Lucr. 2.1164–74), so I would argue
does Virgil. He explores the fears that lead mankind to construct systems
of meaning that give a more palatable order to the world, but he does so
without endorsing the truth value of such creations. On the contrary, the
voices in the *Georgics* that express a confidence in divine help or in the easy
and moral life of the farmer are shown to be mistaken, as *religio* fails to stave
off disaster and the life of the farmer turns into a battlefield. Unlike Varro,
Virgil does not present these "mistaken" voices or characters as superficial
moralizers or hypocrites deserving of satire, but instead as very human and
worthy of his pity.[59]

---

[58] Gale (2000) 61 calls it "perhaps the most controversial section of the whole poem." The bibliography
is immense, but Gale lists many of the sources in her discussion (61–67), to which could be added
La Penna [1962]/(1999) and Perkell (1986). See also Farrell (1991) 182 n. 24 for further bibliography.

[59] Indeed, Virgil's sympathy for his ignorant farmers is highlighted at the end of the proem: "Pity with
me the rustics ignorant of the way" (*ignarosque viae mecum miseratus agrestis*, 1.41).

THE ACTIVE LIFE

In analyzing the *Oeconomicus* and *De Re Rustica*, I argued that the goal of Xenophon's and Varro's examination of farming ethics was not to chastise greedy farmers *per se* so much as to connect farming metaphorically with politics and thereby to critique the active life. Varro's critique of the active life is most clearly seen in books 2 and 3 of his work: book 2 displays Varro during his stint in the active life as a "shepherd of the people" (ποιμὴν λαῶν) (2.5.1) and takes place in the context of war. It uses pastoral analogies to drive home the point that politicians are like greedy shepherds, who treat people like animals and care only for the profit that can be made from the flock. Book 3 makes similar points, this time in a domestic political setting, and utilizes aviaries for profit and pleasure to contrast the active and contemplative life. Book 3 also satirizes the tradition of using the beehive to model an ideal state by pointing out the many unideal aspects of bee society. Virgil transports Varro's political critique into books 3 and 4 of the *Georgics* via discussion of the pastoral arts and beehives. Virgil also presents a contrast between the active and contemplative lives, but because his exploration of this contrast has such a pervasive presence in the *Georgics* and is more nuanced than Varro's, I will reserve my analysis of it for the next chapter.

Virgil begins book 3 by taking on his own poetic version of an active military role akin to Varro's role in *De Re Rustica* 2. Virgil expresses his desire to earn fame as a poet (3.8–11) and describes a temple he will build on the banks of the Mincius with Caesar in the middle (3.12–16). Virgil will drive around the temple as a triumphing *victor* (17–18). There will be games in Virgil's honor (19–21), and he will enjoy watching the parades and the dead cattle (22–23). He will depict battles on the doors of the temple, including Actium (26–36), and there will be statues of Trojan ancestors and Apollo. In doing so, he will conquer *Invidia* ("Envy"), which will be condemned to Hades (37–39). There have been different interpretations of what this temple symbolizes, but most interpret it as a sign that Virgil will soon write a martial epic like the *Aeneid*;[60] thus, his "active" persona

---

[60] Cf. Thomas (1983) 95–96: "The most extended portion of Virgil's proem, and the most striking, is his description of the temple and statuary he will create (12–36), a metaphorical allusion, as most would now agree, to a future poetic project." Klingner (1963) 136–42, 242 outlines (and rejects) previous arguments that the temple refers to the *Georgics*. See also Wilkinson (1969) 323–24. Morgan (1999) 53 has recently suggested that "the evocation of triumphal ritual in the prologue to Book 3 thus seems to double as anticipation of the details of the *Aristaeus*, and it is a strong encouragement to associate what is predicated at the opening of Book 3 with what happens towards the end of Book 4."

is a writer of epic martial poetry. "Optimistic" readers of the *Georgics* have made much of this passage and have suggested that it depicts Virgil working together with Octavian to bring salvation to Rome.[61] Counter-arguments have emphasized the aggressive and ambiguous nature of Caesar's victories compared to the poet's,[62] and the fact that the "utopia" imagined in the proem of book 3 destroys the "utopia" at the end of book 2 by requiring the existence of many items that were condemned earlier, such as dyed clothing and ostentatious wealth, slaughtered cattle, and war.[63] Indeed, putting this passage in the wider context of the *Georgics* complicates its tone, but more

---

[61] This is the argument of Buchheit (1972), emphatically restated by Morgan (1999), and less emphatically so by Gale (2000) 190: "The proem to book 3 strikes the most confident note of all the passages in the poem which reflect on the role of and the relationship between poet and *princeps*. But it does not entirely resolve the tensions between public and private, active and passive which we have been tracing through the first two books." Gale (2000) 44 has also noted Virgil's appropriation of "the triumphant mental 'flight' of Epicurus depicted in *DRN* 1.62–79; but where the philosopher's triumph is presented as a *challenge* to conventional Roman ideology, Virgil portrays poetic and military glory as interdependent rather than opposed to each other. Once again, the poet seems to express his faith in a political solution to the problems which for Lucretius could only be solved by eschewing ambition and public life altogether." I think such a conclusion is too much to draw from Virgil's temple. If anything, I would suggest that the motif of appropriating the language of military victory for the contemplative sphere, whether as an epic poet like Ennius, an elegist like Propertius and Ovid, or a philosopher like Lucretius, is an *inherent* challenge to the active life. Virgil, after all, is the one triumphing, and his victory is an intensely poetic one, drawing together "conquered" poets into his intertextual net – not conquered peoples as Octavian does. On the complex network of allusions to Ennius, Lucretius, Pindar, and Callimachus in these lines, see Wilkinson (1970), Buchheit (1972) 148–59, Lundström (1976), Thomas (1983), (1998), and Gale (2000) 11–15.

[62] E.g. Perkell (1989) 62: "By juxtaposing his name to that of Caesar and by attributing the epithet *victor* as well as the nominative case to himself, he implies that his victory compares favorably with Caesar's . . . He reveals that the significant feature of his victory in contrast to Caesar's is that it is achieved through song (3.1, 3.3; cf. 4.471), hence without aggression – unlike the farmer's or soldier's"; Putnam (1976) 281: "Does Octavian's temple in this lovely spot necessarily mean that he brings a confirming blessing to the landscape or that in fact the bank of the Mincius may prove equally valuable in civilizing the conqueror? B[uchheit] sees only the initial possibility, but there are aspects of Virgil's setting that suggest the *lene consilium* which Horace too offers through the Muses to the soldier Octavian, tired from warring"; Muecke (1979) 103: "[B]y linking the role of the poet as closely as he does with the role of the political reformer Buchheit does not allow Virgil to question the direction the reform is taking, nor indeed the part played by Augustus in the producing of those very conditions that need to be cured. Neither does he give full weight to the threats which oppose the realisation of the *aetas aurea Augusti* and this detracts from the complexity and profundity of Virgil's understanding of the world."

[63] See Miles (1980) 175–81, who notes that "Virgil concludes the introduction to *Georgic* 3 by postponing indefinitely the celebration of a utopia" (181). Cf. also Boyle (1979b) 78: "Observe also in respect of the proem to *Georgic* 3 the contiguity of the proem's laudation of 'the arms of victorious Romulus' (3.27) to the sullen condemnation of war, emblem of postlapsarian man, in the final lines of Book 2 (536–40) – a contextual irony underscored by the imagistic association of the poet and the poetic temple he will build to honour Caesar with the indices of urban artifice, excess and *contra naturam* values only recently condemned (2.459ff., 495ff.) . . . [T]he poet *qua* political, military panegyricist seems disturbingly close to the second georgic's paradigm of psychological, spiritual dislocation. Even Book 2's other concluding emblem of post-Saturnian impiety, 'slaughtered bullocks' (*caesis iuvencis*, 2.537), insinuates itself into the poet's Caesarian fantasy."

importantly, I would argue that reading it with the *De Re Rustica* expands the possibilities of its interpretation.

Critics have noted the great amount of Varronian influence on book 3 of the *Georgics* but have focused only on the technical thematic similarities and not the deeper symbolic connections.[64] I would suggest that Virgil's "active" persona at the beginning of book 3 and his dedication of the temple to Caesar have a parallel function to Varro's appearance as ποιμὴν λαῶν and his dedication of book 2 to the cattle-lover Turranius Niger. Like Varro, Virgil ends the work ensconced back in the contemplative life ("flourishing in the pursuits of ignoble ease," *studiis florentem ignobilis oti*, 4.564), but his temporary foray into the active life as an epic poet prepares for his parody of military/political life and the animalization it entails in book 3. Thus, I would argue that when he mentions at the end of the proem his intention to tell of flaming battles of Caesar (3.46–47), he is referring to the "battles" in book 3 of the *Georgics* as much as to the *Aeneid*.[65] The "slaughtered cattle" (*caesosque... iuvencos*, 3.23) in front of the temple take on new meaning, too, as the difference between man and animal disappears in the course of the book.

Virgil begins the didactic portion of the work not with sheep, as Varro does, but with horses and bulls – animals that immediately fit with the military theme of the preface. He spends half of the book detailing the care of these animals and, in the process, anthropomorphizes their behavior and training even more than Varro does. For instance, he begins by discussing the importance of good breeding and uses blatantly human terms: "The age to undergo childbirth ('Lucina') and lawful marriage ends before the tenth year, and begins after the fourth" (*aetas Lucinam iustosque pati hymenaeos | desinit ante decem, post quattuor incipit annos*, 3.60–61). He goes on to mention the importance of finding a "foal of noble herd" (*pecoris generosi pullus*, 75) with noble (*honesti*, 81) coloring and of branding the calves with the "marks and names of their race" (*notas et nomina gentis*, 158). Later, he talks of choosing the "leader" (*ducem*, 125) and "husband" (*maritum*, 125) of the flock, and when love among animals is mentioned, rival bulls are described like human fighters in a duel over a woman (209–41).

Much emphasis is placed on how to manipulate the animals into obeying (e.g. 3.205–08), and the training of the calves is described as if they were

---

[64] E.g. Van de Woestijne (1931) 910.

[65] Virgil himself connects the two works by importing the book 3 duel between bulls (209–41) into book 12 of the *Aeneid* as a simile to describe the duel between Aeneas and Turnus (12.715–24).

children (163–65).[66] Of course, what they are really being trained for is slavery ("when their free necks have gotten used to slavery . . ." *ubi libera colla | servitio adsuerint . . .* , 167–68). Like Socrates' guardians and Varro's horses, Virgil's horses are trained to be military and Olympic victors by being manipulated with praise and inured to loud noises and labor (e.g. 179–86). Thus, despite the dramatic humanization of these animals, they are still treated like slaves whose only purpose is to maximize the profit of their master, who cares for his animals' well-being only to the extent that their well-being brings him profit (e.g. 295–99, 305–07). When an animal no longer profits his master because of sickness or old age, he is instructed to shut him indoors, "nor grant indulgence to his ugly old age" (*nec turpi ignosce senectae*, 96).

Just as Virgil intensified Varro's conflation between man and beast in his discussion of the pastoral arts, so he exaggerates even further the connections between beehives and human political communities in book 4 of the *Georgics*. As Dahlmann and Thomas have noted, Virgil's treatment of the bee society owes much to the tradition of ethnographical writing – "a tradition otherwise applied exclusively to human societies."[67] This ethnographical approach begins in the first few lines of the book:

> admiranda tibi levium spectacula rerum
> magnanimosque duces totiusque ordine gentis
> mores et studia et populos et proelia dicam.
>
> (4.3–5)
>
> I will tell you of the marvelous spectacles of a small world:
> I will speak in order of the great-hearted leaders, and the
> customs, pursuits, peoples, and battles of their entire race.

While commentators have noted the potentially humorous and "mock-heroic" style of these lines,[68] I would suggest that the parodic tone is directed not just at epic but at political philosophy and its tradition of idealizing the community of bees. Virgil picks up the image of the utopian bee state from Ischomachus, Appius, and, presumably, Cicero, but treats it with the anti-utopian slant of Socrates and Varro (and Mandeville) by

---

[66] Cf. Thomas (1988) II.71 (*ad* 3.163–65): "The language is applicable to the education of children, as at 2.362–3 (of the 'training' of young vines)."

[67] Thomas (1988) II.147 (*ad* 4.1–7). See also Dahlmann [1954]/(1999) and Thomas (1982) 70–92.

[68] Cf. Thomas (1988) II.148 (*ad* 4.3): "The juxtaposition of large and small and the very choice of the bees as subject clearly create a danger of producing an amused response, what is normally regarded as 'mock-heroic' . . . He certainly intends that the reader notice the disparity between size and tone . . . but that need not imply humorous intent." Mynors (1990) 259 (*ad* 4.3–5) compares the *Batrachomyomachia* in connection with the bees' *proelia* (4.5).

emphasizing the materialistic motives and discord that lie behind this supposed ideal.

Varro had Appius present the idealized account of the bee community before Merula presented a more realistic version, which emphasized the fragility of the bees, the conflicts within their communities, and the way in which to profit most from them. Virgil reverses the order of this presentation, with the effect of making the idealized vision of the bees seem even more artificial. So, before describing the utopian features of the bee community, he emphasizes the many dangers to it, such as goats, lizards, or birds, and also gives an epic description of a bee civil war (67–87). The focus of this first half of the discourse on bees, then, is not on the ideal qualities of their community, but on how to profit from and control them. Despite the anthropomorphic language used to depict them, their lives are described as quite meaningless and subject to the whims of the beekeeper. For instance, after the great civil war, the beekeeper is instructed that "these passions and great conflicts will be laid to rest with the toss of a little dust" (*hi motus animorum atque haec certamina tanta | pulveris exigui iactu compressa quiescent*, 86–87). The beekeeper is also instructed to kill the lesser, ugly bee to prevent further conflict (88–90), and to rip the wings off the bee king in order to keep the bees hard at work in the hive and away from "idle play" (*ludo . . . inani*) (105–07).[69] As in the *De Re Rustica*, there is a stark contrast between the human qualities given to the animals and the heartlessness with which they are treated.

Virgil begins describing the utopian aspects of the bee community in line 149, when he introduces the topic of the bees' "natures" (*naturas*), which Jupiter gave them. What follows is a description of their community that, even more than Varro's, picks up on utopian political writing like Plato's *Republic* (esp. *R.* 457c–473c). The bees are said to have children and houses in common (153), to live under laws in a fixed homeland (154), and to share their labor and their profits (157–59). Virgil goes into great detail about how the bees divide up their labor (159–75) and adds an explicit explanation for their motivation: "an innate love of gain urges on the Athenian bees" (*Cecropias innatus apes amor urget habendi*, 177). The purpose of the bee community, both from the bees' point of view and from the beekeeper's, is a material one – namely, to make honey and profit. The profit motive

---

[69] The phrase *ludo . . . inani* ("idle play," 105) is close to how Virgil describes his own activity at the end of the *Georgics*: " . . . flourishing in ignoble ease, I who dallied in the songs of shepherds . . ." *. . . studiis florentem ignobilis oti | carmina qui lusi pastorum . . .* (4.564–65) . Cf. also the description of the "bad" kind of bee, who is *inglorius* ("without glory") (4.94) like Virgil in 2.486.

of the beekeeper is not surprising, but the focus on the bee's materialism is bold and punctures the moral mystique of the bee community.[70]

Despite Virgil's revelation of the bees' materialistic and self-interested motivation, he still piles on allusions to political utopias in which the self-interest of the individual is seemingly sacrificed to that of the group or the ruler. This juxtaposition anticipates Mandeville's point that successful states depend upon the psychological manipulation of the ruled into thinking it is in their self-interest to serve the group or ruler[71] and recapitulates Xenophon's demonstration of how a ruler like Ischomachus utilizes material rewards and praise or blame to accomplish just that. Like Kallipolis, the bee state suppresses *eros*,[72] and the bee-citizens, believing that a "beautiful death" (*pulchramque . . . mortem*, 218) compensates for the loss of life, sacrifice their lives for the community.[73] Like the Persians idealized by Ischomachus, the bees show great obeisance to their king, akin to that of the Egyptians, Lydians, Parthians, and Medes (210–12), and also like the Persians and Spartans written about by Xenophon, the death of their king brings chaos (213–14).[74] Like Cicero's perfect state (cf. *Rep.* 3.34 and 3.41), the hive is said to be immortal ("the immortal race remains," *genus immortale manet*, 208). However, there seems to be irony in this statement since it is soon followed by a description of what to do if a plague wipes out the entire hive (281–82).[75]

It is not just the hive that is immortal: Virgil relates the more extreme belief of some people that individual bees take part in the "divine mind"

[70] Mynors' (1990) 281 (*ad* 4.176–78) attempt to explain away the bees' materialism is revealing of the discomfort it engenders: "[P]oets, who rarely have much themselves, are agreed that the 'love of having' is a very bad thing . . . In bees this is not so, because it is innate, and is the call of duty. And perhaps *Cecropias*, which at first sight is merely, as in 270, an ornamental allusion to the 'nobile nectar' (Martial 13.104) of Mt. Hymettus in Attica, plays a part in lifting the bees above any suggestion of either avarice or drudgery."
[71] Cf. *The Fable of the Bees* 1.42 [28]: "The Chief Thing, therefore, which Lawgivers and other wise Men, that have laboured for the Establishment of Society, have endeavour'd, has been to make the People they were to govern, believe, that it was more beneficial for every Body to conquer than indulge his Appetites, and much better to mind the Publick than what seem'd his private Interest."
[72] As is frequently noted, for the bees, *labor* literally replaces *amor*: cf. *labor omnibus unus* (4.184) with *amor omnibus idem* (3.244). In addition, *contra* Varro, Virgil denies his bees any form of sexual reproduction (4.197–202).
[73] Cf. Xenophon's recognition of Lycurgus' ability to convince the Spartans to prefer "a beautiful death to a shameful life," (τὸν καλὸν θάνατον ἀντὶ τοῦ αἰσχροῦ βίου, *Lac.* 9.1).
[74] As discussed in Part I, Xenophon writes of the decline of the Spartan and Persian states after the deaths of Lycurgus and Cyrus, respectively (and the decline of Ischomachus' household after his death is implied if the Ischomachus of Andocides' *On the Mysteries* is to be identified with him).
[75] Cf. Thomas (1982) 83: "And so, with characteristic irony, Virgil has undercut his suggestions about the immortality of the bees' society. Their race fails in spite of its social complexity and its high level of organization; ultimately the susceptibility which they share with the animal world is realized in precisely the same manner."

(*divinae mentis*, 220), and that instead of dying, they return to the heavens (226–27). As commentators note, this belief is traditional and not exactly vouched for by Virgil;[76] his inclusion of it, however, further elides any distinction between human and bee communities. While this elision may exalt the bees, it has the effect of reducing human beings to the level of insects. It also has the effect of making the bee-keeper's harsh treatment of these divine animals seem worse: immediately after the discussion of the bees' immortality, the beekeeper is described like an enemy invader, who breaks into the bees' "august dwelling" (*sedem augustam*) to steal the honey stored up in their treasury (228–29), and the bees lose their lives in defending it (238).[77]

Nelson (1998) reacted against those critics who find in the bees either an ideal or a repulsive symbol and notes, "This is rather hard on the bees, who are neither ideal nor flawed human beings, but just bees" (224 n. 95). While I agree that in one sense the bees are "just bees," I would also argue that Virgil is entering into a dialogue with ancient authors who *did* use them as an ideal model for mankind. Virgil's bees are given many nationalities: they are referred to as Athenian (4.177) and Roman (4.201), compared to Eastern peoples (4.210–11), and have many Spartan tendencies. They are, then, not just bees, but a pastiche of idealized political communities. Virgil joins Varro and Xenophon (and Mandeville) in using bees to make the point that political communities, even in their "ideal" form, are motivated by self-interest and reduce people to animals. In the next chapter, I will explore Virgil's own version of a "contemplative" alternative to political life.

---

[76] Cf. Thomas (1988) II.187 (*ad* 4.219–27): "It also must be pointed out that the present lines are completely in indirect speech (219–21n.), forming the equivalent of a footnote, a citation of the views of some people (219 *quidam*)." Certainly this is how Servius interprets the line when he notes (*ad* 4.219–21) that while some criticize Virgil here for departing from his Epicurean views, he thinks that Virgil is simply reporting the "opinions of philosophers" (*sententias philosophorum*).

[77] After the description of the beekeeper's invasion of the hive, the beekeeper is instructed to help the bees when it becomes winter and to "pity their crushed fortunes" (*res miserabere fractas*, 240) by fumigating, but it is difficult to interpret this pity as genuine or admirable since the beekeeper is the most immediate reason for their crushed fortunes, and he is also the one who will ultimately benefit from the fumigated hive.

CHAPTER 7

Farmers and poets

Lieber will noch der Mensch *das Nichts* wollen, als *nicht* wollen.
Man would rather will *nothingness* than *not* will.
Nietzsche, On the Genealogy of Morals 3.28

Nor I, nor any man that but man is
With nothing shall be pleas'd, till he be eas'd
With being nothing
Shakespeare, Richard II 5.5

My underlying goal in showing how many of the *Georgics*' themes are anticipated by Xenophon and Varro is to highlight not how Virgil repeats their points but how he builds upon them and creates a new focus in the *Georgics*. This new focus is best examined via the last major theme from their works that is incorporated into the *Georgics*, namely the contrast between the active and the contemplative lives. Whereas Varro presented the contrast between these two modes of life primarily in the last book of his work through his discussion of aviaries, Virgil exploits the contrast at several key points in each book. His conceptualization of the active and contemplative lives, loosely represented by the figures of the farmer and the poet, undergoes several transformations throughout the work. In the first three books, the similarities between them are underscored more than the differences.[1] It is only in Virgil's final formulation of the contrast between these modes of life, which takes place in the epyllion at the end of book 4, that Virgil makes an ultimate distinction between the farmer and the poet.

As I have already mentioned, one of the major differences between the *Georgics* and the *De Re Rustica* is that Virgil focuses on the emotional life of the farmer and particularly on how he reacts to the eruption of chaos in his life. He goes beyond Varro's satire to look at the underlying

---

[1] Cf. Gale (2003) 331: "Throughout the poem, then, Virgil offers us a series of different and conflicting models for the relationship between poet and *princeps*, or between the active and the contemplative life. Sometimes it is suggested that the two can cooperate harmoniously, sometimes they are mutually opposed."

forces that generate the false beliefs and systems that Varro attacked. While Virgil's conception of the contemplative life changes throughout the text, as does the farmer's relationship to it, one aspect of the farmer that is consistent is his determination to make sense of the world in an ordered and comforting way. Virgil's farmer reacts to physical and emotional chaos by trying to recreate order on both levels; the pessimistic voices that express disillusionment lead directly to the optimistic ones that attempt to project a more palatable understanding of the world, and the cycle begins again. Thus, I would argue that this cycle of pessimistic and optimistic voices creates a narrative drama and does not simply represent disembodied or alternative perspectives on the world. Each book of the *Georgics* highlights a different strategy for finding meaning in human life and compensating for death and destruction, and Virgil's poetry reveals both the strengths and weaknesses of these approaches. Virgil's poet figures initially strive for a similar, ordered understanding of the world, but the poet eventually comes to represent the abandonment of this quest for secure happiness and the acceptance of the chaotic uncontrollability of life.

BOOK I: *RELIGIO*

In book 1, the main ordering force is *religio*, and I have already looked in some detail at how Virgil gives prominence to a religious world view in this book. I would now like to show how Virgil contextualizes the farmer's religious understanding of the world and directly connects it to the fears that generate it. Virgil does not explicitly differentiate himself as a poet from the farmer figures he is discussing in the body of book 1, but he does speak as a poet in the preface, and here he aligns himself with the farmers as needing the beneficence of the godlike Caesar ("grant me an easy course and give favor to my bold beginnings; pitying with me the rustics ignorant of the way, approach and become accustomed even now to be called in prayer," *da facilem cursum atque audacibus adnue coeptis,* | *ignarosque viae mecum miseratus agrestis* | *ingredere et votis iam nunc adsuesce vocari,* 1.40–42). Thus, in book 1, both the poet Virgil and the farmers try to find guidance in different kinds of *religio*, particularly in times of crisis and desperation.

The first moment of crisis in book 1 comes in lines 118–21, when the farmer recognizes nature's unrelenting obstruction of his efforts ("nevertheless, despite all the efforts of men and oxen to do these things in turning the land, the wicked goose, Strymonian cranes and endive with bitter fibers get in the way and the shade is harmful," *nec tamen, haec cum sint hominumque boumque labores | versando terram experti, nihil improbus anser | Strymoniaeque grues et amaris intiba fibris | officiunt aut umbra nocet).* This recognition in turn leads directly to the first extensive theological passage, in which the farmer tries to make sense of his difficult situation by relying on a comforting religious explanation: Jupiter himself designed life to be difficult so that mankind would develop useful skills and avoid laziness (121–24). While this "theodicy of labor" initially seems reassuring, the end of the description of man's progress in the arts and sciences, brought about by the difficult conditions imposed by Jupiter, reverts back to the depressing tone of the beginning: "wicked labor conquered all and urgent need in dire circumstances" (*labor omnia vicit | improbus et duris urgens in rebus egestas,* 145–46). Even if the reader chooses to interpret lines 145–46 in a positive way, as some scholars have done,[2] La Penna [1962]/(1999) has noted the relative weakness of Virgil's theodicy when compared to Hesiod's version:

> If one looks closely, in Virgil the providential justification is either not there at all or is very weak. For Hesiod, Zeus hides fire and the other benefits, making work necessary, because he has been tricked by Prometheus: he condemns man as punishment for a crime; even humanity's gloomy decadence in the Iron Age (*Op.* 174–201) is caused by a moral degeneration for which man is responsible. But Virgil leaves out the myth of Prometheus, and does not introduce, at least into this passage, the important element of guilt . . . [O]ne cannot see a reason for man's decline from the golden age or what benefits civilisation brings. (33)

Thus, Virgil seems to intentionally present some cracks in the farmer's attempt to make sense of the world in a theological manner, and he makes it appear an imperfect construct motivated by an emotional recognition of man's difficult place in the world.

A religious view of the world is again explicitly connected to recognition of nature's destruction of man's efforts in the passage following the great autumn storm, which destroyed all of the labor of farmers and oxen (324–26). In fear of another storm arising (*hoc metuens,* 335), the farmer is instructed to "observe the months and stars of the sky" (*caeli mensis et sidera serva,* 335) and "especially worship the gods" (. . . *in primis venerare deos,* 338). Yet, Jupiter himself had taken part in the storm (328–29), and so the potential problems with a religious solution are apparent, especially since divine worship has done nothing to prevent the storm. The reader

---

[2] E.g. Wilkinson (1969) 141: "It is true that Virgil sums up, 'labor omnia vicit *improbus*', and that is an epithet which is always pejorative. But the word represents what the individual toiler would say about his work at the time – it does not belie the overall impression of the value of civilised activity." See chapter 6, "The amorality of farming," for further bibliography on the theodicy of labor.

might be reminded of Lucretius' explanation for why mankind prays to the gods during storms even though the prayers do not avert the disaster: despite the futility of the prayers, it is still comforting to believe that the gods are in control of things (5.1218–40).

Another type of chaotic storm breaks out at the end of book 1, namely the political storm that follows the death of Julius Caesar. This time, the moral chaos that accompanies the physical is even more clearly expressed, as "right and wrong are confounded" (*fas versum atque nefas*, 505). However, the narrator still tries to express a moralized view of the chaos and to understand the conflict as a tale of crime and divine punishment. He calls the current generation of Romans "impious" (*impiaque . . . saecula*, 468) and implies that the series of civil wars that occurred was according to the will of the gods ("And the gods deemed it fitting that Emathia and the wide plains of Haemus grow fertile twice with our blood," *nec fuit indignum superis, bis sanguine nostro | Emathiam et latos Haemi pinguescere campos*, 491–92).

The reason for the punishment of the Romans is clarified a few lines down when the narrator mentions the perjury of Laomedon ("Long enough have we atoned for the perjuries of Laomedon's Troy with our blood," *satis iam pridem sanguine nostro | Laomedonteae luimus periuria Troiae*, 501–502). Yet, this crime is so loosely connected to the current generation of Romans that it seems a weak explanation for the current misery (and the narrator's protest in lines 501–02 makes a similar point). Indeed, by the end of the book, the only thing that is labeled impious is Mars, as a personification of war ("impious Mars rages over the whole world," *saevit toto Mars impius orbe*, 511). Still, despite the narrator's questioning of the gods' rationale for the continuing punishment of the Romans, he is resistant to abandoning a theological understanding of the world. Instead, he expresses hope that the gods will send a savior to rescue the Romans (498–501), and this savior's job is clearly to reinstill not just physical order to Rome but moral and spiritual. Thus, in book 1, *religio* does not prevent disaster, but the farmers (and poet) in the text still try to cling to its comforting explanations of disaster, even as Virgil allows the flaws in its theological logic to appear.

BOOK 2: *RATIO*

The failures of *religio* in book 1 lead to the dominance of *ratio* in book 2. However, as discussed in chapter 6, the confident reliance on *ratio* is eventually shaken by the end of book 2, particularly after the tremendous amount of labor required for vine tending is acknowledged (2.397–419), as well as the potentially negative effects of the vine (2.454–57). The *vituperatio vitis* leads directly into the idealizing Praise of the Farmer, which I argued needs to be contextualized as part of the dialogue between *ratio* and *religio* in books 1 and 2: coming as it does at the end of a book dominated by *ratio*, the Praise of the Farmer reflects a desire to be reconnected with the spiritual world of nature. It includes a digression (475–94) that reflects the juxtaposition of *ratio* and *religio* but also produces a conflation of them, as parallel attempts to make sense of the world in a comforting way. I shall now look further at the Praise of the Farmer and particularly at the juxtaposition it presents between farmers and poets. Indeed, it is in this passage that Virgil most explicitly contrasts the two, while at the same time expressing the similar features that make each mode of life attractive: each is envisioned as finding secure happiness and meaning in life and eliminating death and destruction.

The initial portrait of the farming life in lines 458–74 presents it as a life of golden-age *otium*, which is far distant from war (459), politics (461–62), and luxury (463–66). It is a life of simple pastoral beauty (467–71), hard work (472), religion (473), and justice (474). The further description of the farming life in lines 493–531 continues to define it by the absence of iron-age ills, such as war (495–98), greed (498–99), politics (501–02), and luxury (506–07). In contrast, rustics live a life of *labor* (513–18), virtue (524), and simple pleasures (523–31). As many readers have noted, the life of the farmer in these two sections of the praise is defined more by a consistent description of what is absent from it than by any consistency in what is present, and the "praise" is a patchwork of idealized motifs that alternate between images of *otium* and *labor*.[3] What the praise seems to represent, then, is not a realistic appraisal of farming, but an attempt to locate a meaningful and ordered way of life after the disillusionment brought on by the *vituperatio vitis*.

As discussed in the last chapter, the Praise of the Farmer does not just praise the farmer: embedded within the two halves of the Praise is an intrusion by Virgil's persona in the first person (475–94), in which he seems to discuss his own poetic desires and to praise two different kinds of poets/intellectual figures. I have already suggested that while these two kinds of poet-figures initially seem to represent the opposition between *religio* and *ratio*, upon closer analysis, they also represent the conflation of that opposition. I would now like to look more at how the internal poet figures contrast (or compare) with the farmer figure in the outer frame of

---

[3] Cf. Gale (2000) 38–40 and 170–73.

this passage. La Penna (1995) has suggested that the *agōn* from Euripides' *Antiope*, in which Zethus and Amphion debate the relative merits of the socially useful farming life and the inwardly directed life of the poet, serves as a model for the end of book 2. I find this suggestion persuasive, especially because of the *agōn's* engagement with the contrast between the active and contemplative life, but I would argue that Virgil's particular presentation of this contrast in fact underscores the similarities before the poet and farmer more than their differences.[4]

One way in which Virgil merges the internal description of his poet figure(s) with the external description of the farmer is through an imperceptible segue back to the outer frame via an ambiguous *illum* ("that man," 495):

> fortunatus et ille deos qui novit agrestis
> Panaque Silvanumque senem Nymphasque sorores.
> <u>illum</u> non populi fasces, non purpura regum
> flexit et infidos agitans discordia fratres.   (493–96)

> Fortunate also is that man who knows the rustic gods:
> Pan, old Silvanus and the Nymph sisters.
> no *fasces* of the people have influenced <u>that man</u>, nor the purple
> of kings, nor Discord agitating unfaithful <u>brothers</u>.

This passage proceeds to mention all the iron-age ills absent from the life of *illum*, but the "farmer" is not specified explicitly until line 513; thus, until that point, it seems as if these lines are referring back to the "*fortunatus*" poet-figure.[5] I believe the ambiguity is intentional and in effect conflates the *fortunatus* with the farmer by underscoring their common resistance to iron-age ills. The "*felix*" poet-figure, the Epicurean-sounding philosopher, is evoked in this second part of the praise, as well, through allusions to Lucretius' diatribes against luxury (Lucr. 2.20–36) and ambition, greed, and cruelty (Lucr. 3.59–86) – the cure for all of which is the rational philosophy of Epicurus.[6] Thus, the end of book 2 does not so much juxtapose the poet

---

[4] Of course, it is possible that Euripides' fragmentary debate emphasized some similarities between Amphion and Zethus, as well. As Carter (1986) 170 notes, Amphion defends his lifestyle and attacks his brother's "entirely on [Zethus'] own ground – of advantage to house and city." In addition, by the end of the play, Amphion's contemplative lifestyle has a close connection to the active life, since Hermes tells him that his music will eventually build the walls of Thebes.

[5] Most scholars read lines 495 ff. as referring just to the farmer, though Ryberg (1958) and Clay (1976) would extend the praise of the *fortunatus* through line 502.

[6] Cf. Gale (2000) 40 "[T]he critique of urban violence and futile ambitions in 495–512 recalls the proems to *DRN* 2 and 3." For fuller discussion of the many allusions to Epicureanism and Lucretius in the Praise of the Farmer, see Gale (2000) 38–43 and 170–73. See also Fenik (1962) 77 n. 1.

and farmer as merge them and present them as parallel manifestations of the desire to find order and meaning in the world – a fitting conclusion to the cycles of optimism and pessimism that structure books 1 and 2.

BOOK 3: *GLORIA*

The beginning of book 3 is usually read in close connection with the end of book 2, not only because it has been seen as completing the discussion of Virgil's literary *oeuvre*, but because it provides an "active" counterpart to the contemplative poet in book 2 as Virgil conflates his role of triumphing poet with Caesar's role of triumphing politician. While I discussed the potential irony of this conflation in the previous chapter and its connections to Varro's *De Re Rustica*, I would now like to explore the further meaning of Virgil's "active" poet persona, particularly in connection with his conflation of the farmer and poet at the end of book 2. In book 3, Virgil satirizes military and political life as Varro did, but he also presents military glory and heroism as a force that can give meaning to life, just as *religio* and *ratio* did in books 1 and 2. Virgil's poet figure, then, shares with the farmer, politician, and soldier the quest to find order and meaning in life through immortal glory; however, as in the previous two books, *gloria* falls short as a successful strategy for defeating chaos and death.

Virgil begins the book by emphasizing the importance of obtaining poetic glory and primacy:

> . . . temptanda via est, qua me quoque possim
> tollere humo victorque virum volitare per ora.
> primus ego in patriam mecum, modo vita supersit,
> Aonio rediens deducam vertice Musas.   (8–11)

> A path must be tried, whereby I might also lift myself
> from the ground and as victor fly on the lips of men.
> I will be the first, returning from the Aonian height,
> to lead down the Muses into my country, provided life remain.

Virgil shows himself caught up in the need for glory, just like a military hero, and this desire for glory is directly connected to conquering death. Not only is line 9 an almost direct quotation from Ennius' epitaph (*var.* 18), but Gale (2000) notes that the "extended metaphor of lines 8–12 also recalls the triumphant mental 'flight' of Epicurus depicted in *DRN* 1.62–79" (44). Thus, these lines allude to poetic contexts in which death is conquered through intellectual activity, and by the end of this passage,

Virgil makes explicit his own version of conquering death by sending Envy
to the Underworld:

> Invidia infelix Furias amnemque severum
> Cocyti metuet tortosque Ixionis anguis
> immanemque rotam et non exsuperabile saxum.
>
> (37–39)
>
> Unhappy envy will fear the furies and the grim river
> of Cocytus, the twisted snakes of Ixion,
> the giant wheel and the unconquerable rock.

Thomas (1988) notes that "Envy's fear of the Underworld recalls the van-
quishing of that same fear by the man who understands the workings of
the universe at 2.490–2 (including V. himself?)" (II.47 [*ad* 3.37–39]). In
effect, then, Virgil is conflating yet another kind of poetic persona, that of
the triumphing epic poet, with that of the *felix* and *fortunatus*.

After the proem, book 3 turns to the discussion of pastoral activity,
but there still remains a focus on glory as an organizing principle in life.
The opening line of the didactic portion references the motivating force
of Olympic victory in raising horses (49–50), and the horses themselves
are valued for their desire for glory (102), praise, and victory (112). Yet,
just as *religio* was directly connected to the fear of destruction in book 1,
so the desire for glory is connected with recognition of the fragility and
transience of life. For instance, the first didactic portion of the book inter-
rupts the discussion of what animals to breed with a brief lament about
life's transience:

> optima quaeque dies miseris mortalibus aevi
> prima fugit; subeunt morbi tristisque senectus
> et labor, et durae rapit inclementia mortis.
>
> (66–68)
>
> Each best day of life flees first for miserable mortals;
> diseases and grim old age and hardship approach,
> and harsh death's lack of mercy snatches us away.

Disease and death overwhelm the second half of the book as the plague
of the Norici is described, and the overwhelming devastation of this plague
makes the power of glory seem weak in comparison. The description of
the treatment of plague begins with an optimistic scientific tone ("I will
also teach you the causes and signs of diseases," *morborum quoque te causas
et signa docebo*, 440), but this tone soon changes to one of desperation and
disillusionment as all of the organizing principles of life thus far examined

fail to combat death. *Religio* fails in a dramatic fashion: the *pastor* is said to help the disease thrive by eschewing medicine in favor of prayer (454–56), and the sickness of the cattle interfere with the Norici's attempt to use them in religious rituals (486–93). *Ratio* is also a complete failure, as medicine finds no cure for the plague and even at times helps it to progress (549–50). Finally, the pointlessness of glory and military renown is highlighted by the pathetic death of the *victor equus* ("victorious horse," 499), who stumbles down and paws the ground in his sickness from the plague (498–500). In addition, it is emphasized that the plague does not kill just individual members of a herd, but the entire group (471–73); thus, there is no one left to remember or perpetuate an individual's glorious deeds.

As usual, the *Georgics* focuses not just on the physical destruction but on the emotional disillusionment that accompanies an outbreak of chaos when all systems for controlling and understanding the world fail. Appropriately for book 3, the creature who most clearly expresses this human need to make sense of disaster is not a human at all but a steer, who is mourning the death of his brother:

> . . . it tristis arator,
> maerentem abiungens fraterna morte iuvencum,
> atque opere in medio defixa reliquit aratra.
> non umbrae altorum nemorum, non mollia possunt
> prata movere animum, non qui per saxa volutus
> purior electro campum petit amnis; at ima
> solvuntur latera, atque oculos stupor urget inertis
> ad terramque fluit devexo pondere cervix.
> quid labor aut benefacta iuvant? quid vomere terras
> invertisse gravis? atqui non Massica Bacchi
> munera, non illis epulae nocuere repostae:
> frondibus et victu pascuntur simplicis herbae,
> pocula sunt fontes liquidi atque exercita cursu
> flumina, nec somnos abrumpit cura salubris.
>
> (517–30)

> . . . The ploughman sadly goes,
> unyoking the steer, grieving over his brother's death,
> and abandoned the plough fixed in the middle of its work.
> Neither the shade of the deep woods, nor the soft fields
> are able to move his mind, nor the river which, rolling over
> the rocks, more pure than amber, seeks the plain; but his
> lowest flanks are limp, a stupor presses down his eyes, glazed
> over, and his neck droops to the ground under the pressing weight.
> What use his labor or his good deeds? Why turn the heavy

fields with the plough? But neither the Massic gifts of Bacchus,
nor stretched out feasts harmed them: they feed on foliage
and are nourished by simple grass, their cups are spring water and
coursing rivers, nor does anxiety disrupt their healthful sleep.

This Epicurean-sounding bull loses faith in the philosophy he relied on
to find happiness in life when he cannot control the death and grief that
have overwhelmed him. In the end, all of the forces of destruction that the
human arts of explanation have struggled to make sense of and contain in
books 1–3 are let loose: "Pale Tisiphone rages, and, sent into the light from
the Stygian shadows, she drives before her disease and death" (*saevit et in
lucem Stygiis emissa tenebris | pallida Tisiphone Morbos agit ante Metumque*,
551–52).

Yet, even though the plague has disrupted the sense of moral order
among the Norici, the drive to recreate it and make sense of the disaster
goes on, and, as in the previous books, there is a resistance to accepting
an amoral and chaotic natural world in which human happiness cannot be
secured. For instance, despite the failure of religion to stop the plague, the
narrator still makes a desperate plea to the gods to help out the pious (513).
Religious rituals go on, as well, even if with mismatched animals (531–33).
Some readers of the text have also felt a need to make sense of the disaster in
a moral way. For instance, Harrison (1979) has maintained that the Norici
were in fact being punished with the plague for a ritual error. Though
scholars have critiqued his argument,[7] I would emphasize that Harrison's
attempt to make sense of the plague as a tale of crime and punishment
parallels the desires of the voices in the text to find moral order, even if
Virgil ultimately resists confirming their point of view.[8] Book 3, then, like
books 1 and 2, shows that poets, farmers, and political/military heroes all

---

[7] See Thomas (1988) II.137–38 (*ad* 3.513): "Harrison (1979) finds in *errorem* a reference to an error in ritual on the part of the Noric farmer (531–3n.); but the word precedes the purported error by some 18 lines, and the actions of those lines occur *after* the plague has had its effects (see n.). The search for a rational cause for the plague is reasonable, but as with the unseasonable storm of Book 1, so here there exists none; that is in the nature of the world of *labor improbus*." See also Mynors (1990) 251 (*ad* 3.476): "Harrison (1979) rightly points out that a disaster on this scale might well be regarded as a manifestation of divine wrath, as the loss of Aristaeus's bees, though due to natural causes, was a visitation from the Nymphs . . . and that this would have led to the consultation of an oracle in Greece and to special propitiatory rites in Rome. There is no trace of such a feeling here, not merely because we are in neither Greece nor Rome (though there are details which look purely Roman, such as the *extispicium* of 490 f.), but because the plague is only a massive example of the ills that await every farmer potentially, and any suggestion that his misdeeds or divine wrath are responsible is to be avoided."

[8] Cf. Gale (2000) 77: "It is far from clear whether the plague is to be seen as a natural occurrence or as a divine punishment, and it is significant, I think, that we are in the same position as the Norici themselves in this respect."

share a drive to find order and happiness in life, and that *religio, ratio*, and *gloria*, despite their bouts of success, are ultimately unsuccessful "answers" to the pains of life.

BOOK 4: *GENUS IMMORTALE*

If books 1 and 2 formed a pair, in which the failure of *religio* leads to the rise of *ratio* and eventually a return to *religio*, then I would also argue that books 3 and 4 form a similar narrative pair: the failure of *gloria* and individual heroism in book 3 leads to book 4, in which the focus is instead on literal life after death and the immortality of the group. One study has used book 4 to argue that the *Georgics* presents an optimistic and politicized message about the constructive and regenerative power of death and violence.[9] I would caution, however, that while resurrection and rebirth are important themes of book 4, it is important to contextualize them with the rest of the *Georgics*. Virgil presents them as one more order-producing strategy that the farmer has at his disposal in his fight against physical destruction and emotional disillusionment, but it is a strategy that, like the others, does not appear successful as a permanent solution. At the same time, Virgil uses book 4 to define a new role for the poet and to finally distinguish him from the farmer or politician. This new type of contemplative figure is symbolized by the character of Proteus, who resists the urge to find meaning and order in life and instead tells a story of chaos and failure.

The mystical focus of book 4 is emphasized from the first line of the book: "Next I will pursue the heavenly gifts of celestial honey" (*protinus aërii mellis caelestia dona | exsequar*, 4.1–2). The emphasis on the heavens continues in discussion of the bees: Virgil relates the belief that they partake of the "divine mind" (*divinae mentis*, 220) and do not die ("nor is there a place for death," *nec morti esse locum*, 226).[10] He focuses in particular on the immortality of the hive, which makes up for the short lifespan of the individual bee ("but the immortal race remains," *at genus immortale manet*,

---

[9] Morgan (1999).

[10] There are also various connections between bees and divinity in Greek mythology and religion, on which, see Cook (1895) and Thomas (1978), who notes that "in [Virgil's] time and world the bee, and honey too, carried with them a magico-religious import quite foreign to modern thought and allegorical intent. Merely for the poet to bring up the subject of the bee must have caused some religious associations to begin slipping through the minds of his audience and readers" (35). She cites in particular the evidence of Porphyry's *De Antro Nympharum* 18 on Orphic rites, which says that "souls of the dead on their way to rebirth were called μέλισσαι" (Thomas [1978] 32). In addition, she notes that honey is connected with death and divinities (e.g. Hom. *Il.* 23.170 and Eur. *Ba.* 710–11), several priestesses were called Melissa, and the infant Zeus was nourished by bees (Call. *Jov.* 1.45–53, D.S. 5.70, and Verg. *G.* 4.150–52) (Thomas [1978] 33).

208). Of course, the bees *do* die in the course of book 4, so the second half of the book is dedicated to explaining the ritual of *bugonia*, through which a new hive can be reborn out of the dead carcass of a steer. In the myth explaining the origin of the *bugonia*, more resurrection imagery is present via the story of Orpheus, who tries to resurrect Eurydice from the dead, and through the attendant allusions to mystery religion and Dionysiac ritual in the epyllion.[11]

Very literally, then, the art of resurrection is born from devastation – both the emotional devastation of Aristaeus upon the loss of his bees and the physical devastation of the steer who creates the new bees. I would suggest that the myth attached to the *bugonia*, which explains its origin, also has a meta-literary purpose: using Aristaeus as the archetypal farmer and Orpheus as the archetypal poet, it mirrors the drama of the *Georgics*, as each figure tries to conquer death and find happiness, this time via resurrection. The epyllion also introduces a new kind of poet in the figure of Proteus, who presents Orpheus' story to Aristaeus. The story of Proteus on one level seems to mirror the emotional work of the farmer through-out the *Georgics*: it tries to make sense of Aristaeus' pain and disaster in an understandable, moralized way, as a tale of sin and punishment. On another level, however, Proteus' song might be interpreted as a story of chaos and failure since its moralizing introduction is soon overshadowed by the tragic tale of Orpheus' double loss of his wife. Proteus' poetic art, then, perfectly represents Virgil's own dual focus in the *Georgics* on the attempts of farmers and poets to make sense of the world and compen-sate for death, and on the tendencies of the natural world to resist these efforts.

Before looking at the epyllion in more detail, I would like to look at one more contrast between the active and contemplative life that occurs in the first half of book 4 via the juxtaposition between the politicized bee state and the "Old Man of Tarentum." The bees are not just mini-citizens, as discussed in the previous chapter, but their activities mirror the ordering efforts of the farmer in the *Georgics*. Like the farmer, the bees are not immune to death and destruction; on the contrary, they have a short lifespan, are constantly exposed to natural and human dangers and engage in wars among themselves. Also like their human counterparts, they react emotionally to the eruption of chaos in their lives: they feel excessive anger when the beekeeper tries to take their honey, and they react to this injury

---

[11] On the relation between the epyllion and mystery religions, see Wender (1969), Chomarat (1974), Johnston (1977), Thomas (1978), Campbell (1982), and Morgan (1999) esp. 141–202.

by seeking vengeance (236–38). In addition, the bees suffer from depression when physical disaster strikes (240), and they are motivated to work all the harder to recreate order in their lives ("the more they are drained, the more fiercely will they all strive to repair the ruins of their fallen race," *quo magis exhaustae fuerint, hoc acrius omnes | incumbent generis lapsi sarcire ruinas*, 248–49). Finally, the narrator also suggests that the bees share the same order-producing strategies as the farmer: *religio* (43), *ratio* (56–57), *gloria* (205), and even immortality (208, 225–27, and 281–314) are all a part of their lives.

Yet, just as the farmer's quest for order is undermined in books 1–3, so is the bees' in the course of the narrator's discourse. Not only are they "just bees," and so, from a human perspective, the supposed great meaning of their lives appears absurd, but the narrator instructs the beekeeper to treat them as insignificant creatures: as discussed previously, the great emotions and conflicts of the bees can be easily quashed with a bit of dust (86–87). In addition, their entire hive is liable to extinction, and the beekeeper seems perfectly happy to replace them with a completely different set of bees through the art of *bugonia* (281–314). Because the bees have been so humanized in the course of book 4, the sudden insignificance of their lives has ramifications for human life, as well: one can easily imagine a "beekeeper's perspective" of human life, which sees it as equally meaningless. Thus, in the end, the civilized political life of the bee and its faith in the *genus immortale* does not seem an "answer" to the problem of finding meaning and order in apian or human life.

There is an alternative model of life presented in the middle of the discourse on bees, and that is the life of the old Corycian gardener of Tarentum. While there have been many different interpretations of what this gardener represents in the scholarly literature, most readers view him as a figure sharply opposed to the values of the bee state: whereas the bees are politicized and materialistic, the old man is solitary and unmaterialistic. He has been called a symbol of philosophical *autarkeia*,[12] a philosophical and, most likely, Epicurean ideal,[13] an embodiment of the pastoral ideal,[14] a gardener who "pursues (like the poet) an esthetic and spiritual ideal which ignores material function or profit,"[15] and "a portrayal of the successful workings of private man within the terms of the age of *labor*."[16] Combining all these interpretations together, one might read him as an over-determined symbol of the contemplative life – one that ties together all the different

---

[12] La Penna (1977) esp. 60–66.   [13] Gale (2000) 180–83 and W. R. Johnson (2004).
[14] Davis (1979) 31.   [15] Perkell (1981) 168.   [16] Thomas (1988) 11.169 (*ad* 4.125–48).

strands of it, poetic, philosophical, and pastoral, that were evoked at the end of book 2.

I will briefly summarize the evidence for the Old Man's contemplative pedigree before suggesting what Virgil is doing with him. The philosophical aspect of the *senex* is perhaps the most noticeable part of his portrayal. Virgil notes that he "equaled the wealth of kings in his mind" (*regum aequabat opes animis*, 132), and this phrase particularly brings to mind a Cynic or Stoic ideal in its devaluation of material wealth;[17] however, this transferal of wealth from the material to spiritual plane could also describe the generic sage, as could the self-sufficiency or *autarkeia* provided by his unbought meal ("he would load his table with unbought feasts," *dapibus mensas onerabat inemptis*, 133).[18] While the garden of the Old Man may symbolize Epicureanism,[19] it may also call to mind Cicero's idealized image of Cato the philosopher-farmer,[20] who speaks of his love of gardens, flowers, and bees (*Sen.* 15.54). Cicero also sets his *De Re Publica* in the *horti* of Scipio (*Rep.* 1.14), and in the preface of *De Finibus* book 5, "nearby gardens" (*propinqui hortuli*, 5.2) are said to bring Plato to mind. Thus, gardens are not the exclusive preserve of the Epicureans but can be a generic setting for philosophical discussion.[21]

There are a few other philosophical aspects of the Old Man's portrayal that, as far as I know, have not been emphasized in other interpretations. One is the philosophical connotation of Tarentum itself, known as a center of Pythagoreanism,[22] which is a philosophy that would fit well with the theme of rebirth and immortality in book 4. The most famous Pythagorean of Tarentum was Archytas. Cicero mentions him frequently in his philosophical works (*Sen.* 12.39–41, *Rep.* 1.16, *Fin.* 5.87, *Tusc.* 4.78, and 5.64)

---

[17] Cf. Antisthenes' declaration in Xenophon's *Symposium*: "Because, men, I believe that people have riches and poverty not in their property but in their souls," ὅτι νομίζω, ὦ ἄνδρες, τοὺς ἀνθρώπους οὐκ ἐν τῷ οἴκῳ τὸν πλοῦτον καὶ τὴν πενίαν ἔχειν ἀλλ᾽ ἐν ταῖς ψυχαῖς (4.34).

[18] Cf. La Penna (1977) 60.

[19] Cf. Gale (2000) 181–82: "Can we perhaps go further and see a specific reference here to the Epicurean ideals of autarchy and withdrawal from society? Certainly, these principles were not exclusively Epicurean; but is it simply coincidence that Epicurus' school was also a Garden, situated just outside the city of Athens?. . . If Servius is right to claim that the old man should be identified as an ex-pirate, his change of state might be seen as a powerful symbol of the process the Epicureans called *galenismos* (literally, 'becalming') . . . Finally it is worth noting that flowers, bees and honey occur more than once in the *DRN* as symbols for (Epicurean) pleasure."

[20] Novara (1980) 261 even dubs Cicero's Cato the "elder brother" of the Old Man of Tarentum.

[21] Cf. also the end of one of Cicero's letters to Varro: "if you have a garden in your library, nothing will be lacking" (*si hortum in bibliotheca habes, deerit nihil, Fam.* 9.4).

[22] Cf. Huffman (1993) 6: "It is certainly clear that Croton was the main Pythagorean center up to the attack on the society in 454, whereas Tarentum grows in importance later and as the home of Archytas is important in fourth-century Pythagoreanism."

and emphasizes his friendship and influence on Plato, who Cicero suggests came to Tarentum in his old age. Though Archytas is usually associated today with abstract, mathematical philosophy, the vignettes that Cicero relates involve him in "down to earth," ethical philosophy.[23] More importantly for the *Georgics*, Varro cites him prominently in his catalogue of Greek sources as an author of a treatise on farming (*R.* 1.1.8).[24] Finally, I would note that Archytas, like the *senex* (if Servius' information is correct about the *senex*'s Cilician origin),[25] is a transplant from Asia Minor, or at least is said to be descended from the Myrians (Pl. *Ep.* 12), and of course Pythagoras himself migrated from Asia Minor (Samos) to Southern Italy (Croton). While I am not suggesting that our *senex* actually *is* Archytas, I would suggest that the location of Tarentum might call Archytas and Pythagoreanism to mind, especially since our *senex* already bears the marks of a sage and seems to live as a vegetarian.

   Another philosophical aspect of the *senex* appears in the last line of the description, when the Old Man is said to have planted an elm, pear, plum, and "plane tree, now providing shade to drinkers" (*iamque ministrantem platanum potantibus umbras*, 146). Indeed, one could argue that the only natural setting more conducive to philosophy than a garden is a plane tree providing shade. While no doubt the plane tree is an emblem of pastoral as well,[26] Plato forever joined pastoral imagery (and the plane tree) to philosophy in his famous, idyllic setting of the *Phaedrus* (229a and 230b–c), which Cicero brought to Rome as a setting in the *De Oratore* (1.28).[27] That said, the *senex* has as good a pastoral pedigree as a philosophical one, and these two genres are not mutually exclusive. Thomas (1992) has detailed the complex pastoral genealogy of the *Corycius senex* and ultimately posits a Philitean model. I would suggest that the epigrams of Leonidas of Tarentum, whom Gutzwiller (1998) has called the "most influential of all Greek epigrammatists" (88), might have shaped the *senex*, as well.

---

[23] E.g. *Sen.* 12.39–41, in which Cato relates Archytas' discourse on the evils of carnal pleasures.

[24] Both Varro and Columella believe that the Pythagorean Archytas of Tarentum authored a work (unnamed) on agriculture, though Diogenes Laertius believes a different Archytas wrote *On Agriculture*. On this issue, see Huffman (2005) 27–28.

[25] On the debate about the meaning of Servius' note (*ad G.* 4.127), see Ross (1987) 204–206, Marasco (1990), Thomas (1992), Leigh (1994), and Thibodeau (2001) 185–86.

[26] See Thomas (1992) 41–42 and Van Sickle (2000) 33–34.

[27] Gutzwiller (1991) 73 notes that the "analogy of Socrates to a herdsman" in the *Phaedrus* "goes a long way toward explaining the prominent position of this dialogue in the development of Theocritean pastoral." See Gutzwiller (1991) 233 n. 18 for further bibliography on the link between the *Phaedrus* and Theocritean pastoral. She also suggests that "[t]he ascription to Plato of epigrams very like those of Anyte and Leonidas indicates that the *Phaedrus* was perceived as the spiritual antecedent of the whole series" (74).

It is not just Leonidas' location that reminds one of the Old Man of Tarentum; Leonidas also frequently writes of gardens and impoverished rustics, with moralistic reflections on the vanity of human riches and the value of the simple and humble life.[28] Indeed, the following epigram about the small but sufficient domain of the old Cleiton could well describe the *Corycius senex*. Compare the description of the Old Man of Tarentum's little plot of land ("who had a few acres of abandoned land, which was not fertile for bullocks, and not suitable for the herd or vine," *cui pauca relicti* | *iugera ruris erant, nec fertilis illa iuvencis* | *nec pecori opportuna seges nec commoda Baccho*, 127–29) with Cleiton's:

τοῦτ' ὀλίγον Κλείτωνος ἐπαύλιον ἤ τ' ὀλιγαῦλαξ
σπείρεσθαι λιτός θ' ὁ σχεδὸν ἀμπελεὼν
τοῦτό τε ῥωπεύειν ὀλιγόξυλον· ἀλλ' ἐπὶ τούτοις
Κλείτων ὀγδώκοντ' ἐξεπέρησ' ἔτεα.[29]
(*AP* 6.226, G–P 87)

This is the little homestead of Cleiton, with little arable land to sow,
a scanty vineyard nearby and little wood for cutting down.
But Cleiton passed eighty years on this.

In another epigram (*AP* 6.302, G–P 37), Leonidas portrays *himself* as a "self-sufficient old man" (αὐτάρκης ὁ πρέσβυς, *AP* 6.302.3), who tells the mice to find another house to search for food in, since his is humble and his resources are few. As Gutzwiller (1998) notes, "The persona projected in this playful epigram – that of a poor but contented old poet – is designed, then, to connect Leonidas himself with the elderly poor who are the heroes of his epitaphs and his dedications" (111). The quality of self-sufficiency connects him also to Diogenes the Cynic, "who was said to have learned the art of self-sufficiency . . . by observing the behavior of a mouse."[30] Indeed, Cynic themes were popular with Leonidas, in particular the contrast between wealthy kings and poor philosophers and the leveling

---

[28] As Gutzwiller (1998) 91 notes, "Leonidas modified the customary use of the inscriptional epigram – to celebrate and commemorate the well-to-do or at least the moderately well off – to present detailed portraits of lower-class individuals in their workaday world and to convey a philosophical position, heavily influenced by Cynic tenets, that valued the lives of such people." She also notes that in some epigrams, "Leonidas speaks directly in his own poetic persona to provide moral instruction of a Cynic cast and to associate his own life with the lives of lower-class characters" (92).

[29] Gow and Page (1965) (*ad loc.*) call this a "troublesome quatrain though the general sense is clear," and I aimed more for that general sense than perfect accuracy in my translation since the text is problematic. There is another interesting epigram on a certain "old Cleiton" (γηραιὸς Κλείτων, *AP* 6.239.2) by Apollonides, a poet writing in the second half of Augustus' reign and during Tiberius'. This Cleiton specifically is a beekeeper, and the poem describes him collecting honey.

[30] Gutzwiller (1998) 111. She attributes this point to Geffcken (1896) 126–27.

effect that death has on all.[31] Thus, the description of the Old Man's ability
to equal the wealth of kings in his mind (*regum aequabat opes animis*, 132)
could easily find a home in a Leonidan style epigram. Finally, like the
transplanted Corycian, Leonidas adopts the persona of a wanderer, though
one who much prefers the settled life in Tarentum.[32] Leonidas' epigrams
and his poetic persona, then, present exactly the conflation of pastoral,
philosophical, and poetic themes that critics have located in the Old Man
of Tarentum. Indeed, Tarentum itself conjures up this intersection between
philosophical pastoral and pastoral philosophy through the figures of both
Archytas and Leonidas.[33]

While I have focused primarily on the philosophical and pastoral connotations of the *Corycius senex*, the metapoetic imagery is intense, as well.
Perkell has suggested that the gardener's "pursuit of beauty identifies him
most significantly as a poet," and she has commented on the "noncommercial and miraculously vital" garden of the Corycian, which has a "simultaneous profusion of flowering plants possible only in the imagination."[34]
I would go even further to suggest that his flower garden brings to mind
the Garland of Meleager and particularly the preface in which he associates the different epigrammatists with flowers and trees (*AP* 4.1). The
plants common to the Garland and the garden, starting with the general
description of gardens in *G.* 4.109, include (in the order they appear in the
epigram) lilies, roses, narcissus, crocus, hyacinth, ivy, pine,[35] plane, myr-
tle, pear, apple, celery, and thyme. Gutzwiller (1998) has noted a similar
metapoetic aspect of Leonidas' "poor old rustic" persona: she suggests that
in *AP* 6.300, which she believes formed the prologue to the collection, "the
agricultural products symbolize Leonidas' epigrams, which in style exhibit
qualities of richness, choiceness, and freshness but in subject matter mirror
the humbleness of his poetic offerings" (109).

Of course, in all of this, the important question is, how does the *senex* fit
into Virgil's dialogue on the role and nature of the contemplative life? As
already mentioned, the *senex* seems to embody all of the different strands of

---

[31] E.g. *AP* 7.740 (G–P 75), *AP* 7.67 (G–P 59), and *AP* 7.655 (G–P 17), on which, see Gutzwiller (1998)
  100–02.
[32] Cf. *AP* 7.715 (G–P 93), *AP* 6.300 (G–P 36), and Gutzwiller (1998) 108–09.
[33] Gigante (1971) 65–67 has even suggested a symbolic connection between Archytas and Leonidas
  by supposing that Leonidas' celebration of the working class and banausic arts derives from the
  tradition of Archytas as artisan-philosopher, instead of from the Platonic and Aristotelian tradition
  in which such crafts are devalued.
[34] Perkell (1989) 135 (first quotation) and Perkell (1981) 172 (second and third quotations). See also
  Perkell (1981) 172 nn. 19 and 22 for further bibliography on the wondrous garden.
[35] If *pinus* is read instead of *tinus* in *G.* 4.141.

the contemplative life that Virgil's persona yearned for at the end of book 2, where again the poetic, pastoral, and philosophical came together.[36] Yet, Virgil's longing for some sort of initiation into an ideal contemplative life seemed to indicate that he did not yet possess it but was searching for it. I would suggest that Virgil's description of the Old Man of Tarentum, and particularly his indication that he must pass over this discussion of gardens and leave it for others to tell (147–48), represents Virgil's relinquishing of this search: Virgil abandons the *senex* because he has abandoned the quest for the elusive contemplative ideal that can bring order and happiness to life. This is essentially Perkell's (1981) conclusion:

> The ways in which the gardener differs from the farmer are largely those in which he resembles the poet, as we may see from comparing the gardener to Orpheus and to the *Georgic* poet, the two poet figures in the poem. From them we learn of Vergil's unidealized, ambivalent view of the poet's experience. As was noted above, the *Georgic* poet implies a melancholy distinction between himself and the gardener when he indicates that he is not free to pursue his vision of the gardener as he would wish (4.116 ff., 147–48). The gardener's appeal seems precisely to be his freedom from the limiting realities, internal and external, which torment the *Georgic* poet. (175)

I would suggest, however, that there is a third poet figure in the poem, namely Proteus, and it is with Proteus that Virgil ultimately identifies himself.

I would also suggest that within the description of the Old Man of Tarentum, there are clues that this contemplative ideal is not a realistic one and does not hold up to close scrutiny. For one thing, though the Old Man is presented as living in the mind and completely separate from materialistic desires, he certainly labors long hours in his garden.[37] His labor is presumably part of his self-sufficient manner of providing himself with food (132–33), but gardens are also presented in the agricultural literature as extremely profitable, especially if they are near a city, as the Old Man's seems to be.[38] In addition, as has been frequently noted, the

---

[36] Cf. Nelson (1998) 148: "In his [the Old Man's] retirement and self-sufficiency he lives, unselfconsciously, the Epicurean ideal, reconciling the philosopher and the lover of nature whose opposition closed Book 2."

[37] Cf. Ross (1987) 201: "[H]e puts in an inordinately long day, for someone who so often is made to represent the ease of the sane rustic existence."

[38] Cato calls the watered garden (*hortus inriguus*) the second best kind of farm to have (*Agr.* 1.7). Cicero has "Cato" praise the profitability gardens in *Sen.* 16.56. Columella also emphasizes the profit that can be made from gardens (10.308–10) in his own continuation of Virgil's garden digression. Varro notes the profit that can be made from a garden, particularly if it is near a city (1.16.3). Perkell (1981) 171 points out that *G.* 4.125 ("beneath the towers of the Oebalian citadel," *sub Oebaliae . . . turribus*

passage on the *Corycius senex* is essentially a substitution for a memory of Varro, recounted by Merula, in book 3 of the *De Re Rustica*. Merula says he heard Varro once speak of two brothers in Spain, who had only a small villa, but had an aviary and a garden and made a huge profit from it (3.16.10–11).[39] While Perkell (1981) notes that "the character of this passage [on the *senex*] emerges clearly when contrasted with Varro's Veianius brothers who turned their very small holding into a profitable apiary" (172 n. 21), I would suggest instead that this substitution raises the possibility that the *senex* is as motivated by profit as any garden owner and that the pastoralizing *de-emphasis* on materialism may be just that: the fantasy of the pastoral vision. There is nothing inherently "noncommercial" about a flower garden; quite the contrary, as the ancient evidence suggests, and the Old Man might not be as different from the bees as he initially appears.

Another way in which the idealized image of the Old Man might be compromised is by Virgil's emphasis on the time-bound nature of his activities. Far from living an ethereal existence in the mind, the Old Man's daily life is dictated by rhythms of nature that he cannot control. Indeed, Thibodeau's recent study (2001) has emphasized the extent to which the description of the *senex*'s activities in his garden "provides a record of the old man's struggle against something of profound concern to him – the evanescence of time" (175–76). He notes the Old Man's impatience with the slow coming of summer ("chiding the late summer and the delaying Zephyrs," *aestatem increpitans seram Zephyrosque morantis*, 138),[40] and also "his habit of cultivating way ahead of schedule and outside normal work hours" (176). Virgil's language emphasizes the passing of time and the seasons (134–38), and Thibodeau also shows how the description of his cultivation of his garden implies a passage of time:

arcis) implies the Old Man is indeed near a city. Cf. also Jashemski's (1979) 411 description of a real commercial flower garden found in Pompeii: "The proprietor of this garden may well have found the advice of the ancient agricultural writers very sound – flowers can be a very profitable crop."

[39] There are other ways, too, in which the Old Man of Tarentum might bring Varro to mind, and particularly Varro's elderly and contemplative persona in the *De Re Rustica*. Macrobius tells us that Varro connected his *nomen* Terentius etymologically to Tarentum (see Macr. 3.18.13). In addition, the designation of the *senem* as *Corycium* might reference Varro's stint overseas fighting Cilician pirates (as opposed to an actual retired Cilician pirate, as proposed by Servius; see discussion earlier in this section). Of course, the pedigree of the Old Man is too complex to be reduced to one figure, so I am suggesting only that a contemplative Varronian figure might be added to the mix of contemplative models already adduced.

[40] I would note, too, that *increpitans* is a rather strong word to indicate anger, especially when the object of his rebuke is the season and the wind; it creates an image of frustration and futility that belies his philosophical coloring.

His tasks are not those of a single day or even a single year, but span several years, during which he is able to bring to perfection ever more ambitious forms of cultivation. (179) . . . Thus, the maturation of the trees measures the passage of time . . . It also marks the fulfillment of the gardener's ultimate aim, the complete conversion of the things in his garden to productive ends. Every tree produces something useful. (182)

Thibodeau's *senex* seems to be a farmer who has essentially followed Ischomachus' direction to buy uncultivated land and improve it (*Oec.* 20.22–23).

Perkell (1989) and Thibodeau (2001) in many ways have opposite ways of interpreting the Old Man of Tarentum, a fact which Thibodeau notes:

I agree with [Perkell] that the passage thematizes artistic practice, and shows the Corycian's garden to be in effect a piece of art. However, rather than being «timeless,» as she says (art. cit. 177), the garden, just as much as the narrative about the garden, displays profound accommodations to the demands of time, as I have tried to show. (183 n. 20)

Indeed, interpretations of the passage in general seem split between those which emphasize the Old Man's idealizing features and those which focus on the realism of his portrayal. I would suggest that the reason there are such conflicts is because the text itself provides for two visions of the Old Man, one in which he is a realistic, time-bound creature, and another in which he is an idealized, timeless, and *un*materialistic figure. Another way to read these conflicts, however, is to suggest that the ideal vision is punctured by the underlying reality and shown to be a fiction or even a parody.

Ross (1975) has made the suggestion that the pseudo-Virgilian *Moretum* is a parody of the "triteness of poetic reflections on the rewards of rustic self-sufficiency" and of the "artificiality of the way such passages must have been clumsily sewn onto the fabric of a poem by bad poets so as to appear, not as the digressions they so obviously were, but as a part of the narrative" (259, both quotes). The close connections between the moralizing description of Simylus' garden in the *Moretum* (61–86) and the Old Man of Tarentum's have been recognized,[41] but a parodic tone has generally been denied to Virgil's version.[42] I would argue that the Old

---

[41] E.g. Fitzgerald (1996) 406.

[42] Thomas (1988) II.172 (*ad* 4.133) notes that 4.133 ("he would load his table with unbought feasts," *dapibus mensas onerabat inemptis*) calls to mind Hor. *Epod.* 2.48 ("[if she should] prepare unbought feasts," *dapes inemptas apparet*) and that "presumably one imitated the other." Of course, *Epode* 2 is the famously ironic Alfius epode, in which it is revealed at the end that the pastoral fantasy depicted throughout is spoken by a moneylender who has no real desire to lead the life of a farmer. Thomas suggests that despite the irony of the epode, "the statement in itself is not parodistic either

Man of Tarentum is in fact a parody, but one with a serious purpose. Virgil is parodying his own previously stated desire at the end of book 2 to find happiness and an ability to transcend the difficulties of life through a contemplative ideal. His description of the Old Man of Tarentum posits that no such ideal exists – except in a hazy memory of the past that loses coherence if examined too closely.

Now that Virgil has left behind the quest for a contemplative ideal that can provide secure happiness and order in human life, he can finally craft a form of the contemplative life that is different from the active life in its overall aims. As already indicated, he does so through the epyllion that ends book 4 and explains the origins of the ritual of *bugonia*, the art that is the "salvation" of Egypt (294) and that produces a new hive from the dead body of a calf (*vitulus*). While the *bugonia* itself is a technical device that restores physical order after the destructive plague, the *myth* of the *bugonia* provides a paradigm for how the farmer attempts to recreate physical and moral order after disaster and thus represents in miniature the major theme of the *Georgics*. More than that, however, it displays how the work of a poet (Proteus) can subvert or add complexity to an orderly and moralized view of the world. It thus also presents a model of the *Georgic* poet and of the different ways in which his poem might be read.[43]

The narrator begins the myth by recounting Aristaeus' emotional devastation upon the loss of his hive to "sickness and famine" (*morboque fameque*, 318):

> mater, Cyrene mater, quae gurgitis huius
> ima tenes, quid me praeclara stirpe deorum
> (si modo, quem perhibes, pater est Thymbraeus Apollo)
> invisum fatis genuisti? aut quo tibi nostri
> pulsus amor? quid me caelum sperare iubebas?
> en etiam hunc ipsum vitae mortalis honorem,
> quem mihi vix frugum et pecudum custodia sollers
> omnia temptanti extuderat, te matre relinquo.
> quin age et ipsa manu felicis erue silvas,
> fer stabulis inimicum ignem atque interfice messis,
> ure sata et validam in vitis molire bipennem,
> tanta meae si te ceperunt taedia laudis.   (321–32)

---

for Horace or V" (2.172, *ad* 4.133). However, I would note that the irony of the epode comes not just from Alfius' lack of sincerity about being a rustic, but also from his idealization of that life. His description of "the unbought feasts" (*dapes inemptas*) has more than just a literal meaning but connotes a sort of golden-age existence that in reality does not describe the life of a rustic. Thus, I would argue that the attribution of these "unbought feasts" (*dapibus... inemptis*) to the *senex* connotes a similar (and possibly ironic) idealization of his life.

[43] Batstone (1997) 128 calls the epyllion "a story of interpretation."

> Mother, mother Cyrene, you who dwell in the lowest
> depths of this abyss, why did you bear me, hated by the fates,
> from the brilliant race of the gods (if indeed Thymbraean
> Apollo is my father as you maintain)? Or whither has your
> love for me been driven? Why did you order me to hope
> for heaven? Lo even this very glory of my mortal life,
> which the skillful tending of crops and herds has
> scarcely wrought for me trying everything, I abandon
> despite the fact that you are my mother.
> But come and destroy with your very hand my fertile woods,
> fling hostile fire on my stables and destroy my crops.
> Burn my fields and wield the mighty ax against my vines,
> if such weariness of my praise has seized you.

Aristaeus voices all of the frustrations that have been scattered throughout the *Georgics* when man's expectations have been dashed by natural disaster. Aristaeus faces the loss not just of his bees but of his faith in a morally ordered world in which good deeds are rewarded and there is compensation for death.[44] He responds to this loss not with acceptance but with anger and an increased desire to rectify the situation. Thus, he is the archetypal farmer not just in his livelihood but in the way he reacts to disaster.[45]

Cyrene responds by telling Aristaeus to seek advice from Proteus, "for the seer knows everything, what is, what has been, and what will soon come about" (*novit namque omnia vates,* | *quae sint, quae fuerint, quae mox ventura trahantur*, 392–93). Yet, Cyrene warns Aristaeus that he will have to trap him with bonds and force him with violence to reveal the "cause of the plague" (*morbi causam*), to "make the results favorable" (*eventusque secundet*) and to give "instructions" (*praecepta*) (396–400). In addition, Proteus will try to elude him with his "vain tricks" (*doli . . . inanes*, 400), which involve turning into "various shapes and appearances of wild beasts" (*variae . . . species atque ora ferarum*, 406), including a boar, a tiger, a snake, a lioness, fire, and water (407–10). Aristaeus follows his mother's orders and binds Proteus until he agrees to give him oracles (*oracula*, 449). The binding of Proteus has many symbolic connotations which critics have well explored, and it is frequently taken to represent the farmer's struggle to order nature on a physical level.[46] While this is no doubt one aspect of

---

[44] Cf. Campbell (1982) 110: "We hear no mention of bees; Aristaeus questions rather the meaning of his life: *quid me . . . genuisti* (*G.* 4.322 ff). 'Why have you borne me?'" Cf. also Nappa (2005) 194: "Aristaeus has lost not only a swarm but also the place he has made for himself in the world."

[45] His words also imply that he has relied upon all of the different strategies of the farmer for creating meaning and order in the *Georgics*, namely *religio* and a hope for immortality (*quid me caelum sperare iubebas?*, 325) *ratio/ars* (*custodia sollers*, 327) and *gloria* (*meae . . . laudis*, 332).

[46] E.g. Miles (1980) 267: "The struggle to subdue Proteus in all his varied forms might be interpreted in almost any context as symbolic of mankind's efforts to subdue the forces of disorder and destruction

Aristaeus' struggle as a farmer and of his conquest of Proteus, I would like
to emphasize the other aspect of the farmer's struggle that is also symbolized
here, and that is the attempt to force a *moral* order on the world and to
force Proteus to reveal an understandable and meaningful reason for the
disaster.

In addition to being a symbol of chaotic nature, Proteus, as *vates* (392), is
also designated a poet-figure. He responds to Aristaeus' force with *oracula*,
but his poetry, like Virgil's, also contains a vision of chaos that resists
Aristaeus' desire for a moralized understanding of events. Proteus begins
with the following enigmatic words:

> non te nullius exercent numinis irae;
> magna luis commissa: tibi has miserabilis Orpheus
> haudquaquam ob meritum poenas, ni fata resistant,
> suscitat, et rapta graviter pro coniuge saevit.
>
> $$(453-56)$$

> The anger of a not inconsiderable spirit harasses you;
> You are atoning for great crimes; miserable Orpheus stirs up these punishments
> for you, not because of what is deserved, if the fates should not resist,
> and he rages sorrowfully on behalf of his wife snatched away.

The surface meaning of these lines implies that Orpheus has sent the
plague on Aristaeus' bees to punish him for trying to rape Eurydice, an
act which led to her death. Such an interpretation would reflect a moral
universe in which the events of the natural world can be comprehended
in a meaningful way and there are repercussions for sins. Yet, on closer
examination, Proteus' words are not so straightforward. The great sin that
Aristaeus committed has never been mentioned before now and so comes
across as a contrivance of narrative. The explanation becomes more suspect
when the cause of Aristaeus' punishment is later contradicted by Cyrene,
who attributes the cause of disease to the nymphs instead of to Orpheus
(532).

In addition, despite the fact that Aristaeus has supposedly already suffered the punishment, Proteus adds in a strange conditional: *ni fata resistant*
("if the fates should not resist," 455) – if the fates should not resist what?
If it is the "punishment," then it seems a strange clause because they have
not resisted that. It is usually taken to mean that Orpheus' punishment

---

in nature. In the *Georgics* such a symbolic conflict effectively epitomizes in a single scene one of
the major themes of the entire poem." Morgan (1999) 84–93 presents a more specific philosophical
interpretation of Aristaeus' conquering of Proteus and suggests it represents the Stoic theory of
creation, with Proteus representing inactive matter and Aristaeus cause or reason.

will still be resisted by the fates since Aristaeus will get new bees, but that turn of events does not mean the punishment did not occur, and if they really had resisted the punishment, there would be no need for atonement. While certainly there are ways to explain the conditional without calling the narrative of events into question, I would argue that it forces the reader to struggle to make sense of the chain of events, which are presented in such an oracular manner by Proteus. Further confusion is caused by the enigmatic phrase *haudquaquam ob meritum* ("not because of what is deserved," 455). Commentators have noted the many possible meanings of this phrase and come to different conclusions about which is intended:

> *haudquaquam ob meritum poenas*: taken in three ways: (a) 'penalties which you have by no means deserved [because you did not intend Eurydice's death]'; (b) (with the Palatinus reading *ad* for *ob*) 'penalties which are by no means as severe as you deserve'; (c) (taking the phrase with *miserabilis*) 'Orpheus, wretched by no means according to his deserts'; (b) seems excessive and (c) somewhat harsh grammatically. (Thomas [1988] 2.226 [*ad* 4.455])

> *haudquaquam ob meritum poenas*: with *ob*, the reading of all our witnesses save one, the sense is clear: 'punishment which you have not deserved' . . . This will not do for Aristaeus, who has 'magna commissa' to his discredit and has, if anything, been let off rather lightly. Serv. makes it mean 'not up to the level of what you deserve' ('non tales quales mereris'), and so does Norden; but this is contrary to the obvious sense of the words. We must therefore read *ad* for *ob* with the Palatinus, and translate 'by no means up to your deserts'. To separate *haudquaquam ob meritum* from *poenas* and take it in retrospect with *miserabilis* gives an impossible order of words, and if it were possible, we are not concerned with what Orpheus deserves. (Mynors [1990] 315 [*ad* 4.455–56])

> The fates are on Aristaeus' side . . . but there is a hint that the wise seer is not wholly in agreement, for his phrase *haudquaquam ob meritum* in 455, implying that Orpheus' suffering [*sic*] are 'undeserved,' places the weight of moral judgment against Aristaeus. (Segal [1989] 76)

Why should this crucial phrase be so unclear when the moral message of the punishment is at stake? I would argue that its lack of clarity is precisely the point, or, to quote Clint Eastwood, "Deserve's got nothing to do with it."[47] Readers who want to mold Proteus' words into a clear story of sin, punishment, and atonement, must actively force the narrative into that shape, just as Aristaeus must force Proteus to provide *oracula*.

---

[47] *Unforgiven*, Dir. Clint Eastwood. Cf. Nappa (2005) 201: "Yet attempting to place or remove blame here obscures a more important aspect of the story: Eurydice fails to see a poisonous serpent and so it kills her. Guilt is quite irrelevant in the natural world."

Proteus never does tell Aristaeus how to get his bees back, nor does he explicitly create a favorable outcome (*eventusque secundet*, 397). Instead, he follows up his enigmatic opening words with the tragic story of Orpheus' grief, which leads Orpheus to try to win Eurydice back from the underworld through his song. In Proteus' shocking version of the tale,[48] Orpheus ends up killing her again when "madness" (*dementia*, 488) seizes his mind and causes him to break the seemingly arbitrary rule that he cannot look back at Eurydice (488–91). Proteus' tale, then, is a story of failure, and particularly of the failure of human beings to change the laws of nature and conquer death. The *Manes* ("spirits of the Underworld") do not know how to forgive (489) and can only temporarily be manipulated to serve human needs. Orpheus, the second poet figure in the tale, initially shares with Aristaeus the characteristics of the farmer, who struggles against chaos and tries to repair the damage caused by death and destruction.[49] In that respect, he also resembles the version of the contemplative life that merged with that of the active life in the earlier sections of the *Georgics*.[50] After his complete failure to succeed at changing nature, however, Orpheus comes to resemble Proteus more,[51] as he responds to the second eruption of chaos

[48] As Thomas (1988) II.225 (*ad* 4.453–527) notes, "Orpheus traditionally succeeds." See also Gale (2003) 333–34 for a list of sources for the Orpheus myth and discussion of Virgil's innovation in having Orpheus fail. She concludes, "[M]ost, if not all, pre-Virgilian accounts of Orpheus' *catabasis* ended with the successful restoration of Eurydice to life" (333).

[49] *Contra* Segal (1989) 45: "[Orpheus] makes no attempt to use nature for his own ends, to work upon it."

[50] While Aristaeus and Orpheus are frequently deemed opposites of each other in critical discussions of the epyllion, Batstone (1997) 127 recognizes their deeper similarities: "The figures merge as they separate: both are passionate, self-absorbed, and destructive of others; both destroy Eurydice but remain indifferent to guilt . . . Both recall the farmer, staving off the backward pull of entropy (see 1.199–203). Both seek to dominate nature and death." For further bibliography on their characters and particularly their symbolic relation to each other, see Kronenberg (2000) 357–59, to which could be added Gale (2003) 331–33 and Nappa (2005) 201. One could even argue that Proteus and Aristaeus have something in common in that they are both shepherd figures (cf. 4.317, *pastor Aristaeus* ["shepherd Aristaeus"] with the simile in 4.433–36, which, drawing on Homer's brief shepherd-Proteus comparison in *Od*. 4.413, compares Proteus to a shepherd), though the figure of the *pastor* in the context of the *Georgics* is multivalent and might connote the *otium* of pastoral poetry as much as the political allegories of book 3. Thus, in the absence of other parallels, Proteus and Aristaeus seem to remain opposing types of figures in the *Georgics*.

[51] As Morgan (1999) 151 has nicely pointed out, Orpheus and Proteus are nearly anagrams: "It has been noted by Thomas that Proteus has much in common with the protagonist of the story he tells . . . To begin with, the names Orpheus and Proteus are almost anagrams of each other. But perhaps more cogently, at 4.509 the two seem to coalesce even in respect of the telling of the story: Proteus describes Orpheus singing *haec*, that is, apparently, precisely the content of Proteus' story. Thomas writes, 'Orpheus is more than just a character in the action; Proteus suggests that he is responsible for the actual poem – *haec* refers to the entire song.'" The Thomas quotation is from Thomas (1988) II.233 (*ad* 4.509).

in his life not with a renewed attempt at order but by singing tragic songs (507–15) until Bacchants tear him apart (520–22).[52]

Proteus' song, then, like Orpheus', is not ultimately about the moral order of the world, but about the chaos of life. As Cyrene had warned (398–99), Proteus does not willingly reveal causes or create favorable outcomes, and Proteus is not a willing didactic poet in the deepest sense: unless he is forced to, he will not package the world into a comprehensible tale of cause and effect with a happy ending. Even when he is forced to do so, his language creates gaps in the logic of his explanation (453–56), and he follows his short moralistic explanation of the plague with a longer, more affecting story of inexplicable failure. I would argue that in Proteus we have a model of Virgil as a didactic poet. The sea-god's *doli . . . inanes* are Virgil's deceptive games, his recalcitrance against Maecenas' "not gentle commands" (*haud mollia iussa*, 3.41), and his attempt to subvert his own narrative of the causes of things.[53] Virgil presents two visions in the *Georgics*: one from the perspective of farmers and poets who struggle to mold the world both intellectually and physically such that it produces "favorable outcomes," and one from the perspective of a different type of poet figure, who pokes holes in the logic of the first vision and presents an alternative image of an amoral and, from a human perspective, tragic universe.

"But not Cyrene . . ." (*at non Cyrene*, 530). While Proteus' song is over, Virgil's is not. As soon as Proteus leaves the scene, Cyrene takes over and the lesson of Orpheus' grief and loss is superseded by religious ritual. It

---

[52] Cf. Gale (2003) 332: "It is significant, too, that, once his attempt to recover Eurydice has failed, he puts the power of his song to no practical end."

[53] Gale (2003) suggests other ways in which Proteus' poetry compares with Virgil's: "What Proteus offers is neither prophecy nor advice, but an *aetiology* of the disease. In this respect, he acts as a *vates* in the Augustan sense of the word, as a poet rather than a prophet. Despite the overtly practical aspect of the *Georgics*, Virgil, too, has been concerned with aetiology through the poem" (335); "Virgil's portrayal of Proteus resembles his self-depiction in the *sphragis* and elsewhere in other ways, too. Like both the poet himself and his counterpart Orpheus, Proteus is a detached figure. He is depicted as a shepherd enjoying his noonday *otium*, as a prophet whose knowledge must be extorted from him and is not bestowed willingly on those who require it" (336). Schiesaro (1997) 67 prefers to identify Virgil with Cyrene: "Although it is tempting to identify Proteus with the poetic narrator of the *Georgics*, this solution entails considerable difficulties. Unlike Proteus, the narrator shows his ability to deliver a complete and understandable answer to the question he asks of the Muses at the beginning of the epyllion. It is Cyrene who, like the narrator, imparts *praecepta* both when she orders Aristaeus to seek Proteus' advice and when she explains what to do in order to restore the bees (548) . . . Similar in this respect to Cyrene, the narrator of the *Georgics* is not only the indispensable link to a world of knowledge which lies outside the reach of the common mortal, the knowledge of the Muses or of Proteus, but he is also able to distill it into practical and valuable *praecepta*." Ultimately, of course, it is up to each reader to decide whether the poet of the *Georgics* bestows practical *praecepta* like Cyrene or whether he fails, like Proteus, to deliver "a complete and understandable answer" to the questions raised by the text.

is Cyrene, and not Proteus, who finally fixes things and allows Aristaeus to "remove the grim cares from his spirit" (*tristis animo deponere curas*, 531). She gives him a new cause of disease, which is now attributed to angry nymph friends of Eurydice (532–34), and, better yet, a ritual with which to appease the nymphs' anger and get new bees (534–47). Aristaeus performs the ritual and sees a miraculous portent (*dictu mirabile monstrum*, 554): new bees burst forth from the rotting flesh of the oxen (555–58) and thus fulfill the promise of book 4 – the rebirth of the group, if not of the individual. "Pessimistic" readings of this narrative frequently focus on the extreme violence that is required in the ritual for the restoration of the bees, as well as on Aristaeus' lack of repentance for Eurydice's death and the lingering sadness of Orpheus' tale (e.g. Boyle [1986]); "optimistic" readings privilege the happy ending and the act of rebirth, which can compensate for death, as well as the constructive aspects of the violence in the tale – with political implications for Octavian (e.g. Morgan [1999]); and "ambivalent" readings point to the unresolved tensions between the forces of sadness and hope, success and failure, in the epyllion (e.g. Gale [2003]). While all of these readings find support in the text, I would suggest that a more complicated attitude towards the contrast between Orpheus' and Aristaeus' fates emerges if placed in the context of the dialectic between farmers and poets that goes throughout the *Georgics*.

    The contrast between the fates of Orpheus and Aristaeus is really a contrast between the *praecepta* of Proteus and Cyrene. Proteus and Cyrene equip Aristaeus with very different kinds of information: Proteus' account is primarily a poetic description of the failure of an individual to conquer death and has no apparent practical purpose for Aristaeus, who also gives no indication that he has learned or understood anything that Proteus has said. In contrast, Cyrene tries to turn Aristaeus away from sad thoughts (531) and diverts his attention with a ritual, which is intended to give him new bees.[54] Aristaeus' exact repetition of Cyrene's instructions provides a sense of order and accomplishment, and the appearance of new bees seems to validate Cyrene's approach. Yet, as many have noted, there are also ways in which her *praecepta* are called into question. For one thing, Proteus gives a *morbi causa* that differs from Cyrene's; since the former possesses

---

[54] As Segal (1989) 42 notes, "As far as the narrative itself is concerned, Proteus is really superfluous. Aristaeus' mother, Cyrene, does indeed say (398) that Proteus will give *praecepta*, the needed practical instructions. But, as has been seen above, he leaps abruptly away at the crucial moment (527 ff.), and it is Cyrene who in fact gives the *praecepta* (531 ff.), which forthwith prove their efficacy. Thus Cyrene has known what to do all along. She has not needed Proteus at all."

"universal knowledge,"[55] this difference calls into question Cyrene's own access to or willingness to convey true knowledge of the universe. Her ritual instructions also differ from the technical description of *bugonia* that leads into the epyllion (4.295–314), a fact that has led Habinek and others to suggest that the second version of the bugonia has been fashioned into a ritual sacrifice that restores order.[56]

If the *bugonia* is fashioned into a sacrifice, then Virgil shows sacrifice and *religio* to be diversions that act to deflect attention away from sadness and the nature of things. The *bugonia* may not "work" as an actual scientific device, but it does seem to work for now as a device of *religio*.[57] Whether it works as a permanent solution to the problems humans face in the universe is, I think, answered by the previous three books of the *Georgics*. Indeed, the ending focus on Aristaeus and *religio* sends the reader back to the beginning again, where Aristaeus finally finds his deification by being mentioned obliquely as the inhabitant of the woods of Ceos (1.14–15). The cycles of pessimism and optimism in the *Georgics* show that the farmer's attempts to order the world are never permanent accomplishments because they try to shape nature into something it is not. *This* knowledge

---

[55] Cf. Boyle (1986) 75: "And Proteus – it should not be forgotten . . . possesses universal knowledge (392 f.): a fact which both associates his narrative with Virgil's Hesiodic ideal (and thus with Ascraean Virgil himself) and endows it with the status of an existential paradigm."

[56] Habinek (1990) 211–12: "And indeed, it is through an account of conventional animal sacrifice, the central and defining ritual of Roman, as of Greek religion, that Vergil completes the history of the bees, and celebrates the potential for renewal of human society as well." Cf. also Bettini (1991) 209, Dyson (1996) 280–81, Gale (2000) 110–11, and Nappa (2005) 212 and 268 n. 91. Thomas (1991) has noted the many ways in which Aristaeus' "sacrifice" is not precisely a sacrifice and, more importantly, not a simple affirmation of order and renewal. Morgan's (1999) 112–13 modification of Habinek's thesis, that "the details of Aristaeus' ritual . . . are at least very strongly *reminiscent* of sacrificial practice," seems reasonable, but does not solve the problem of interpreting these sacrificial allusions. As Thomas (1991) 215 notes, "the only *actual* instance of a formal sacrifice in the poem" (i.e. *G.* 3.486–93) is a miserable failure, and "[a]ny interpretation of the poem, then, that claims resolution to the problems of this world through sacrifices which are not real sacrifices, and at the same time fails to confront the only actual sacrifice the poem contains, must be found wanting" (216).

[57] Critics have noted that Virgil introduces the *bugonia* as a *thauma* with suspect scientific credentials. See Gale (2000) 229: "The *bugonia*, which forms the climax of the poem and the connecting link between the two halves of book 4, is elaborately framed as the ultimate *thauma*. Not only is it explicitly called a *monstrum* ('prodigy', 554) and explained only in mythological terms, with no hint of a scientific explanation, but the phenomenon is located in Egypt, the archetypal setting for wonders and romance" and Thomas (1988) II.196 (*ad* 4.281–314): "Though the practice is mentioned by technical writers (not, however, by Aristotle), since it is a fiction and an impossibility, it is not described in any detail by, for instance, Varro (*R.R.* 2.5.5; 3.16.4), who regards it as a piece of traditional lore (at 2.5.5 it is included with Jupiter's metamorphosis into a bull to abduct Europa). V. himself knew it was an impossibility, and he says as much by presenting it as an eastern θαῦμα ('marvel'); 287–94, 309 nn. And who in the Mediterranean world would kill an ox in order to gain a hive?" See also Boyle (1986) 74 n. 83 and Ross (1987) 216–18.

is ultimately the lesson of Proteus' (and Virgil's) poetry, and it is a lesson that Aristaeus must ignore if he is to find success and a happy ending.

In his analysis of the epyllion, Nappa (2005) emphasizes how heavily the text depends "on what readers bring to it. Salvation can only be found here by those who already believe that it is possible; the hostility of the universe and the futility of life do not exist for those who do not believe in them" (213). I agree that Virgil has crafted his text in such a way as to separate readers themselves into "farmers" and "poets," and Virgil ends his work with a final "sphragis" that might suggest two such opposed readers of his poem (4.559–66): while great Caesar was fulminating by the Euphrates, giving laws to willing people as victor, and attempting to reach Olympus, Virgil was singing of crops, cattle, and trees, and enjoying his pursuit of ignoble *otium.* Caesar utilizes *religio* ("he strives after the path to Olympus," *viamque adfectat Olympo*, 562), *ratio* ("he gives laws," *dat iura*, 562) and *gloria* ("and as victor," *victorque*, 561) to conquer the world, while Virgil pursues a contemplative life with no obvious goal beyond *ignobile otium.*

Virgil seems committed at the end to a contemplative life that resists the ordering impulses of the farmer or politician. He does reflect, however, on his earlier pastoral activity and calls himself "bold in his youth" (*audaxque iuventa*, 565) for singing of Tityrus. Perhaps this line reflects his own previous desire to find an "answer" to life in poetry, a desire that was poignantly recalled at the end of *Georgics* book 2. Thus, while the *Georgics* expresses a Menippean sort of distrust of dogmatic systems and over-arching solutions and often portrays the farmer's attempts to restructure the world as violent and mistaken, it also expresses much sympathy and understanding for those who try to hang onto a meaningful world and presents its author as once implicated in the same struggle.

Epilogue

I have designed my readings of Xenophon's, Varro's, and Virgil's agricultural dialogues to work independently of each other, though I hope to have shown ways in which they may also have been in dialogue with each other and with the genre of philosophical or Menippean satire. Viewing the *Georgics* as an outgrowth of philosophical dialogue, and not just of various genres of poetry, presents new ways of thinking about the poem's polyphony, as well as its allegorical and ironic aspects. Allowing Varro's dialogue the importance of a philosophical satire forces the reader to come up with explanations for the many contradictory and surprising aspects of the text that are too easily swept beneath the rug of Varro's old age, professed haste, and pedantic tendencies. Finally, granting Xenophon's *Oeconomicus* the status of a true Socratic dialogue integrates it with Plato's more famous renditions of his master's conversations and with a tradition of dialectical philosophy that requires careful reading and a literary sensibility to decipher. When each work is read in such a manner, a remarkably similar allegorical use of farmers, herds, and beehives emerges, one that questioned the foundations of politics and morality long before Mandeville scandalized Europe with his greedy bees.

Bibliography

Adkins, A. W. H. (1960) *Merit and Responsibility: A Study in Greek Values.* Oxford: Clarendon Press.

Adolf, R. (1975) "'What Pierces or Strikes': Prose Style in The Fable of the Bees," in Primer (1975) 157–67.

Ahbel-Rappe, S. and R. Kamtekar, eds. (2006) *A Companion to Socrates.* Malden, MA: Blackwell Publishing.

Alfonsi, L. (1961–64) "La tradizione ciceroniana dell'«Economico» di Senofonte," *Ciceroniana* 3–6: 7–17.

Algra, K., J. Barnes, J. Mansfeld, and M. Schofield, eds. (1999) *The Cambridge History of Hellenistic Philosophy.* Cambridge University Press.

Allen, D. (2004) "Burning *The Fable of the Bees*: The Incendiary Authority of Nature," in Daston and Vidal (2004) 74–99.

Ambler, W. H. (1996) "On the *Oeconomicus*," in Bartlett (1996) 102–31.
    trans. (2001) *Xenophon: The Education of Cyrus.* Ithaca, NY: Cornell University Press.

André, J.-M. (1966) *L'Otium dans la vie morale et intellectuelle romaine, des origines à l'époque augustéenne.* Paris: Presses universitaires de France.

Angeli, A. (1990) "La critica filodemea all'*Economico* di Senofonte," *CErc* 20: 39–51.

Annas, J. (1992) "Ancient Ethics and Modern Morality," *Philosophical Perspectives* 6: 119–36.
    (1993) *The Morality of Happiness.* New York: Oxford University Press.
    (1999) *Platonic Ethics, Old and New.* Ithaca, NY: Cornell University Press.
    (2002) "What are Plato's 'Middle' Dialogues in the Middle of," in Annas and Rowe (2002) 1–23.

Annas, J. and C. Rowe, eds. (2002) *New Perspectives on Plato, Modern and Ancient.* Cambridge, MA: Harvard University Press.

Arieti, J. A. (1991) *Interpreting Plato: The Dialogues as Drama.* Savage, MD: Rowman & Littlefield Publishers.

Armstrong, D., J. Fish, P. A. Johnston, and M. B. Skinner, eds. (2004) *Vergil, Philodemus, and the Augustans.* Austin: University of Texas Press.

Ax, W. (1995) "*Disputare in utramque partem.* Zu literarischen Plan und zur dialektischen Methode Varros in *de lingua Latina* 8–10," *RhM* 138: 146–77.

Badian, E. (1970) "Additional Notes on Roman Magistrates," *Athenaeum* 48: 3–14.
  (1996) "Tremelius Scrofa, Gnaeus," *OCD* 3rd edn.: 1549.
Baier, T. (1997) *Werk und Wirkung Varros im Spiegel seiner Zeitgenossen: Von Cicero bis Ovid.* Stuttgart: Franz Steiner.
Bakhtin, M. M. (1981) *The Dialogic Imagination: Four Essays.* Ed. M. Holquist, trans. C. Emerson and M. Holquist. Austin: University of Texas Press.
  (1984) *Problems of Dostoevsky's Poetics.* Ed. and trans. C. Emerson. Minneapolis: University of Minnesota Press.
Balansard, A. (2001) *Technè dans les Dialogues de Platon: l'empreinte de la sophistique.* Sankt Augustin: Academia.
Balot, R. K. (2001) *Greed and Injustice in Classical Athens.* Princeton University Press.
Barnes, J. and M. Griffin, eds. (1997) *Philosophia Togata II: Plato and Aristotle at Rome.* Oxford: Clarendon Press.
Bartlett, R. C., ed. (1996) *Xenophon: The Shorter Socratic Writings; Apology of Socrates to the Jury, Oeconomicus, and Symposium.* Ithaca, NY: Cornell University Press.
Batstone, W. (1997) "Virgilian Didaxis: Value and Meaning in the *Georgics*," in Martindale (1997) 125–44.
Bayet, J. (1967) *Mélanges de littérature latine.* Rome: Edizioni di storia e letteratura.
Bernard, J. D., ed. (1986) *Vergil at 2000: Commemorative Essays on the Poet and His Influence.* New York: AMS Press.
Betensky, A. (1972) "The Literary Use of Animals in Lucretius' *De Rerum Natura* and Virgil's *Georgics*," Dissertation Yale University.
Bettini, M. (1991) *Anthropology and Roman Culture: Kinship, Time, Images of the Soul.* Trans. J. Van Sickle. Baltimore: Johns Hopkins University Press.
Blondell, R. (2002) *The Play of Character in Plato's Dialogues.* Cambridge University Press.
Bloom, A., trans. (1968) *The Republic of Plato.* New York: Basic Books.
Bloomer, W. M. (1997) *Latinity and Literary Society at Rome.* Philadelphia: University of Pennsylvania Press.
Blössner, N. (2007) "The City-Soul Analogy," in Ferrari (2007) 345–85.
Bobonich, C. (1994) "Akrasia and Agency in Plato's *Laws* and *Republic*," *AGPh* 76: 3–36.
Boissier, G. (1861) *Étude sur la vie et les ouvrages de M. T. Varron.* Paris: L. Hachette et cie.
Booth, W. C. (1974) *A Rhetoric of Irony.* The University of Chicago Press.
Bosman, P. (2006) "Selling Cynicism: The Pragmatics of Diogenes' Comic Performances," *CQ* 56: 93–104.
Boyle, A. J., ed. (1979a) *Virgil's Ascraean Song: Ramus Essays on the Georgics.* Berwick, Vic.: Aureal Publications.
  (1979b) "*In Medio Caesar.* Paradox and Politics in Virgil's *Georgics*," in Boyle (1979a) 65–86.
  (1986) *The Chaonian Dove: Studies in the Eclogues, Georgics, and Aeneid of Virgil.* Leiden: E. J. Brill.

Boys-Stones, G. R., ed. (2003a) *Metaphor, Allegory, and the Classical Tradition.* Oxford University Press.

(2003b) "Introduction," in Boys-Stones (2003a) 1–5.

Brandenburg, P. (2006) "Review of *Varro. Über die Landwirtschaft. Texte zur Forschung 87* by D. Flach, ed.," *BMCR* 2006.07.19.

Branham, R. B. (1996) "Defacing the Currency: Diogenes' Rhetoric and the Invention of Cynicism," in Branham and Goulet-Cazé (1996) 81–104.

Branham, R. B. and M.-O. Goulet-Cazé, eds. (1996). *The Cynics: The Cynic Movement in Antiquity and Its Legacy.* Berkeley and Los Angeles: University of California Press.

Braund, S. H. (1988) *Beyond Anger: A Study of Juvenal's Third Book of Satires.* Cambridge University Press.

ed. (1989a) *Satire and Society in Ancient Rome.* University of Exeter.

(1989b) "City and Country in Roman Satire," in Braund (1989a) 23–47.

(1996) *The Roman Satirists and Their Masks.* London: Bristol Classical Press.

Brickhouse, T. C. and N. D. Smith (2000) *The Philosophy of Socrates.* Boulder, CO: Westview Press.

Bruell, C. (1987) "Xenophon," in Strauss and Cropsey (1987) 90–117.

Brunt, P. A. (1972) "Cn. Tremellius Scrofa the Agronomist," *CR* 22: 304–08.

Bryant, J. M. (1996) *Moral Codes and Social Structure in Ancient Greece: A Sociology of Greek Ethics from Homer to the Epicureans and Stoics.* Albany: State University of New York Press.

Buchheit, V. (1972) *Der Anspruch des Dichters in Vergils Georgika: Dichtertum und Heilsweg.* Darmstadt: Wissenschaftliche Buchgesellschaft.

Burck, E. (1929) "Die Komposition von Vergils *Georgika*," *Hermes* 64: 279–321.

Cairns, D. (1993) *Aidōs: The Psychology and Ethics of Honour and Shame in Ancient Greek Literature.* Oxford: Clarendon Press.

Campbell, J. S. (1982) "Initiation and the Role of Aristaeus in *Georgics* Four," *Ramus* 11: 105–15.

Cardauns, B. (2001) *Marcus Terentius Varro: Einführung in sein Werk.* Heidelberg: C. Winter.

Carter, L. B. (1986) *The Quiet Athenian.* Oxford: Clarendon Press.

Cascardi, A. J., ed. (1987) *Literature and the Question of Philosophy.* Baltimore: Johns Hopkins University Press.

Cèbe, J.-P. (1972) *Varron, Satires ménippées: Édition, traduction et commentaire.* vol. 1. Rome: École française de Rome.

Chandler, A. R. (1934–35) "The Nightingale in Greek and Latin Poetry," *CJ* 30: 78–84.

Chomarat, J. (1974) "L'initiation d'Aristée," *REL* 52: 185–207.

Christ, M. R. (2006) *The Bad Citizen in Classical Athens.* Cambridge University Press.

Christmann, E. (1982) "Zur Antiken Georgica-Rezeption," *WJA* 8: 57–67.

Cima, M. and E. La Rocca, eds. (1998) *Horti Romani: Atti del Convegno Internazionale, Roma, 4–6 maggio 1995.* Rome: "L'Erma" di Bretschneider.

Clay, D. (1994) "The Origins of the Socratic Dialogue," in Vander Waerdt (1994) 23–47.

(2002) "*Reading the Republic*" in Griswold Jr. (2002a) 19–33.

Clay, J. S. (1976) "The Argument of the End of Vergil's Second Georgic," *Philologus* 120: 232–45.

Clayman, D. L. (1980) *Callimachus' Iambi*. Leiden: E. J. Brill.

Colebrook, C. (2004) *Irony*. New York: Routledge.

Collart, J. (1963) "Analogie et anomalie," in Reverdin (1963) 117–40.

ed. (1978) *Varron, grammaire antique et stylistique latine*. Paris: Les Belles Lettres.

Connor, P. (1979) "The *Georgics* as Description: Aspects and Qualifications," in Boyle (1979a) 34–58.

Connors, C. (1997) "Field and Forum: Culture and Agriculture in Roman Rhetoric," in Dominik (1997) 71–89.

Conte, G. B. (1994) *Latin Literature: a History*. Trans. J. B. Solodow, rev. D. Fowler and G. W. Most. Baltimore: Johns Hopkins University Press.

Cook, A. B. (1895) "The Bee in Greek Mythology," *JHS* 15: 1–24.

Cossarini, A. (1976–77) "*Dominus* e *praedium* in Catone. Elementi di una ideologia," *AIV* 135: 71–86.

(1979–80) "Il prestigio dell'agricoltura in Sallustio e Cicerone," *AIV* 138: 355–64.

Cramer, R. (1998) *Vergils Weltsicht: Optimismus und Pessimismus in Vergils Georgica*. Berlin: De Gruyter.

Crowther, N. B. (1979) "Water and Wine as Symbols of Inspiration," *Mnemosyne* 32: 1–11.

Curtis, R. I., ed. (1989) *Studia Pompeiana & Classica in Honor of Wilhelmina F. Jashemski*. 2 vols. New Rochelle, NY: A. D. Caratzas.

Dahlmann, H. (1935) "M. Terentius Varro," *RE* Suppl. 6: 1172–1277.

[1954]/(1999) "Der Bienenstaat in Vergils Georgica," in Hardie (1999) II.253–67 = *Abhandl. der Akad. der Wiss. & der Lit. Mainz, Geistes- & Sozialwiss. Kl.* (1954) 10: 547–62.

Danzig, G. (2003) "Why Socrates was not a Farmer: Xenophon's *Oeconomicus* as a Philosophical Dialogue," *G&R* 50: 57–76.

Daston, L. and F. Vidal, eds. (2004) *The Moral Authority of Nature*. The University of Chicago Press.

Davies, J. K. (1971) *Athenian Propertied Families, 600–300 BC*. Oxford: Clarendon Press.

Davis, P. J. (1979) "Vergil's *Georgics* and the Pastoral Ideal," in Boyle (1979a) 22–33.

Decleva Caizzi, F. (1999) "Protagoras and Antiphon: Sophistic Debates on Justice," in Long (1999) 311–31.

Della Corte, F. (1970) *Varrone, il terzo gran lume Romano*. 2nd edn. Florence: La nuova Italia.

Dentith, S. (2000) *Parody*. New York: Routledge.

Descat, R. (1988) "Aux origines de l'*oikonomia* grecque," *QUCC* 28: 103–19.

Destrée, P. and N. D. Smith, eds. (2005) *Socrates' Divine Sign: Religion, Practice and Value in Socratic Philosophy*. Kelowna, BC: Academic Printing & Publishing.

Diederich, S. (2007) *Römische Agrarhandbücher zwischen Fachwissenschaft, Literatur und Ideologie.* Berlin: Walter de Gruyter.

Dillon, J. M. and A. A. Long, eds. (1988) *The Question of "Eclecticism": Studies in Later Greek Philosophy.* Berkeley and Los Angeles: University of California Press.

Dominik, W. J., ed. (1997) *Roman Eloquence: Rhetoric in Society and Literature.* New York: Routledge.

Doody, A. (2007) "Virgil the Farmer? Critiques of the *Georgics* in Columella and Pliny," *CP* 102: 180–97.

Dorion, L.-A. (2006) "Xenophon's Socrates," in Ahbel-Rappe and Kamtekar (2006) 93–109.

Dover, K. J. (1974) *Greek Popular Morality in the Time of Plato and Aristotle.* Reprint, 1994. Indianapolis: Hackett Publishing Company.

Dudley, D. R. (1937) *A History of Cynicism: From Diogenes to the 6th Century AD.* Reprint. Chicago: Ares Publishers Inc.

Duff, J. W. (1936) *Roman Satire: Its Outlook on Social Life.* Berkeley and Los Angeles: University of California Press.

Dutton, D. (1987) "Why Intentionalism Won't Go Away," in Cascardi (1987) 192–209.

Dyson, J. T. (1994) "*Georgics* 2.503–12: The Temple's Shadow," *Vergilius* 40: 3–18.
    (1996) "*Caesi Iuvenci* and *Pietas Impia* in Virgil," *CJ* 91: 277–86.

Earl, D. C. (1967) *The Moral and Political Tradition of Rome.* Ithaca, NY: Cornell University Press.

Edmunds, L. (2001) *Intertextuality and the Reading of Roman Poetry.* Baltimore: Johns Hopkins University Press.
    (2004) "The Practical Irony of the Historical Socrates," *Phoenix* 58: 193–207.

Edwards, C. (1993) *The Politics of Immorality in Ancient Rome.* Cambridge University Press.

Engelke, C. (1912) *Quae ratio intercedat inter Vergilii Georgica et Varronis Rerum Rusticarum libros.* Blankenburg: Typis O. Kircher.

Faraguna, M. (1994) "Alle origini dell'*oikonomia*: dall'Anonimo di Giamblico ad Aristotele," *RAL* 9.5: 551–89.

Farrell, J. (1991) *Vergil's Georgics and the Traditions of Ancient Epic: The Art of Allusion in Literary History.* New York: Oxford University Press.

Fehling, D. (1956–57) "Varro und die grammatische Lehre von der Analogie und der Flexion," *Glotta* 35: 214–70 and 36: 48–100.

Fenik, B. (1962) "Horace's First and Sixth Roman Odes and the Second Georgic," *Hermes* 90: 72–96.

Ferrari, G. R. F. (1997) "Strauss's Plato," *Arion* 5: 36–65.
    ed. (2007) *The Cambridge Companion to Plato's Republic.* Cambridge University Press.

Ferrary, J.-L. (1984) "L'archéologie du *De re publica* (2, 2, 4–37, 63): Cicéron entre Polybe et Platon," *JRS* 74: 87–98.
    (1995) "The Statesman and the Law in the Political Philosophy of Cicero," in Laks and Schofield (1995) 48–73.

Field, G. C. (1967) *Plato and His Contemporaries: A Study in Fourth-century Life and Thought.* 3rd edn. London: Methuen.

Figueira, T. (forthcoming) "Xenophon and the Spartan Economy," in Powell and Richer (forthcoming).

Firpo, L., ed. (1970) *Storia delle idee politiche economiche e sociali.* Vol. 1. Turin: Unione tipografico-editrice torinese.

Fitzgerald, W. (1996) "Labor and Laborer in Latin Poetry: the Case of the *Moretum*," *Arethusa* 29: 389–418

Flach, D., ed. (1996) *Marcus Terentius Varro: Gespräche über die Landwirtschaft.* Buch 1. Darmstadt: Wissenschaftliche Buchgesellschaft.

    ed. (1997) *Marcus Terentius Varro: Gespräche über die Landwirtschaft.* Buch 2. Darmstadt: Wissenschaftliche Buchgesellschaft.

    ed. (2002) *Marcus Terentius Varro: Gespräche über die Landwirtschaft.* Buch 3. Darmstadt: Wissenschaftliche Buchgesellschaft.

Fox, M. (2007) *Cicero's Philosophy of History.* New York: Oxford University Press.

Freudenburg, K. (1993) *The Walking Muse: Horace on the Theory of Satire.* Princeton University Press.

    ed. (2005) *The Cambridge Companion to Roman Satire.* Cambridge University Press.

Frye, N. (1957) *Anatomy of Criticism: Four Essays.* Princeton University Press.

Gale, M. (1991) "Man and Beast in Lucretius and the *Georgics*," *CQ* 41: 414–26.

    (1994) *Myth and Poetry in Lucretius.* Cambridge University Press.

    (2000) *Virgil on the Nature of Things: The Georgics, Lucretius and the Didactic Tradition.* Cambridge University Press.

    (2003) "Poetry and the Backward Glance in Virgil's *Georgics* and *Aeneid*," *TAPA* 133: 323–52.

Geffcken, J. (1896) *Leonidas von Tarent.* Leipzig: B. G. Teubner.

Giannantoni, G. and M. Gigante, eds. (1996) *Epicureismo greco e romano: Atti del congresso internazionale, Napoli, 19–26 maggio 1993.* 3 vols. Naples: Bibliopolis.

Gigante, M. (1971) *L'Edera di Leonida.* Naples: Morano.

Glucker, J. (1988) "Cicero's Philosophical Affiliations," in Dillon and Long (1988) 34–69.

Goldsmith, M. M. (1985) *Private Vices, Public Benefits: Bernard Mandeville's Social and Political Thought.* Cambridge University Press.

    (2000) "Mandeville's Pernicious System" in Prior (2000) 71–84.

Gonzalez, F., ed. (1995) *The Third Way: New Directions in Platonic Studies.* Lanham, MD: Rowman & Littlefield Publishers, Inc.

Gordon, J. (1996) "Against Vlastos on Complex Irony," *CQ* 46: 131–37.

Gottschalk, H. B. (1980) "Varro and Ariston of Chios," *Mnemosyne* 33: 359–62.

Gow, A. S. F. and D. L. Page, eds. (1965) *The Greek Anthology: Hellenistic Epigrams.* Cambridge University Press.

Gray, V. J. (1998) *The Framing of Socrates: The Literary Interpretation of Xenophon's Memorabilia.* Stuttgart: Franz Steiner.

    (2000) "Xenophon and Isocrates," in Rowe and Schofield (2000) 142–54.

(2004) "A Short Response to David M. Johnson 'Xenophon's Socrates on Law and Justice'," *AncPhil* 24: 442–46.

ed. (2007) *Xenophon on Government*. Cambridge University Press.

Green, C. M. C. (1997) "Free as a Bird: Varro *De Re Rustica* 3," *AJP* 118: 427–48.

Griffin, D. (1994) *Satire: A Critical Reintroduction*. Lexington: The University Press of Kentucky.

Griffin, J. (1979) "The Fourth *Georgic*, Virgil, and Rome," *G&R* 26: 61–80.

Griffith, M. and D. J. Mastronarde, eds. (1990) *Cabinet of the Muses: Essays on Classical and Comparative Literature in Honor of Thomas G. Rosenmeyer*. Atlanta: Scholars Press.

Grilli, A. (1953) *Il problema della vita contemplativa nel mondo greco-romano*. Milan: Fratelli Bocca.

Griswold, C. L., Jr., ed. (2002a) *Platonic Writings, Platonic Readings*. University Park: The Pennsylvania State University Press. Originally published: New York: Routledge, 1988.

(2002b) "Irony in Platonic Dialogues," *Philosophy and Literature* 26: 84–106.

(2002c) "Comments on Kahn" in Annas and Rowe (2002) 129–44.

Gruen, E. S. (1974) *The Last Generation of the Roman Republic*. Berkeley and Los Angeles: University of California Press.

Guiraud, C., ed. (1985) *Varron: Économie rurale*. Livre 2. Paris: Les Belles Lettres.

ed. (1997) *Varron: Économie rurale*. Livre 3. Paris: Les Belles Lettres.

Guthrie, W. K. C. (1971) *Socrates*. Cambridge University Press.

Gutzwiller, K. J. (1991) *Theocritus' Pastoral Analogies: The Formation of a Genre*. Madison: The University of Wisconsin Press.

(1998) *Poetic Garlands: Hellenistic Epigrams in Context*. Berkeley and Los Angeles: University of California Press.

Habinek, T. N. (1990) "Sacrifice, Society, and Vergil's Ox-Born Bees," in Griffith and Mastronarde (1990) 209–23.

(1998) *The Politics of Latin Literature: Writing, Identity, and Empire in Ancient Rome*. Princeton University Press.

Habinek, T. and A. Schiesaro, eds. (1997) *The Roman Cultural Revolution*. Cambridge University Press.

Hardie, P. R. (1986) *Virgil's Aeneid: Cosmos and Imperium*. Oxford: Clarendon Press.

ed. (1999) *Virgil: Critical Assessments of Classical Authors*. 4 vols. New York: Routledge.

Harrison, E. L. (1979) "The Noric Plague in Vergil's Third *Georgic*," *PLLS* 2: 1–65.

Harrison, S. J., ed. (1995) *Homage to Horace: A Bimillenary Celebration*. Oxford: Clarendon Press.

Hart, R. and V. Tejera, eds. (1997) *Plato's Dialogues: The Dialogical Approach*. Lewiston, NY: E. Mellen Press.

Harth, P. (1969) "The Satiric Purpose of *The Fable of the Bees*," *Eighteenth-Century Studies* 2: 321–40.

Harvey, F. D. (1984) "The Wicked Wife of Ischomachus," *EMC* 28: 68–70.

Haubold, J. (2000) *Homer's People: Epic Poetry and Social Formation.* Cambridge University Press.

Heath, M. (2002) *Interpreting Classical Texts.* London: Duckworth.

Heisterhagen, R. (1952) "Die literarische Form der Rerum rusticarum libri Varros." Diss. Philipps-Universität Marburg.

Hemmenway, S. R. (1999) "The Techne-analogy in Socrates' Healthy City: Justice and the Craftsman in the *Republic*," *AncPhil* 19: 267–84.

Henderson, J. (2002) "Columella's Living Hedge: The Roman Gardening Book," *JRS* 92: 110–33.

    (2005) "The Turnaround: A Volume Retrospect on Roman Satires," in Freudenburg (2005) 309–18.

Henrichs, A. (1967) "Zwei Fragmente über die Erziehung (Antisthenes)," *ZPE* 1: 45–53.

    (1975) "Two Doxographical Notes: Democritus and Prodicus on Religion," *HSCP* 79: 93–123.

    (1984) "The Sophists and Hellenistic Religion: Prodicus as the Spiritual Father of the Isis Aretalogies," *HSCP* 88: 139–58.

Heurgon, J. (1950) "L'effort de style de Varron dans les *Res rusticae*," *RPh* 76: 57–71.

    (1978) *Varron: Économie rurale.* Livre 1. Paris: Les Belles Lettres.

Higginbotham, J. (1997) *Piscinae: Artificial Fishponds in Roman Italy.* Chapel Hill: University of North Carolina Press.

Higgins, W. E. (1977) *Xenophon the Athenian: The Problem of the Individual and the Society of the Polis.* Albany: State University of New York Press.

Hillman, T. P. (1993) "When did Lucullus Retire?" *Historia* 42: 211–28.

Hind, G. (1968) "Mandeville's *Fable of the Bees* as Menippean *Satire*," *Genre* 1: 307–15.

Hinds, S. (1998) *Allusion and Intertext: Dynamics of Appropriation in Roman Poetry.* Cambridge University Press.

Hirzel, R. (1895) *Der Dialog: Ein literarhistorischer Versuch.* 2 vols. Leipzig: S. Hirzel.

Hofmann, H. and A. Harder, eds. (1991) *Fragmenta Dramatica: Beiträge zur Interpretation der griechischen Tragikerfragmente und ihrer Wirkungsgeschichte.* Göttingen: Vandenhoeck & Ruprecht.

Hooley, D. M. (2007) *Roman Satire.* Malden, MA: Blackwell Publishing.

Hooper, W. D. and H. B. Ash, trans. (1934) *Marcus Porcius Cato: On Agriculture. Marcus Terentius Varro: On Agriculture.* Cambridge, MA: Harvard University Press.

Horne, T. A. (1978) *The Social Thought of Bernard Mandeville: Virtue and Commerce in Early Eighteenth-Century England.* London: Macmillan.

Howland, J. (1991) "Re-reading Plato: The Problem of Platonic Chronology," *Phoenix* 45: 189–214.

    (1993) *The Republic: The Odyssey of Philosophy.* New York: Twayne Publishers.

    (2000) "Xenophon's Philosophic Odyssey: On the *Anabasis* and Plato's *Republic*," *The American Political Science Review* 94: 875–89.

Huffman, C. A. (1993) *Philolaus of Croton: Pythagorean and Presocratic.* Cambridge University Press.

(2005) *Archytas of Tarentum: Pythagorean, Philosopher, and Mathematician King.* Cambridge University Press.

Humble, N. (2004) "The Author, Date and Purpose of Chapter 14 of the *Lakedaimoniōn Politeia*," in Tuplin (2004) 215–28.

Hundert, E. J. (1994) *The Enlightenment's Fable: Bernard Mandeville and the Discovery of Society.* Cambridge University Press.

Hunter, R. L. (1985) *The New Comedy of Greece and Rome.* Cambridge University Press.

(1995) "Written in the Stars: Poetry and Philosophy in the *Phainomena* of Aratus," *Arachnion* 2: www.cisi.unito.it/arachne/num2/hunter.html.

Hutcheon, L. [1985]/(2000) *A Theory of Parody: The Teachings of Twentieth-Century Art Forms.* Urbana: University of Illinois Press.

(1995) *Irony's Edge: The Theory and Politics of Irony.* New York: Routledge.

Hyland, D. A. (1995) *Finitude and Transcendence in the Platonic Dialogues.* Albany: State University of New York Press.

Innes, D. (2003) "Metaphor, Simile, and Allegory as Ornaments of Style," in Boys-Stones (2003a) 7–27.

Irwin, T. (1995) *Plato's Ethics.* New York: Oxford University Press.

Jack, M. (1975) "Religion and Ethics in Mandeville," in Primer (1975) 34–42.

(1987) *The Social and Political Thought of Bernard Mandeville.* New York: Garland Publishing.

(2000) "Mandeville, Johnson, Morality and Bees," in Prior (2000) 85–96.

Jashemski, W. F. (1979) "'The Garden of Hercules at Pompeii' (II.viii.6): The Discovery of a Commercial Flower Garden," *AJA* 83: 403–11.

Jenkyns, R. (1998) *Virgil's Experience: Nature and History, Times, Names, and Places.* Oxford: Clarendon Press.

Jocelyn, H. D. (1982) "Varro's *Antiquitates Rerum Divinarum* and Religious Affairs in the Late Roman Republic," *BRL* 65: 148–205.

Johnson, D. M. (2003) "Xenophon's Socrates on Law and Justice," *AncPhil* 23: 255–81.

(2004) "Reply to Vivienne Gray," *AncPhil* 24: 446–48.

Johnson, J. W. (1961) "That Neo-Classical Bee," *Journal of the History of Ideas* 22: 262–66.

Johnson, W. R. (2004) "A Secret Garden: *Georgics* 4.116–148," in Armstrong, Fish, Johnston, and Skinner (2004) 75–83.

Johnston, P. A. (1977) "Eurydice and Proserpina in the *Georgics*," *TAPA* 107: 161–72.

Johnstone, S. (1994) "Virtuous Toil, Vicious Work: Xenophon on Aristocratic Style," *CP* 89: 219–40.

Joly, R. (1956) *Le thème philosophique des genres de vie dans l'antiquité classique.* Brussels: Palais des Académies.

Jones, R. E. (1939) "Cicero's Accuracy of Characterization in His Dialogues," *AJP* 60: 307–25.

Jowett, B. and L. Campbell, eds. (1894) *Plato's Republic: The Greek Text*, vol. III. Oxford: Clarendon Press.

Kambylis, A. (1965) *Die Dichterweihe und ihre Symbolik: Untersuchungen zu Hesiodos, Kallimachos, Properz und Ennius*. Heidelberg: Carl Winter.

Kanelopoulos, C. (1993) "Les techniques et la cité: les positions de Xénophon," *ASNP* 23: 33–70.

Kaplan, C. (2000) *Critical Synoptics: Menippean Satire and the Analysis of Intellectual Mythology*. Madison, NJ: Fairleigh Dickinson University Press.

Kaye, F. B. (1924) *Bernard Mandeville: The Fable of the Bees, Or Private Vices, Publick Benefits*. With a Commentary, Critical, Historical, and Explanatory by F. B. Kaye. 2 vols. Oxford: Clarendon Press.

Keaveney, A. (1992) *Lucullus: A Life*. New York: Routledge.

Kerferd, G. B. (1981) *The Sophistic Movement*. Cambridge University Press.

Kirk, E. P. (1980) *Menippean Satire: An Annotated Catalogue of Texts and Criticism*. New York: Garland Publishing, Inc.

Klingner, F. (1963) *Virgils Georgica*. Zürich: Artemis Verlag.

Knox, P. E. (1985) "Wine, Water, and Callimachean Polemics," *HSCP* 89: 107–19.

Knox, P. E. and C. Foss, eds. (1998) *Style and Tradition: Studies in Honor of Wendell Clausen*. Stuttgart: Teubner.

Kraut, R., ed. (1997) *Plato's Republic: Critical Essays*. Lanham, MD: Rowman & Littlefield Publishers.

Kretschmar, M. (1938) *Otium, studia litterarum, Philosophie und βίος θεωρητικός im Leben und Denken Ciceros*. Würzburg-Aumühle: Konrad Triltsch.

Kronenberg, L. (2000) "The Poet's Fiction: Virgil's Praise of the Farmer, Philosopher, and Poet at the End of *Georgics* 2," *HSCP* 100: 341–60.

Kumaniecki, K. (1962) "Cicerone e Varrone. Storia di una conoscenza," *Athenaeum* 40: 221–43.

Laird, A. (2003) "Figures of Allegory from Homer to Latin Epic," in Boys-Stones (2003a) 151–75.

Laks, A. and M. Schofield, eds. (1995) *Justice and Generosity: Studies in Hellenistic Social and Political Philosophy*. Proceedings of the Sixth Symposium Hellenisticum. Cambridge University Press.

La Penna, A. [1962]/(1999) "Hesiod in the Culture and Poetry of Virgil," in Hardie (1999) II.25–40 = *Hésiode et son influence*, Entretiens sur l'antiquité classique Tome 7, Fondation Hardt, Vandœuvres-Geneva (1962) 225–47.

(1977) *"Senex Corycius,"* in *Atti del Convegno virgiliano sul bimillenario delle Georgiche (Napoli 17–19 Dicembre 1975)*: 37–66.

(1995) "Towards a History of the Poetic Catalogue of Philosophical Themes," in Harrison (1995) 314–28.

Laughton, E. (1956) "Varro the Grammarian. Review of *Varron Grammairien Latin* and *De Lingua Latina, livre v* by J. Collart," *CR* 6: 38–41.

(1960) "Observations on the Style of Varro," *CQ* 10: 1–28.

(1978) "Humour in Varro," in Collart (1978) 105–11.

Laurenti, R. (1973) *Filodemo e il pensiero economico degli epicurei*. Milan: Istituto editoriale cisalpino-La goliardica.

Leach, E. W. (1981) "*Georgics* 2 and the Poem," *Arethusa* 14: 35–48.

(1999) "Ciceronian '*Bi-Marcus*': Correspondence with M. Terentius Varro and L. Papirius Paetus in 46 BCE," *TAPA* 129: 139–79.

Le Bonniec, H. and G. Vallet, eds. (1980) *Mélanges de littérature et d'épigraphie latines, d'histoire ancienne et d'archéologie: Hommage à la mémoire de Pierre Wuilleumier*. Paris: Les Belles Lettres.

Lehmann, Y. (1997) *Varron théologien et philosophe romain*. Brussels: Latomus.

Leigh, M. (1994) "Servius on Vergil's *Senex Corycius*: New Evidence," *MD* 33: 181–95.

Liebeschuetz, W. (1965) "Beast and Man in the Third Book of Virgil's *Georgics*," *G&R* 12: 64–77.

Linderski, J. (1985) "The Dramatic Date of Varro, *De re rustica*, Book iii and the Elections in 54," *Historia* 34: 248–54.

(1989) "Garden Parlors: Nobles and Birds," in Curtis (1989) ii.105–27.

Löbl, R. (1997) *TEXNH–Techne: Untersuchung zur Bedeutung dieses Wortes in der Zeit von Homer bis Aristoteles*. 2 vols. Würzburg: Königshausen & Neumann.

Long, A. A. (1978) "Timon of Phlius: Pyrrhonist and Satirist," *PCPS* 204: 68–91.

(1995) "Cicero's Politics in *De officiis*," in Laks and Schofield (1995) 213–40.

(1996a) "The Socratic Tradition: Diogenes, Crates, and Hellenistic Ethics," in Branham and Goulet-Cazé (1996) 28–46.

(1996b) *Stoic Studies*. Berkeley and Los Angeles: University of California Press.

ed. (1999) *The Cambridge Companion to Early Greek Philosophy*. Cambridge University Press.

Long, A. A. and D. N. Sedley, eds. (1987) *The Hellenistic Philosophers*. 2 vols. Cambridge University Press.

Lundström S. (1976) "Der Eingang des Proömiums zum dritten Buche der Georgica," *Hermes* 104: 163–91.

Lyne, R. O. A. M. [1974]/(1999) "*Scilicet et Tempus Veniet . . . Virgil, Georgics* 1.463–514," in Hardie (1999) ii.162–83 = T. Woodman and D. West, eds. *Quality and Pleasure in Latin Poetry*, Cambridge University Press (1974) 47–66.

MacIntyre, A. (1984) *After Virtue: A Study in Moral Theory*. 2nd edn. University of Notre Dame Press.

Mackie, J. L. (1977) *Ethics: Inventing Right and Wrong*. New York: Penguin Books.

Maggiulli, G. (1994) "*Utilitas/delectatio, utilitas/voluptas* nell'ideologia delle *Res rusticae*," *BstudLat* 24: 487–99.

(1995) "*Dixi in eo libro quem de rebus rusticis scripsi* (Cic. *Cato* 54)," *RCCM* 37: 205–19.

Marasco, G. (1990) "*Corycius Senex* (Verg. *Georg.* 4.127)," *RFIC* 118: 402–07.

Marchant, E. C. and O. J. Todd, trans. (1923) *Xenophon: Memorabilia, Oeconomicus; Symposium, Apology*. Reprint, 2002. Cambridge, MA: Harvard University Press.

Martin, R. (1971) *Recherches sur les agronomes latins et leurs conceptions économiques et sociales*. Paris: Les Belles Lettres.

(1995) *"Ars an quid aliud?* La conception Varronienne de l'agriculture," *REL* 73: 80–91.

Martindale, C., ed. (1997) *The Cambridge Companion to Virgil*. Cambridge University Press.

McPherran, M. L. (1996) *The Religion of Socrates*. University Park: Pennsylvania State University Press.

Miles, G. B. (1975) *"Georgics* 3.209–294: *Amor* and Civilization," *CSCA* 8: 177–97.

(1980) *Virgil's Georgics: A New Interpretation*. Berkeley and Los Angeles: University of California Press.

Minyard, J. D. (1985) *Lucretius and the Late Republic: An Essay in Roman Intellectual History*. Leiden: E. J. Brill.

Monro, H. (1975) *The Ambivalence of Bernard Mandeville*. Oxford: Clarendon Press.

Moore, T. J. (1998) *The Theater of Plautus: Playing to the Audience*. Austin: University of Texas Press.

Morgan, L. (1999) *Patterns of Redemption in Virgil's Georgics*. Cambridge University Press.

Morrison, D. R. (1987) "On Professor Vlastos' Xenophon," *AncPhil* 7: 9–22.

(1994) "Xenophon's Socrates as Teacher," in Vander Waerdt (1994) 181–208.

Morson, G. S. (1989) "Parody, History, and Metaparody," in Morson and Emerson (1989) 63–86.

Morson, G. S. and C. Emerson, eds. (1989) *Rethinking Bakhtin: Extensions and Challenges*. Evanston, IL: Northwestern University Press.

(1990) *Mikhail Bakhtin. Creation of a Prosaics*. Stanford University Press.

Muecke, F. (1979) "Poetic Self-Consciousness in *Georgics* ii," in Boyle (1979a) 87–107.

Münzer, F. (1937) "Scrofa," *RE* 6A: 2287–89.

Myles, M. (2006) *Roman Manliness: Virtus and the Roman Republic*. Cambridge University Press.

Mynors, R. A. B., ed. (1990) *Virgil: Georgics*. Oxford: Clarendon Press.

Nadon, C. (2001) *Xenophon's Prince: Republic and Empire in the Cyropaedia*. Berkeley and Los Angeles: University of California Press.

Nagle, D. B. (2006) *The Household as the Foundation of Aristotle's Polis*. Cambridge University Press.

Nappa, C. (2005) *Reading after Actium: Vergil's Georgics, Octavian, and Rome*. Ann Arbor: The University of Michigan Press.

Natali, C. (1995) *"Oikonomia* in Hellenistic Political Thought," in Laks and Schofield (1995) 95–128.

Nehamas, A. (1998) *The Art of Living: Socratic Reflections from Plato to Foucault*. Berkeley and Los Angeles: University of California Press.

Nelson, S. (1998) *God and the Land: The Metaphysics of Farming in Hesiod and Vergil*. New York: Oxford University Press.

Nicolet, C. (1970) "Le livre III des 'Res rusticae' de Varron et les allusions au déroulement des comices tributes," *REA* 72: 113–37.

Nightingale, A. W. (1992) "Plato's *Gorgias* and Euripides' *Antiope*: A Study in Generic Transformation," *CA* 11: 121–41.

(1993) "The Folly of Praise: Plato's Critique of Encomiastic Discourse in the *Lysis* and *Symposium*," *CQ* 43: 112–30.

(1995) *Genres in Dialogue: Plato and the Construct of Philosophy*. Cambridge University Press.

Noè, E. (1977) "L'agronomo Cneo Tremellio Scrofa," *NAC* 6: 119–33.

Norden, E. [1898]/(1983) *Die antike Kunstprosa vom VI. Jahrhundert v. Chr. bis in die Zeit der Renaissance*. 2 vols. 9th edn. Stuttgart: B. G. Teubner.

Novara, A. (1980) "Le vieux Caton «aux champs» ou le plaisir exceptionnel de l'agriculture pour un sage vieillard (a propos de Cic., *Cato Maior*, 51–56)," in Le Bonniec and Vallet (1980) 261–68.

Nussbaum, M. C. (1986) *The Fragility of Goodness: Luck and Ethics in Greek Tragedy and Philosophy*. Cambridge University Press.

(1990) *Love's Knowledge: Essays on Philosophy and Literature*. New York: Oxford University Press.

(2003) "Philosophy and Literature," in Sedley (2003) 211–41.

O'Hara, J. J. (2005) "Trying Not To Cheat: Responses to Inconsistencies in Roman Epic," *TAPA* 135: 15–33.

Osgood, J. (2006) *Caesar's Legacy: Civil War and the Emergence of the Roman Empire*. Cambridge University Press.

O'Sullivan, T. M. (2006) "The Mind in Motion: Walking and Metaphorical Travel in the Roman Villa," *CP* 101: 133–52.

(2007) "Walking with Odysseus: The Portico Frame of the Odyssey Landscapes," *AJP* 128: 497–532.

Pagán, V. E. (2006) *Rome and the Literature of Gardens*. London: Duckworth.

Pangle, T. L. (1994) "Socrates in the Context of Xenophon's Political Writings," in Van der Waerdt (1994) 127–50.

Parry, A. (1972) "The Idea of Art in Virgil's *Georgics*," *Arethusa* 5: 35–52.

Parry, R. D. (1996) *Plato's Craft of Justice*. Albany: State University of New York Press.

Pendrick, G. J., ed. (2002) *Antiphon the Sophist: The Fragments*. Cambridge University Press.

Perkell, C. (1981) "On the Corycian Farmer of Vergil's Fourth *Georgic*," *TAPA* 111: 167–77.

(1986) "Vergil's Theodicy Reconsidered," in Bernard (1986) 67–83.

(1989) *The Poet's Truth: A Study of the Poet in Virgil's Georgics*. Berkeley and Los Angeles: University of California Press.

Perl, G. (1980) "Cn. Tremelius Scrofa in Gallia Transalpina. Zu Varro, *RR* 1,7,8," *AJAH* 5: 97–109.

Pomeroy, S. B. (1984) "The Persian King and the Queen Bee," *AJAH* 9: 98–108.

(1994) *Xenophon: Oeconomicus; A Social and Historical Commentary*. Oxford: Clarendon Press.

(1996) "Review of *Xenophon: The Shorter Socratic Writings; Apology of Socrates to the Jury, Oeconomicus, and Symposium* by R. C. Bartlett," *BMCR* 96.9.4.

Pöschl, V. [1936]/(1990) *Römischer Staat und griechisches Staatsdenken bei Cicero: Untersuchungen zu Ciceros Schrift De re publica.* Darmstadt: Wissenschaftliche Buchgesellschaft.

Powell, J. G. F., ed. (1995) *Cicero the Philosopher: Twelve Papers.* Oxford: Clarendon Press.

Powell, A. and S. Hodkinson, eds. (1994) *The Shadow of Sparta.* London: Routledge for the Classical Press of Wales.

Powell, A. and N. Richer, eds. (forthcoming) *Xenophon and Sparta.* Swansea: Classical Press of Wales.

Press, G. A., ed. (1993) *Plato's Dialogues: New Studies and Interpretations.* Lanham, MD: Rowman & Littlefield.

(1996) "The State of the Question in the Study of Plato," *The Southern Journal of Philosophy* 34: 507–32.

(1997) "Introduction: The Dialogical Mode in Modern Plato Studies," in Hart and Tejera (1997) 1–28.

ed. (2000) *Who Speaks for Plato? Studies in Platonic Anonymity.* Lanham, MD: Rowman & Littlefield.

Primer, I., ed. (1975) *Mandeville Studies: New Explorations in the Art and Thought of Dr. Bernard Mandeville (1670–1733).* The Hague: Martinus Nijhoff.

Prince, S. (2006) "Socrates, Antisthenes, and the Cynics," in Ahbel-Rappe and Kamtekar (2006) 75–92.

Prior, C. W. A., ed. (2000) *Mandeville and Augustan Ideas: New Essays.* Victoria, BC: English Literary Studies, University of Victoria.

Putnam, M. C. J. (1976) "Review of *Der Anspruch des Dichters in Vergils Georgika: Dichtertum und Heilsweg* by V. Buchheit," *CP* 71: 279–82.

(1979) *Virgil's Poem of the Earth: Studies in the Georgics.* Princeton University Press.

Rawson, E. (1985) *Intellectual Life in the Late Roman Republic.* London: Duckworth.

Reay, B. (2005) "Agriculture, Writing, and Cato's Aristocratic Self-Fashioning," *CA* 24: 331–61.

Relihan, J. C. (1984) "On the Origin of 'Menippean Satire' as the Name of a Literary Genre," *CP* 79: 226–29.

(1993) *Ancient Menippean Satire.* Baltimore: Johns Hopkins University Press.

Reshotko, N. (2006) *Socratic Virtue: Making the Best of the Neither-Good-Nor-Bad.* Cambridge University Press.

Reverdin, O., ed. (1963) *Varron: Six exposés et discussions par C. O. Brink et al.* Geneva: Fondation Hardt.

Richardson, J. S. (1983) "The Triumph of Metellus Scipio and the Dramatic Date of Varro *RR* 3," *CQ* 33: 456–63.

Richter, W. (1969) "Einige Rekonstruktions- und Quellenprobleme in Cicero *De re publica*," *RFIC* 97: 273–95.

Rimell, V. (2005) "The Satiric Maze: Petronius, Satire, and the Novel," in Freuden-burg (2005) 160–73.

Ritschl, F. W. [1866]/(1978) *Opuscula Philologica*. 5 vols. Hildesheim: Olms.

Rocca, S. (1983) *Etologia Virgiliana*. Genoa: Istituto di filologia classica e medievale.

Roller, M. B. (2001) *Constructing Autocracy: Aristocrats and Emperors in Julio-Claudian Rome*. Princeton University Press.

Rollinson, P. (1981) *Classical Theories of Allegory and Christian Culture*. Appendix by P. Matsen. Pittsburgh, PA: Duquesne University Press.

Romilly, J. de (1992) *The Great Sophists in Periclean Athens*. Trans. Janet Lloyd. Oxford: Clarendon Press.

Roochnik, D. (1996) *Of Art and Wisdom: Plato's Understanding of Techne*. University Park: The Pennsylvania State University Press.

 (2003) *Beautiful City: The Dialectical Character of Plato's "Republic."* Ithaca, NY: Cornell University Press.

Roscalla, F. (1990) "La dispensa di Iscomaco. Senofonte, Platone e l'amministrazione della casa," *QS* 31: 35–55.

Rösch-Binde, C. (1998) *Vom "δεινὸς ἀνήρ" zum "diligentissimus investigator antiquitatis": Zur komplexen Beziehung zwischen M. Tullius Cicero und M. Terentius Varro*. Munich: Utz.

Rose, M. A. (1993) *Parody: Ancient, Modern, and Post-modern*. Cambridge University Press.

Rosen, R. M. and I. Sluiter, eds. (2006) *City, Countryside, and the Spatial Organization of Value in Classical Antiquity*. Leiden: E. J. Brill.

Ross, D. O., Jr. (1975) "The *Culex* and *Moretum* as Post-Augustan Literary Parodies," *HSCP* 79: 235–63.

 (1979) "Two Rustic Notes," *CP* 74: 52–56.

 (1987) *Virgil's Elements: Physics and Poetry in the Georgics*. Princeton University Press.

Rowe, C. and M. Schofield, eds. (2000) *The Cambridge History of Greek and Roman Political Thought*. Cambridge University Press.

Rudd, N. (1966) *The Satires of Horace: A Study*. Cambridge University Press.

Russell, B. (1945) *A History of Western Philosophy*. New York: Simon and Schuster.

Ryberg, I. S. (1958) "Vergil's Golden Age," *TAPA* 89: 112–31.

Salvatore, A. (1978) *Scienza e poesia in Roma: Varrone e Virgilio*. Naples: Guida.

Saxonhouse, A. W. (1978) "Comedy in Callipolis: Animal Imagery in the *Republic*," *The American Political Science Review* 72: 888–901.

Schaerer, R. (1930). ΕΠΙΣΤΗΜΗ *et* ΤΕΧΝΗ: *étude sur les notions de connaissance et d'art d'Homère a Platon*. Macon: Protat frères.

Schiesaro, A. (1997) "The Boundaries of Knowledge in Virgil's *Georgics*," in Habinek and Schiesaro (1997) 63–89.

Schneider, L. (1987) *Paradox and Society: The Work of Bernard Mandeville*. New Brunswick, NJ: Transaction Books.

Schofield, M. and G. Striker, eds. (1986) *The Norms of Nature: Studies in Hellenistic Ethics*. Cambridge University Press.

Schultz, H. (1911) "Die *Georgica* in Vergils Stilentwicklung," in *Charites: Friedrich Leo zum sechzigsten Geburtstag dargebracht*. Berlin: Weidmann. 359–70.

Seager, R. (2001) "Xenophon and Athenian Democratic Ideology," *CQ* 51: 385–97.

Sedley, D., ed. (2003) *The Cambridge Companion to Greek and Roman Philosophy*. Cambridge University Press.

Segal, C. (1989) *Orpheus. The Myth of the Poet*. Baltimore: Johns Hopkins University Press.

Shorey, P. (1909) "Φύσις, Μελέτη, Ἐπιστήμη," *TAPA* 40: 185–201.

Skydsgaard, J. E. (1968) *Varro the Scholar: Studies in the First Book of Varro's De Re Rustica*. Copenhagen: Einar Munksgaard.

Slings, S. R. (1991) "The Quiet Life in Euripides' Antiope," in Hofmann and Harder (1991) 137–51.

Smith, G. B. (1997) "Leo Strauss and the Straussians: An Anti-Democratic Cult?" *Political Science and Politics* 30: 180–89.

Smith, S. B. (2006) *Reading Leo Strauss: Politics, Philosophy, Judaism*. The University of Chicago Press.

Speranza, F., ed. (1974) *Scriptorum Romanorum de re rustica reliquiae*. Messina: Università degli studi.

Spurr, M. S. (1986) "Agriculture and the *Georgics*," *G&R* 33: 164–87.

Stafford, J. M., ed. (1997) *Private Vices, Publick Benefits? The Contemporary Reception of Bernard Mandeville*. Solihull: Ismeron.

Stevens, J. A. (1994) "Friendship and Profit in Xenophon's *Oeconomicus*," in Vander Waerdt (1994) 209–37.

Strauss, L. (1952) *Persecution and the Art of Writing*. Reprint, 1988. The University of Chicago Press.

(1964) *The City and Man*. Reprint, 1978. The University of Chicago Press.

(1970) *Xenophon's Socratic Discourse: An Interpretation of the Oeconomicus*. Ithaca, NY: Cornell University Press.

Strauss, L. and J. Cropsey, eds. (1987) *History of Political Philosophy*. 3rd edn. The University of Chicago Press.

Stull, W. C. (2002) "Review of *Marcus Terentius Varro: Einführung in sein Werk* by B. Cardauns," *BMCR* 2002.06.40.

Stumpf, T. (2000) "Mandeville, Asceticism, and the Spare Diet of the Golden Age," in Prior (2000) 97–116.

Taragna Novo, S. (1968) *Economia ed etica nell'Economico di Senofonte*. Turin: G. Giappichelli.

Tarver, T. (1997) "Varro and the Antiquarianism of Philosophy," in Barnes and Griffin (1997) 130–64.

Tatum, W. J. (1992) "The Poverty of the Claudii Pulchri: Varro, *De Re Rustica* 3.16.1–2," *CQ* 42: 190–200.

Taylor, C. C. W. (2002) "The Origins of Our Present Paradigms," in Annas and Rowe (2002) 73–84.

Thibodeau, P. (2001) "The Old Man and His Garden (Verg. *Georg.* 4, 116–48)," *MD* 47: 175–95.

Thomas, G. T. (1978) "Religious Background for Virgil's Bee Symbol in the *Georgics*," *Vergilius* 24: 32–36.

Thomas, R. F. (1982) *Lands and Peoples in Roman Poetry: The Ethnographical Tradition*. Cambridge Philological Society.

(1983) "Callimachus, the *Victoria Berenices*, and Roman Poetry," *CQ* 33: 92–113 = Thomas (1999) 68–100.

(1987) "Prose into Poetry: Tradition and Meaning in Virgil's *Georgics*," *HSCP* 91: 229–60 = Thomas (1999) 142–72.

ed. (1988) *Virgil. Georgics.* 2 vols. Cambridge University Press.

(1990) "Ideology, Influence, and Future Studies in the *Georgics*," *Vergilius* 36: 64–70.

(1991) "The 'Sacrifice' at the End of the *Georgics*, Aristaeus, and Vergilian Closure," *CP* 86: 211–18.

(1992) "The Old Man Revisited: Memory, Reference and Genre in Virg., *Georg.* 4, 116–48," *MD* 29: 35–70 = Thomas (1999) 173–205.

(1998) "Virgil's Pindar?" in Knox and Foss (1998) 99–120 = Thomas (1999) 267–87.

(1999) *Reading Virgil and His Texts: Studies in Intertextuality*. Ann Arbor: University Of Michigan Press.

(2000) "A Trope by Any Other Name: 'Polysemy', Ambiguity, and *Significatio* in Virgil," *HSCP* 100: 381–407.

(2001a) *Virgil and the Augustan Reception*. Cambridge University Press.

(2001b) "Review of *Vergils Weltsicht: Optimismus und Pessimismus in Vergils Georgica* by R. Cramer," *Gnomon* 73: 580–85.

(2001c) "The *Georgics* of Resistance: From Virgil to Heaney," *Vergilius* 47: 117–47.

(2004) "Review of *Virgil on the Nature of Things: The Georgics, Lucretius and the Didactic Tradition* by M. Gale," *CR* 54: 371–74.

Tilly, B., ed. (1973) *Varro the Farmer: A Selection from the Res Rusticae*. London: University Tutorial Press.

Too, Y. L. (1998) "Xenophon's *Cyropaedia*: Disfiguring the Pedagogical State," in Too and Livingstone (1998) 282–302.

(2001) "The Economies of Pedagogy: Xenophon's Wifely Didactics," *PCPS* 47: 65–80.

Too, Y. L. and N. Livingstone, eds. (1998) *Pedagogy and Power: Rhetorics of Classical Learning*. Cambridge University Press.

Traglia, A. (1985) "Le *Res rusticae* di Varrone come opera letteraria," *C&S* 94: 89–97.

Tsouna McKirahan, V. (1994) "The Socratic Origins of the Cynics and the Cyrenaics," in Vander Waerdt (1994) 367–91.

(1996) "Epicurean Attitudes to Management and Finance," in Giannantoni and Gigante (1996) II.701–14.

Tsouna, V. (2007) *The Ethics of Philodemus*. Oxford University Press.

Tuplin, C. (1993) *The Failings of Empire: A Reading of Xenophon Hellenica 2.3.11–7.5.27*. Stuttgart: Franz Steiner.

(1994) "Xenophon, Sparta and the *Cyropaedia*," in Powell and Hodkinson (1994) 127–81.

(1996) "Xenophon (1)," *OCD* 3rd edn.: 1628–31.

ed. (2004a) *Xenophon and His World: Papers from a Conference Held in Liverpool in July 1999*. Stuttgart: Franz Steiner.

(2004b) "Xenophon and His World: An Introductory Review," in Tuplin (2004a) 13–31.

Vander Waerdt, P. A., ed. (1994a) *The Socratic Movement*. Ithaca, NY: Cornell University Press.

(1994b) "Socrates in the Clouds," in Vander Waerdt (1994a) 48–86.

Van de Woestijne, P. (1931) "Varron de Réate et Virgile," *RBPh* 10: 909–29.

Van Sickle, J. B. (2000) "Virgil *vs.* Cicero, Lucretius, Theocritus, Callimachus, Plato, and Homer: Two Programmatic Plots in the First Bucolic," *Vergilius* 46: 21–58.

Vasaly, A. (1993) *Representations: Images of the World in Ciceronian Oratory*. Berkeley and Los Angeles: University of California Press.

Vasiliou, I. (1999) "Conditional Irony in the Socratic Dialogues," *CQ* 49: 456–72.

(2002) "Socrates' Reverse Irony," *CQ* 52: 220–30.

Vegetti, M. (1970) "Il pensiero economico greco," in Firpo (1970) 583–607.

Virlouvet, C. (1996) "Une allusion varronienne aux fraudes de Clodius ? À propos de *Res rusticae* III, 5, 18," *MEFRA* 108: 873–91.

Vlastos, G. (1991) *Socrates: Ironist and Moral Philosopher*. Ithaca, NY: Cornell University Press.

Volk, K. (2000) "Review of *Vergils Weltsicht: Optimismus und Pessimismus in Vergils Georgica* by R. Cramer," *Vergilius* 46: 162–67.

(2002) *The Poetics of Latin Didactic: Lucretius, Vergil, Ovid, Manilius*. New York: Oxford University Press.

Wallace-Hadrill, A. (1997) "*Mutatio Morum*: The Idea of a Cultural Revolution," in Habinek and Schiesaro (1997) 3–22.

(1998) "*Horti* and Hellenization," in Cima and La Rocca (1998) 1–12.

Waterfield, R. (1997) "Review of *Xenophon: Memorabilia* by. A. L. Bonnette and *Xenophon: The Shorter Socratic Writings; Apology of Socrates to the Jury, Oeconomicus, and Symposium* by R. C. Bartlett," *CR* 47: 416–17.

Wedeck, H. E. (1929) *Humour in Varro and Other Essays*. Oxford: B. Blackwell.

Weeber, K.-W. (2003) *Die Schwelgerei, das süße Gift: Luxus im alten Rom*. Darmstadt: Primus.

Weinbrot, H. D. (2005) *Menippean Satire Reconsidered: From Antiquity to the Eighteenth Century*. Baltimore: Johns Hopkins University Press.

Weiss, R. (2006) *The Socratic Paradox and its Enemies*. The University of Chicago Press.

Wellman, R. R. (1976) "Socratic Method in Xenophon," *JHI* 37: 307–18.

Wender, D. S. (1969) "Resurrection in the Fourth Georgic," *AJP* 90: 424–36.

White, K. D. (1973) "Roman Agricultural Writers I: Varro and His Predecessors," *ANRW* 1.4: 439–97.

(1977) *Country Life in Classical Times*. London: Elek Books Ltd.

White, N. (2002) *Individual and Conflict in Greek Ethics*. Oxford: Clarendon Press.

Whitman, J. (1987) *Allegory: The Dynamics of an Ancient and Medieval Technique*. Oxford: Clarendon Press.

Wilhelm, R. M. (1976) "The Second *Georgic*: The Sowing of a Republic," *ZAnt* 26: 63–72.

Wilkinson, L. P. (1969) *The Georgics of Virgil: A Critical Survey*. Reprint, 1997. Norman: University of Oklahoma Press.

(1970) "Pindar and the Proem to the Third Georgic," in Wimmel (1970) 286–90.

Williams, B. (1985) *Ethics and the Limits of Philosophy*. Cambridge, MA: Harvard University Press.

(1993) *Shame and Necessity*. Berkeley and Los Angeles: University of California Press.

(1997) "The Analogy of City and Soul in Plato's *Republic*," in Kraut (1997) 49–60.

(2006) *The Sense of the Past: Essays in the History of Philosophy*. Princeton University Press.

Wilms, H. (1995) *Techne und Paideia bei Xenophon und Isokrates*. Stuttgart: B. G. Teubner.

Wimmel, W., ed. (1970) *Forschungen zur römischen Literatur: Festschrift zum 60. Geburtstag von Karl Büchner*. Wiesbaden: F. Steiner.

Wirszubski, C. (1954) "Cicero's *Cum Dignitate Otium*: A Reconsideration," *JRS* 44: 1–13.

Woodruff, P. (1999) "Rhetoric and Relativism: Protagoras and Gorgias," in Long (1999) 290–310.

Zetzel, J. E. G., ed. (1995) *Cicero: De Re Publica; Selections*. Cambridge University Press.

ed. (1999) *Cicero: On the Commonwealth and On the Laws*. Cambridge University Press.

Index of passages cited

General index

Academic philosophy, 30
active life, *see also* contemplative life
    and Cicero, 89, 119–21
    in Roman ideology, 31
    in the *De Re Rustica*, 108–29
    in the *Georgics*, 149–55, 156, 160–62, 184
    in the *Oeconomicus*, 54–62, 65
Adkins, A. W. H., 25–28
agriculture, *see* farming
allegory, 20–23
    ancient definitions of, 20–21
    in the *De Re Rustica*, 21, 108–29
    in the *Georgics*, 21–22, 135, 149–55
    in the *Oeconomicus*, 21, 62–66
    pastoral, 21, 111–16, 128
Allen, D., 1, 2, 23
amor, see Georgics–amor
animals, conflation with humans
    in Plato's *Republic*, 71, 112–13
    in the *De Re Rustica*, 111, 114–17, 125–27
    in the *Georgics*, 143–46, 151–55, 163–68
    in the *Oeconomicus*, 57–58, 60, 65
Annas, J., 26, 28, 29, 31
Aratus, *see Georgics*–influence of Aratus on
Archytas, *see Georgics*–Old Man of Tarentum
Aristaeus, *see Georgics*–Aristaeus
Aristophanes, 108, *see also* comedy;
        Oeconomicus–as comedy;
        Plato–*Republic*–comic elements
    Birds, 71, 108
    Clouds, 41, 57
    Ecclesiazusae, 71
ars, see also farming–as an "art"; *ratio*
    in the *De Oratore*, 82–83, 85
    in the *De Re Rustica*, 82–84, 91–93, 125
    in the *Georgics*, 132, 158
Atticus, T. Pomponius, 88, *see also De Re
    Rustica*–Atticus (as a character)
Augustus, *see Georgics*–Octavian/Augustus
authorial intention, 19
aviaries, *see De Re Publica*–aviaries

Bacchus (Dionysus), *see* religion–Bacchus
Bakhtin, M., 4, 6, 16
Batstone, W., 13, 14, 17, 131, 145, 176, 180
bees
    in Bernard Mandeville, 1–3, 23
    in Cicero, 125–26
    in Plato's *Republic*, 68, 126
    in the *De Re Rustica*, 92–93, 125–27
    in the *Georgics*, 144, 147, 152–55, 166–68
        bugonia, 167–68, 176, 181–84
    in the *Oeconomicus*, 56
Booth, W., 17–20
bugonia, see bees–in the *Georgics*

Callicles, *see* sophists–Callicles
Callimachus, 94, 122, 127, 133, 150
Cardauns, B., 11–13, 87
Cato the Elder
    De Agri Cultura, 22, 77, 94–95, 99, 111, 138,
        173
    in Cicero's *De Senectute*, 22, 79–80, 95, 98
    in Pliny's *Natural History*, 77
    in the *De Re Rustica*, 84
Cicero, *see also* contemplative life; *De Re
    Rustica*–Appius; *De Re Rustica*–parody of
    Cicero; *Georgics*–influence of Cicero on
    Academica, 6, 80, 88, 119, 120, 121
    critique of Epicureanism, 27
    De Finibus, 81, 85, 122, 136, 169
    De Officiis, 27, 30, 92, 97–98, 107, 125
    De Oratore, 20, 79, 81–83, 85, 87, 100, 101,
        108, 119, 145, 170
    De Re Publica, 22, 80, 82, 108–10, 112, 117,
        118–19, 125, 154, 169
    De Senectute, 22, 30, 79–80, 98, 136, 146, 169,
        170, 173
    philosophical views, 30–31
    relationship with Varro, 31, 75, 80, 88–89,
        108
    translation of the *Oeconomicus*, 30, 32, 125–26
civil war, *see also* war

216

Martin, R., 3, 11, 37, 73–79, 81, 82, 95, 98, 102, 105
Menippean satire, 3–7, 33–34
  and Bernard Mandeville, 4, 7
  and Cynicism, 4, 6–7
  and Menippus, 4–5
  and Socratic dialogue, 4, 11, 13, 33–34
  and Varro, 4–7, 11–13, 33, 74, 85–86, 94, 99, 123, 141
  and Virgil, 15, 141, 184
  and Xenophon, 33
  definitions of, 4–7
Miles, G., 3, 12, 102, 140, 144, 146, 150, 177
morality, 23–32, *see also* decline (moral and physical); *delectatio*; *De Re Rustica*–morality; *Georgics*–morality; greed; *honestus*; justice; *kalokagathia*; *Oeconomicus*–*enkrateia*, *sōphrosunē*; pleasure; self-interest; utility; *voluptas*
  ancient vs. modern, 26
  definition of, 27
  Epicurean, 27, 98–99
  foundations of, 25–28
  in classical Athens, 26–27
  in Mandeville's *Fable of the Bees*, 1–2, 23–24
  in Republican Rome, 27, 30
  in the *Cyropaedia*, 44
  in the *De Re Rustica*, 94
  in the *Georgics*, 142–48
  in the *Oeconomicus*, 37
  language of, 26–28, 97–99, 144–48
  moral skepticism, 26, 27
  naturalism, 31
  naturalistic fallacy, 23–25
  shame-culture, 26
  virtue ethics, 26
  vs. ethics, 26
Morgan, L., 13, 14, 149, 150, 166, 167, 178, 180, 182, 183
Morson, G. S., 16–17
Mynors, R. A. B., 135, 139, 140, 143, 145, 152, 154, 165, 179
mystery religion, *see* religion

Nadon, C., 8, 9, 30, 43, 44
Nappa, C., 13–15, 19, 22, 177, 179, 180, 183, 184
naturalistic fallacy, *see* morality–naturalistic fallacy
Nelson, S., 3, 14, 22, 143, 147, 155, 173
Nightingale, A. W., 16, 28, 33, 41, 46

Octavian, *see Georgics*–Octavian/Augustus
Oeconomicus, *see also* active life; allegory; animals, conflation with humans; bees; civil war; contemplative life; decline (moral and physical); diligence; dogs; farming; gardens; greed; horses; justice; *kalokagathia*; luxury; morality; *oikonomia*; pastoralism; plague; pleasure; praise; praise of farming; profit; quincunx rows (of trees); religion; rewards and punishments; sacrifice; self-interest; slavery; storms; *technē*; utility; vines; war
  appearance vs. reality, 41, 45–46, 52–55, 63
  art of ruling, 54–62, 65
  as a response to Plato's *Republic*, 66–72
  as comedy, 41, 57
  banausic arts, 41–42
  bifurcated structure of, 37–38
  Critobulus, 30, 37–42, 49–50, 52–53, 61
    in other dialogues of Xenophon and Plato, 39–40
  Cyrus the Great, 42–44, 49, 60, 98–99
  Cyrus the Younger, 44–47
  enkrateia, 40, 57
  genre, 33–34, 41
  Ischomachus, 21, 29, 30, 32, 37, 38, 41, 52, 53, 54–66, 71, 81, 82, 90, 111, 126, 152, 154, 175
    as the "anti-Socrates", 55–56
    historical Ischomachus, 37–38, 60–61
    similarities to Xenophon, 37
  Lysander, 44–46, 98–99
  marriage, 56–57
  Persia, 30, 42–46, 48, 54, 58, 59, 62
  Socrates, 29–30, 37–66
  sōphrosunē, 56
  wife of Ischomachus, 56–57
oikonomia, 21, 29, 32, 37–41, 43, 52, 55, 66, 67, 72
Old Man of Tarentum, *see Georgics*–Old Man of Tarentum
Orpheus, *see Georgics*–Orpheus
otium, *see also* contemplative life
  in the *De Re Rustica*, 81, 108
  in the *Georgics*, 139, 151, 160, 184

parody, 7, 13, 16–17, *see also De Re Rustica*–parody; *Georgics*–Old Man of Tarentum–as parody
pastio villatica, *see De Re Rustica*–*pastio villatica*
pastoral analogy, *see* allegory–pastoral
pastoral poetry, *see Georgics*–Old Man of Tarentum; *Georgics*–pastoral imagery; Virgil–*Eclogues*
pastoralism, *see also* dogs; *Georgics*–bulls; horses
  in the *De Re Publica*, 113